MY STORY
as told by WATER

Other Books by David James Duncan

The River Why
The Brothers K
River Teeth

MY STORY
as told by WATER

confessions, Druidic rants, reflections, bird-watchings,
fish-stalkings, visions, songs and prayers refracting
light, from living rivers, in the age of the industrial dark

David James Duncan

Sierra Club Books
San Francisco

The Sierra Club, founded in 1892 by John Muir, has devoted itself to the study and protection of the Earth's scenic and ecological resources—mountains, wetlands, woodlands, wild shores and rivers, deserts and plains. The publishing program of the Sierra Club offers books to the public as a nonprofit educational service in the hope that they may enlarge the public's understanding of the Club's basic concerns. The point of view expressed in each book, however, does not necessarily represent that of the Club. The Sierra Club has some sixty chapters coast to coast, in Canada, Hawaii, and Alaska. For information about how you may participate in its programs to preserve wilderness and the quality of life, please address inquiries to Sierra Club, 85 Second Street, San Francisco, CA 94105.

www.Sierra.org/books

A complete list of permissions is on page 294.

Published by Sierra Club Books in conjunction with Crown Publishers, New York, New York. Member of the Crown Publishing Group.

Random House, Inc. New York, Toronto, London, Sydney, Auckland
www.randomhouse.com

SIERRA CLUB, SIERRA CLUB BOOKS, and Sierra Club design logos are registered trademarks of the Sierra Club.

Design by Elina D. Nudelman

Library of Congress Cataloging-in-Publication Data

Duncan, David James.
    My story as told by water : confessions, Druidic rants, reflections, bird-
    watchings, fish-stalkings, visions, songs and prayers refracting light, from living
    rivers, in the age of the industrial dark / David James Duncan.

    1. Environmental protection. 2. Environmentalism. 3. Environmental
    policy.   I. Title.
TD170.3 .D86   2001
333.7'2—dc21   00-051578

ISBN 1-57805-049-9

10 9 8 7 6 5 4 3 2

First Edition

Contents

MY STORY
as told by WATER

Wonder Versus Loss

> . . . Like the water
> of a deep stream, love is always too much. We
> did not make it. Though we drink till we burst
> we cannot have it all, or want it all.
> In its abundance it survives our thirst.
>
> —Wendell Berry

1. Valmiki's Palm

In the Beginning

"In the beginning," says the *Brihadaranyaka Upanisad*—a scripture composed, according to the rishis of ancient India, by no one; a scripture self-created, found floating like mist, or the bands of a rainbow, in the primordial forest air—*"there was nothing here at all. . . ."*

Death alone covered this completely, as did hunger, for what is hunger but death? Then death made up his mind: "Let me equip myself with a body" (atman). So he undertook a liturgical recitation (arc), and as he was engaged in recitation, water (ka) suddenly sprang from him. Amazed, death thought: "While I was reciting, water sprang up for me!" This is what gave the name to and discloses the hidden nature of recitation (ar-ka). Truly, water springs up for he or she who knows the name and nature of recitation. Recitation is water."

Adoration of a Hose

I was born in a hospital located on the flanks of a volcanic cone. This cone, named Mount Taber, looks as innocent as an overturned teacup as it rises over a densely populated section of Southeast Portland, Oregon. Decades before my birth, scientists had of course declared the cone to be unimpeachably extinct. The hospital, however, afforded a nice view of another cone, thirty-five miles away in the same volcanic system, also declared extinct in those days: Mount St. Helens. Forgive my suspicion of certain unimpeachable declarations of science.

My birth-cone's slopes were drained by tiny seasonal streams, which, like most of the creeks in that industrialized quadrant of Portland, were buried in underground pipes long before I arrived on the scene. There were also three small reservoirs on Mount Taber's slopes, containing the water that bathed me at birth, water I would drink for eighteen years, water that gave me life. But this water didn't come from Mount Taber, or from the surrounding hills, or even from the aquifer beneath: it came, via concrete and iron flumes, from the Bull Run River, which drains the slopes of the Cascade Mountains forty miles away.

I was born, then, without a watershed. On a planet held together by gravity and fed by rain, a planet whose every creature depends on water and whose every slope works full-time, for eternity, to create creeks and rivers, I was born with neither. The creeks of my birth-cone were invisible, the river from somewhere else entirely. Of course millions of Americans are now born this way. And many of them grow up without creeks, live lives lacking intimacy with rivers, and become well-adjusted, productive citizens even so.

Not me. The dehydrated suburbs of my boyhood felt as alien to me as Mars. The arid industrial life into which I was being prodded looked to me like the life of a Martian. What *is* a Martian? Does Mars support intelligent life? I had no idea. My early impression of the burgeoning burbs and urbs around me was of internally-combusting hordes of dehydrated beings manufacturing and moving unnecessary objects from one place to another in order to finance the rapid manufacture and transport of more unnecessary objects. Running water, on the other hand, felt as necessary to me as food, sleep, parents, and air. And on the cone of my birth, all such water had been eliminated.

I didn't rebel against the situation. Little kids don't rebel. That comes later, along with the hormones. What I did was hand-build my own rivers—breaking all neighborhood records, in the process, for amount of time spent running a garden hose. In the beginning, in Southeast Portland, there was nothing much there at all. Dehydrated Martians seemed to cover the place completely. So I would fasten the family hose to an azalea bush at the uphill end of one of my mother's sloping flower beds, turn the faucet on as hard as Mom would allow, and watch hijacked Bull Run River water spring forth in an *arc* and start cutting a miniscule, audible river (*ka*) down through the bed. I'd then camp by this river all day.

As my river ran and ran, the thing my mother understandably hated and I understandably loved began to happen: *creation.* The flower-bed topsoil slowly washed away, and a streambed of tiny colored pebbles gradually appeared: a bed that soon looked just like that of a genuine river, complete with tiny point bars and cutbanks, meanders and eddies, fishy-looking riffles, slow pools. It was a nativity scene, really: the entire physics and fluvial genius of Gravity-Meets-Water-Meets-Earth incarnating in perfect miniature. I built matchbook-sized hazelnut rafts and cigarette-butt-sized elderberry canoes, launched them on my river, let them ride down to the gargantuan driveway puddle that served as my Pacific. I stole a three-inch-tall blue plastic cavalry soldier from my brother's Fort Apache set, cut the stock off his upraised rifle so that only the long, flexible barrel remained, tied a little thread to the end of the barrel to serve as fly line, and sent the soldier fishing. I'd then lie flat on my belly, cheek to the ground, and stare at this U.S. Cavalry dropout, thigh-deep in his tiny river, rifle-rod high in the air, line working in the current; stare till I became him; stare till, in the sunlit riffle, we actually hooked and landed tiny sun-glint fish. "Shut off that hose!" my mother would eventually shout out the kitchen window. "You've turned the whole driveway into a mudhole!"

Poor woman, I'd think. *It's not a mudhole. It's a tide flat.*

I'd gladly turn the hose off, though: that's how I got the tide to go out. I'd then march my river soldier out onto the flat, to dig for clams.

Celilo

One Sunday morning when I was five, my siblings, first cousins, and I were loaded into the two family wagons by our parents and driven up the Columbia River past The Dalles, Oregon, where, for hours, we watched the deceptively smooth, one-to-two-mile-wide flow of the lower Columbia squeeze into a single four-hundred-yard-wide basalt chute, and explode, in a long series of rapids and falls, toward the Pacific. The occasion of our coming was a familiar one in the Cold War Northwest: the falls before our eyes—one of the world's great natural wonders, and one of humanity's—home of the longest-inhabited village on the planet, and annually the largest "city," or tribal gathering place, west of the Mississippi for six hundred generations of Indian fishermen and traders—was doomed, in a few weeks, to be inundated by The Dalles Dam.

The first thing I remember, from the moment we sat, is that my big, usually noisy clan was engulfed by the sound and struck silent: Celilo was louder than thunder, more constant than storm surf. The second thing I recall is the way sound and smell, usually two things, were crushed by the falls into one: Celilo smelled, simultaneously, of ozone, intense life, and constant death. The third thing I remember is that the falls were far more complex than one mind or pair of eyes could take in. Rather than tumble, Niagara-style, over a photogenic cliff, Celilo smashed the river open for a mile and a half, charging the air with its energy and fragrance, telling your nose, ears, and skin a thousand-stranded story about the myriad lives those waters had touched, countless places and beings they'd seen and been, countless places and beings they would circle back, as vapor, cloud, and rainfall, to enliven and inhabit again. The Northwest's great river, Celilo Falls revealed, is a convection, not a collection; purest verb, not noun; an intensity that annihilates dispersion, diversion, coercion. A million cubic feet of exploding water per second may be a hydroelectric bonanza, but it is not a river. The Columbia at Celilo was no arithmetical sum. Rain + springs + snowbanks + rills + creeks do not equal River any more than cops + entrepreneurs + fashion designers + shoppers + junkies equal City. You can't part out a great river, because it is both greater and other than its parts: its constancy and immensity of flow are a *union,* the antithesis of parts. The Columbia's ocean-bound heart was utterly exposed at Celilo, and what I saw, smelled, and felt there was inhumanly joyous. The great river at Celilo was a boulevardier, not a pioneer: the grandstand-shaped cliffs from which we gulls, terns, and humans watched, the earthshaking drumroll, endless rainbows and prisms born of water's constant crushing, gave the place the aura, strange to say, of an H_2O Manhattan or Paris on some fabulous holiday, a madcap downtown celebration of the multitudinous whole.

Awed to silence, both by Celilo's power and by its unimaginable doom, my family and I watched Indian men wait, with long-handled dip-nets, on preposterously frail platforms above the bone-crushing white, as they'd done since before the births of Pharoahs. But we expected to see salmon caught, or at least leaping. The fall chinook were running. One reason the Army Corps of Engineers was building these Columbia/Snake system dams, they solemnly told us civilians, was to protect salmon from all those rapacious, dip-netting Indians.

We did not see a fish caught. We did not see one leap. And after a few hours we were exhausted by the brightness and thunder, the wait for nothing, the raging whole. We were then returned to the coffin-quiet of our cars and breezed the hundred miles home, to enjoy the fiercely mandated fruits of cheap hydropower: frozen dinners served on throwaway aluminum trays; pop from throwaway cans; snap-on lamps; a snapped-on TV, and—the detail that froze the day in memory as the strangest of my early life—Elvis the Pelvis on *Ed Sullivan* for the first time, singing "You Ain't Nothin' But a Hound Dog" while he writhed like a salmon in its death throes.

Woe v. Wade

The spiritual and economic overseer of my large suburban family was my maternal grandmother, Ethel Rowe. Gramma Rowe was four feet eleven, but insisted with such vehemence that she was five-one that most of the family felt her missing two inches were surely an oversight on the Lord's part, and should be imagined as real. For my part, I wished Gramma Rowe was three feet eleven, or even two-eleven, since at four-eleven she was overwhelming. In those days we called people like her "firecrackers," but firecrackers explode once and that's it. Gramma Rowe could just keep exploding. She was more like a four-foot-eleven-inch Uzi. When a young nephew who had trouble with *r* sounds one day referred to our matriarch as "Gwamma Woe," it was too perfect. I called her nothing else ever after.

Gwamma Woe's lovingly despotic rule, like her mystical five-foot-oneness, was based on an interpretation of scripture that corrected countless oversights on the part of the Bible's authors. All this "God works in mysterious ways" stuff, for starters, was hooey. Gwamma Woe knew *exactly* how God worked, exactly how humans should work in response, and mystery, garden hoses, rivers, and U.S. Cavalry dropouts had nothing to do with it, thank-you-very-much. A fiercely devout

Seventh Day Adventist, Gwamma Woe had, per her self-bowdlerized Bible's instructions, turned herself into a crackerjack real-estate sales-lady, the better to serve the Lord; she was now spending her life getting rich by the sweat of her brow and enjoying all but a tithe of those riches, just as God ordered, after which she might agree to die, or at least briefly slumber, until such time as Jesus woke her, gave her body the complete rebuild that would make her a true five feet one inch, and whisked her up to the gold mansions and permanent riches of heaven to frolic and sing hymns forever.

I had just one small objection to Gwamma Woe's Gold-Mansion-Track Plan for her life: it was her plan for *my* life too. There were just two incarnational options for a Woe grandchild. You either (1) became a staunch Seventh Day Adventist like Gwamma, spent your life pursuing wealth like Gwamma, and later retired for eternity to the even greater wealth of heaven with Gwamma, or, (2) surprise, surprise: *YOU BURNED IN HELL FOREVER!!!*

Ah, Gwamma Woe! If only I'd been able to embrace her plan for my life, I'd have saved myself a lot of heartbreak. Capitalist fundamentalism, I still believe, is the perfect Techno-Industrial religion, its goal being a planet upon which we've nothing left to worship, worry about, read, eat, or love but dollar bills and Bibles. My boyhood worry, though, was that this world might not *be* techno-industrial. Maybe only the *human* world is techno-industrial. Maybe the world God made is *natural,* its "industry" a bunch of forces like gravitation, solar rays, equinoctial tilt, wind, tides, photosynthesis, sexuality, migration. And if the world *is* natural, I'd fret, if it was the *natural* world God loved enough to send His son to die for it, then it might not be such a God-pleasing thing to spend my life converting that world into industrial waste products, dollar bills, and Bibles.

Needless to say, our matriarch disagreed with every jot and iota of this. She recognized natural beauty in a way: a "beautiful day," for instance, increased the likelihood of selling a house. But the word *nature,* to Gwamma, had an unwashed, unsaved ring to it. Wild Nature, she believed, was basically a bunch of naked, dirty, heathenish creatures having sex with, stalking, and devouring each other—more or less like realtors, she admitted, only in Nature's case there was no post-prandial Gold Mansion to give purpose to the earthly jism and gore. The Natural World's duty, Gwamma Woe was certain, was to be knocked down, processed, and converted ASAP into Industrial Christian World. And unconvertibly wild creatures and wilderness were to be avoided from cradle to coffin, by staying voluntarily shut up in the Adventist fold.

I didn't argue with this. Gwamma would turn the Uzi on an arguer. But from the day I first heard even a garden-hose trout stream deliver a sermon, I began to hear the Adventist word "fold" as the move one makes in poker when one's cards aren't worth a damn. I began to compare the Natural World to the Industrial World, trying to decide for myself which was the more unwashed and unsaved. One day on the lower Columbia River, for instance, in the interests of theological investigation, I poked a stick into the belly of an enormous dead carp—and when the thing flupped open, releasing a riot of vile gases and writhing maggots, it sure enough was an unsaved, sexual, heathenish-looking business in there. But growing up on the same great river we heard rumors of industrial and national defense maggotry writhing in the bellies of the paper mills, aluminum plants, weapons dumps, and nuclear weapons works into which no one could even poke a stick and live to tell the tale. So. Maggots or PCBs? Maggots or anthrax? Maggots or plutonium?

Gwamma Woe believed, prophetically, that her best chance of keeping me on the Heavenly Mansion Track was to keep me as ignorant and suspicious of the nonindustrialized world as she was. But the wonders of my boyhood world—the things that filled me at first sight with awe and yearning—were, in order of preference, (1) Rivers, (2) Mountains, (3) Ancient Forest, (4) the Ocean, and (5) Cute Girls. Gwamma Woe's leading man, Jesus, though I revered him, was so besmirched in my mind by his followers that he merely tied with Disney's Davy Crockett for sixth. When the matriarch got wind of these priorities, she deployed her boundless energy, twisted scripture, bribes, threats, and Uzi to convince me that I was gravitating toward unwashed heathen nonsense. And she was a force: I was convinced, by age six, that I'd eventually become a well-heeled Adventist doctor or lawyer, not because I wanted to, but because any less remunerative, more nature-loving career would result in that formidable annoyance: eternal damnation.

One day when I was still six, though, my religious adviser committed a fatal tactical blunder . . .

We all like doing what we do best. Gwamma Woe also liked showing off while she did it. As a combination matriarch/real-estate whiz, she had an exhibitionistic love for hauling my siblings and me to "Open Houses" at the various properties she had up for sale, and letting us eavesdrop while she hooked and played prospective buyers like fish.

Between clients she delivered impassioned sermonettes on Salesmanship, a biblical virtue that ranked right in there with Cleanliness and Godliness in its power to convert penniless wretches like us kids into Gold-Mansion-track sales experts like her. No matter how many times she explained the key concepts, though—terms like "earnest money," "commandment," "mortgage," "Holy Ghost," "immaculate interior," "redemption," "FHA approval"—I couldn't wrap my nature-smitten mind around them. After a single Open House spent cross-eyed with boredom, I became an extremely reluctant companion.

As I said, though, Gwamma Woe was a great saleslady. One day in October she drove her red Rambler convertible down our driveway, spotted me merged with my garden-hose river and fishing soldier, but instantly conjured three words that made me leap into her car with anticipation. The words were *"Creek-front property!"*

I don't remember a thing about the drive to the Open House, the sermonette en route, the layout of the home. All I remember is hearing—the instant Gwamma parked beside a FOR SALE sign and shut off her engine—the unfamiliar song of unpiped, nonhosed water flowing somewhere behind the house. In the lost Celtic recesses of my bloodstream, a bagpipe and a drum immediately answered. I told Gwamma to holler when she needed me, shot around the house, scrambled down a riprapped embankment into a ribbon of ancient fir and alder—and the world of mortgages and immaculate interiors vanished as a remnant slice of green world, non-man-made world, Ancient World, suddenly shimmered on all sides.

It was just one of Portland's dying creeks. Really, one with a much-needed but long-lost Indian name. Johnson Creek was now its anemic title. But it was twenty-six miles long, hence a little too big to bury. And when you fail to bury Northwest creeks, or to poison them quite to death, a few of them—even now—receive unimaginably non-Adventistic visitors from wild and distant realms. Vigilant though she was, Gwamma Woe had not foreseen this.

I found a walking stick. I began wading a stone streambed for the first time in my life. Because of what ensued, thirty or so pairs of wading shoes later I am wading them still. Love, it turns out, is for me something slippery, arrived at on foot, via lots of splashing.

A creek, given its visual complexity, is a surprisingly simple construction.

Two nouns: Water and Land. One verb: Gravity.

Plant and animal life, growth and decay, the play of light on water, the visual and liturgical improvisations of current, all obscure the simplicity. But the grammar of creeks is the antithesis of complex. The instant it alights on Earth, the first noun—Water—is turned by the verb, Gravity, into a ceaseless search for the lowest possible place while the second noun, Land, does all in its passive power to thwart that search. The result? Riffle; rapid; eddy; pool; scouring sand; sculptured wood and rock; soil-making mud; insects; birds; fish; *ar-ka;* endless music; sustenance; life.

Kids tend to befriend creeks the way adults befriend each other: start shallow, and slowly work your way deeper. So: skippers; water-striders. That's what I noticed first. Inch-long, spraddle-legged, white-walled, black-topped creatures embarrassing Gwamma Woe's man, Saint Peter, by demonstrating that mere bugs not only walk on water, they *run*. Next, deeper down: caddis fly larva. Driving their glued-gravel RV's back an' forth, back an' forth all day across the bottom like it was Arizona down there an' they were sick o' golf, dang it, an' maybe shouldn'a took early retirement after all. Deeper yet—I had to turn submerged stones to flush these—crawdads: designed right there in the fifties by staunch war hawks, it seemed, judging by their attraction to bombproof rock shelters, their preference for traveling backasswards, their armor; Cold War antennae; oversized Pentagon-budget claws.

Then I came to water too deep to wade, too deep to see bottom: a shady black pool, surface-foam eddying like stars in a nebula. And though I wanted to keep exploring, though I'd barely begun, the big pool proved a psychic magnet . . .

Its surface was a night sky in broad daylight . . .

Its depths were another world within this one . . .

The entire frenetic creek stopped here to rest . . .

I was 78 percent water myself . . .

I felt physically ordered to crawl out on a cantilevered log, settle belly-down, and watch the pool gyre directly beneath me, the foam-starred surface eddying, eddying, till it became a vision of night; water-skipper meteors; sun-glint novas. The creek would not stop singing. I spun and spiraled, grew foam-dazed and gyre-headed. Pieces of the mental equipment I'd been taught to think I needed began falling into the pool and dissolving: my preference of light to darkness; sense of rightsideup and upsidedownness, sense of surfaces and edges, sense of where I end and other things or elements begin. The pool taught nothing but mystery and depth. An increasingly dissolved "I" followed the first verb, gravity, down. Yet depth, as the dissolved "I" sees it, is also height.

Then, up from those sunless depths, or yet also down from foam-starred heavens, a totem-red, tartan-green impossibility descended or arose, its body so massive and shining, visage so travel-scarred and ancient, that I was swallowed like Jonah by the sight. I know no better way to invoke the being's presence than to state the naked name:

Coho. An old male coho, *arcing* up not to eat, as trout do, but just to submarine along without effort or wings; just to move, who knows why, through a space and time it created for itself as it glided. And as it eased past my face not a body's length away, the coho gazed—with one lidless, primordial eye—clean into the suspended heart of me: gazed not like a salmon struggling up from an ocean to die, but like a Gaelic or Kwakiutl messenger dropped down from a realm of gods, *Tir na nOg,* world of deathlessness, world of *Ka,* to convey, via the fact of its being, a timeless message of sacrifice and hope. The creek would not stop singing. My bagpipe heart could not stop answering. When you see a magnificent ocean fish confined in small, fresh water, it is always like a dream. And in our dreams, every object, place, and being is something *inside* us. Despite my smallness, ignorance, inexperience, I felt a sudden huge sense of entitlement. This creek and its music, secret world and its messenger, belonged to me completely. Or I to them.

The coho vanished as serenely as it had come, back into depth. But not before its shining eye changed the way I see out of my own. I'd glimpsed a way into a Vast Inside. A primordial traveler through water and time had said, *Come.*

But, ah, the worlds, the overlapped worlds . . .

Not three hundred yards from my first draught of Deep Primordial, Gwamma Woe had found a buyer for the house! She was exultant when she called me up off the water, literally dancing: a four-foot-eleven-inch pot-of-real-estate-hoarding leprechaun. Yet as I stepped from ancient streambank onto neatly mowed lawn, my intensity, for the first time, was a match for hers.

She could see something had happened, and asked about it at once.

I tried to tell. But my words, as I spoke of the coho, were bereft of the yearning that still gripped me.

Being a purveyor of precise square footages for exact amounts, Gwamma Woe had just one question about the salmon. In answer, I held my arms as wide apart as they'd go. She snorted, obviously not believing a good foot-and-a-half of it, then began triumphantly narrating her incomparably more tangible conquest: *They offered twenty-six. I pointed out more features—immaculate interior, garbage disposal, good schools. They wouldn't budge. So I mentioned the other interested parties* (a leprechaun wink)—*even though there weren't any. They panicked! Came all the way up to twenty-seven-five! Four percent of that mine! Except the tithe, of course—for Jesus. Not bad for an hour's work! You're my good-luck charm! You and your* fish. *What say we go get a banana split?*

What a strangeness, our overlapping realities. There was no doubt in my matriarch's mind that she had achieved the day's great feat and was wooing me toward similar greatness. But *I'd just glimpsed a messenger from the Vast Inside!*

Poor Gwamma Woe. Never more certain of our united course in life than at that moment. And I was already gone. Lost to matriarchy, Adventists, Gold Mansion Tracks. Gratefully lost—to deep woods and deeper waters, with a green and crimson compass gripped tight in my fist.

What the Second Troll Showed Me

So now I had an interior coho compass. *Find water*, it told me daily. But mine was hardly a culture, church, or family whose members employed salmon as compasses by which to direct their lives. A salmon, in my family's and culture's view, was a "resource" placed on Earth by God, so that human beings (which in our suburbs meant white folks) could "convert the resource"—via a process of commercial fishing, cooking, chewing, and swallowing—into ever-larger and more numerous white folks. To admire the flavor of the "resource" was allowable. Even to admire the resource's beauty was tolerated, though it might mean you were sexually unusual—hence the typical meat-fisherman's back-pedaling response to a captured salmon's beauty: "What a *hawg!*" But to *revere* the resource; to believe the resource in some sense lived inside us; to fuel this belief by worshiping the waters that spawned both this faith and its salmon—this was all, of course, a lot of unsaved, unwashed, heathen nonsense.

Yet Gwamma Woe's youngest grandson was suddenly full of just that.

I became the Hamlet of the Adventist church, lurking in back pews, haunted by a suspicion that something was rotten in the State of Rote Worship. I managed not to blame the followers on the Leader: I saw Jesus as an expert fisherman and non-Christian, same as I longed to be. But I did notice, as a born river-lover and tree-hugger, how Christ never really got cracking till John the Baptist dunked Him in a river, and never saved the world till He died on a tree. Jesus, as I saw it, needed Christianity and churches the way an ocean needs sailors and ships: i.e., not at all. It made no sense to me to demote the Cause (Jesus/the Ocean) of an effect (churches/ships) to the level of a mere occupant of the effect (Christian/sailor). So I didn't.

And with that conclusion, church became a stagnant pool in which I waited for rain, fresh flow, and escape. The real sacrificial dramas of the Northwest, the Christ-like activity, as I saw it, was taking place not in the buildings where Christians so brackishly tried to worship, but in the lives of the salmon I spontaneously *did* worship, for the way they poured in from the sea in defiance of every threat, predator and pharisee, climbed increasingly troubled mountain streams, nailed their beautiful bodies to lonely beds of gravel, and died there not for anything they stood to gain, but for the sake of tiny silver offspring.

Howell Raines, decades later, nailed my plight pretty well in his book *Fly Fishing Through the Midlife Crisis.* He wrote: "As I reflect more deeply on the fish's history as a mythic symbol and religious icon, I begin to wonder if having fish shapes around me is a way to stay in touch with the ideas of Jesus without having to go near the people who do business in his name." The big difference between Howell and me: I hit the crisis at age seven. One dying creek, one primordial coho, and I was longing to bust out into the natural, God-given world in the hope of further exploring a world within me. And, young though I was, there was no doubt in my mind as to how to go about this: *I needed to fish.* And not just in hose rivers. My intuition blasted me daily with the sense that real rivers had something crucial to teach, that this something lived in fluid darks and deeps, that I needed to lay literal hands on the literal life of these deeps.

My father fished now and then. I began hounding my father—failing to take into account the fact that fishing was what the poor guy did to escape his five kids, endless home fix-it projects, rocky marriage, and tedious electronics-plant job. I was as relentless as a force of nature, believing with the intensity of an Adventist preacher the dogma that nature *must* win in the end. But Dad, to my amazement, proved as resistant to my yearning as a Columbia River dam.

He did take me fishing two, three, maybe four times a year. And his favorite destination was also mine: the Oregon high desert, Crooked and Deschutes rivers. The drive took us up the Doug fir and alder slopes of the Cascades, over the timberline-touching south shoulder of Mount Hood, down the tamarack-and-ponderosa-pined backside of the range, then an impossible burst out of pine forest into vast, stark desert broken only by an occasional flat-topped butte, shockingly deep basalt canyon, stunted junipers, hawks, and sage. Every trip was an ecstasy for me. Each time out I saw places so beautiful I lost all interest in the gold gew-gaws of heaven. And the cast of characters! Raven! Meadowlark! Prairie falcon! Osprey! Eagle! Black bear! Coyote! Porcupine! Beaver! Cougar! Bullsnake! Rattlesnake! Chinook! Steelhead! Sockeye! Lamprey! Sturgeon! Desert rainbow! Salmonfly! Grasshopper! Mayfly! Lupine! Forget-me-not! Black-eyed Susan! I caught fish so magnificent that just to touch them was a healing. I beheld water so wild yet familiar I'd feel, for hours on end, that I was standing in the kingdom Christ said we carry within us. When my father would end these communions with a chipper "Time to head home!" I'd unashamedly weep. The instant we'd arrive home I'd begin begging for the next date of departure. And when Dad would answer with vague, politic phrases like "Couple, three weeks, maybe," I'd be incredulous. Wait "a couple three weeks" for *rivers?* Wait for ecstasy? Wait to revisit the kingdom?

Something had to be done.

My family moved twice during my boyhood. The first time was from the foot of the volcanic cone to a country lane nine miles east of Portland, called Rockwood Road. We had a huge vegetable garden there, a cherry/apple/peach orchard, eight long rows of three kinds of berries, fifty chickens, a yard big enough for baseball if it hadn't been for windows and foul balls, a large rose garden, a thick laurel hedge between us and the quiet road, and a row of stately, climbable maples just inside the hedge. Three Rockwood Road neighbors owned little Jeffersonian farms, and a fourth owned two hundred acres of ancient fir beginning behind our garden, which forest I freely roamed. Our front window faced Mount Hood—my way-marker to high-desert bliss. It took no effort on my part to consider our home an earthly paradise and me the luckiest bounder alive.

Then, one calm country morning, a chunk of basalt the size of a football crashed through the front window and landed on the couch. Turned out it was blown there by the dynamite of "a developer." I didn't know what a developer was. Or a metaphor, either. Over the next few months I found out.

First, we learned that state and federal highway planners had designated Rockwood Road as the main connecting artery between Interstate 84 and U.S. Highway 26. Next, our little road's name was changed to N.E. 181st. As a hydrophile and optimist, I rather liked this reminder that we lived exactly 181 blocks from Portland's east/west divider, the Willamette River. Then the highway department cut down our big maple trees, tore out our sheltering laurel hedge, widened the road to four lanes, ran a concrete sidewalk through our rose garden, traffic increased a hundredfold, and a car ran over my dog, Hunter. My parents got me another dog. I named it Hunter the Second. Two weeks later a bus ran over Hunter the Second. The Jeffersonian farms vanished beneath a multicolored acne of the dynamite developer's housing. Another developer snuck up from behind, converting the two-hundred-acre forest into another vast housing tract. There were suddenly no woods to wander, no dog to wander with, and we no longer knew our neighbors. Bikes began to be stolen, homes robbed or vandalized, the words *rape* and *abduction* entered our vocabularies. A sicko in an old Pontiac tried one day to steal me out of the now-hedgeless, unprotected yard. Another jolly old soul wagged his penis at my little sister while she stood waiting for the school bus. We learned never to leave the yard, never to talk to strangers, never to go anywhere alone, always to lock doors. In recognition of our changed circumstances, my father bought my brothers and me boxing gloves. First time I tried them, I was still just gawking at the bizarre look of the gloves themselves when a sizable new neighbor kid hit me flush on the jaw, I fell onto a concrete floor, hit my head, and was knocked out cold.

When I awoke, I no longer wanted to learn to box; I wanted forests, country roads, dog, trees, gardens, friends, farms, and freedom back.

Amazingly, I got them. When I was eight, my parents moved again to what felt like "country": this time a fir-tree-lined street called Osborne Road, twelve miles east of Portland, five rural miles from the town of Gresham. The population of Gresham, when we moved, was six thousand. Ten years later it was sixty thousand, Osborne Road had become N.E. 205th, my world was again destroyed, and so it keeps on going. But for a six-year hiatus, before Progress had its way with another big piece of the Primordial, I had daily access to a large piece of world more wild than tame.

My coho compass, meanwhile, had been thwarted. A spring a quarter-mile from our new house flowed into a series of backyard trout ponds for neighbors, but these ponds were picture-windowed, guard-dogged, private. The closest fish-inhabited waters to my house, so far as I knew, were the Columbia, three miles due north. But the Columbia was two miles wide, had treacherous currents and even more treacherous human visitors, and I was forbidden to go there. My father's yearning for rivers still maxed out at three or so visits a year. My own yearning beat me up daily. I needed fish shapes to stay in touch with the ideas of Jesus. I needed *Ka*. And one June day, I found it.

Riding my bike a mile east, to the general store in the postage-stamp-sized town of Fairview, I scored my vices of the era: one-cent Bazooka bubble gum, chewed five pieces at a time; five-cents-per-bag sunflower seeds jammed sixty or eighty at a time, in imagined preparation for chewing tobacco, into the corner of my cheek. I had just jammed my face full of this chipmunk chaw and set out for home when I heard—seemingly under the pavement of Halsey Street—a gruff voice yell, *"Son of a bitch! Gotcha! Ow! You shit!"*

I stopped for several reasons. One: I didn't cuss (yet), so the dialect interested me. Two: the voice was a boy's. Three: the boy was invisible. Four: despite his choice of words, he sounded very happy.

Further oaths drew me to a barn-red barber shop perched precariously at the point of a V created by two car-covered thoroughfares. *"You bastard!"* yelled the boy from nowhere. *"Come 'ere, ya lil' fucker! Ha! Gotcha!"* I hopped off my bike, found a cavelike opening under the west wall of the barbershop, peered down under, and there—in 3-D, living fairy tale—stood a rough-looking lout about my age, holding a galvanized bucket in one hand and a coat hanger he'd straightened into a spear in the other—both impressive in themselves. But the shocking thing, the magical thing, was that he was standing knee-deep in clear, lively creek water. A creek surrounded on all sides by briars so dense I'd never noticed it before. "Wanna see?" the troll asked, holding up his bucket.

Without a thought to shoes or clothes, I waded in beside him. His bucket was crawling with speared, mangled, and dying crawdads. The troll boy informed me—as I contemplated multicolored skeins of intestine trailing out of shattered shells—that their tails and claws, once boiled, shelled, and dipped in French's Mustard, were delicious. I laughed. Yeah, right. But his ludicrous suggestion didn't make the prospect of standing in a creek catching some of these exotic creatures any less attractive.

I pedaled the mile back home, grabbed a bucket and a coat hanger of my own, told my mother I was going crawdadding, returned to the preposterous bridge barbershop, heard splashing beneath, slipped under—but this time was alarmed to discover an entirely different troll. Bigger. Wilier-looking. And sneaking away—after a single surly glance back at me—by tramping right down the creekbed through the tunnel of briars. Before he vanished, though, I saw that in one hand he held not a spear but a fishing pole, and in the other not a crayfish but a fresh-caught, still-flopping trout.

No Christmas or birthday moment has ever compared: a mile from my house, beneath a magic barbershop, True North on the coho compass: *a secret trout stream.* I tore back home, ditched the bucket and hanger, grabbed a pole, hooks, and split-shot, rode back to the creek, caught crawdads bare-handed, crushed the life out of them without compunction, used the tails and claw meat for bait, and by suppertime had caught, absolutely solo, my first two native cutthroat trout.

N a t i v e   T e a c h e r

Fairview Creek, it turned out, was five miles long, two-thirds wild, and amazingly full of life. Over the next six years I probed its every side-piddle, run, and pool from the gravel-pit source to the Mud Lake mouth, catching hundreds of its cutthroat. Their size shocked everyone. Though they averaged seven or eight inches, the largest I landed was over eighteen inches, and I caught scores around a foot: quite a specimen in a creek just a yard or two wide.

I discovered other life in the currents. In the gravel pits at the headwaters I caught stocked rainbow trout. Near the Multnomah Kennel Club's greyhound racetrack in Fairview, in a small pond hidden by raspberry rows, I plunked for bullhead catfish, cooling my feet in the water. I then noticed, after catching a few cats, that leeches—two on each ankle—had meanwhile been catching me. In the plunge-pool below the Banfield Freeway culvert, I caught a thirteen-inch Giant Pacific Salamander that stared straight into my eyes, flaring and hissing like something out of Dante Volume One, till I apologized, cut my line, and released it. In the deep, cottonwood-lined meanders down near

Mud Lake, I caught channel cats, enormous carp, bluegill, crappie, perch, bass, and a couple of cutthroat approaching two pounds.

Giving way to full obsession, I fished the creek an easy fifty, sixty times a year. There turned out to be interesting problems to work out. I was chased by police, many times, at the gravel-pit ponds, arrested for trespass near the Mud Lake mouth, and run out of yards and off farms by irate landowners, scary teen bullies, and a variety of militant dogs. Did the chasings and arrests combine to "teach me a lesson"? Absolutely. I learned to be *much* sneakier. The moral ambiguities of private-property issues, though, had been resolved for me in a 1964 publication called *Trout Fishing in America,* in which one Justice Richard Brautigan gave this verdict:

No Trespassing
$^4/_{17}$ of a haiku

The fishing koan for me, ever since, has not been whether to trespass but how not to get caught.

I learned to fish the gravel-pit ponds on moonlit nights or at first light, to avoid the watchmen and cops. I learned to drift a worm and bobber down into the backyards of those who forbade trespass, skiing fish back up to where I legally stood. (This twice so impressed people who had no idea their creek even held trout that they gave me permission to trespass for life.) I learned to clean up a big pile of creekside garbage and hold it sincerely under one arm before knocking on the porch of a landowner to ask permission to fish. I used the mailman's trick—a pocketful of Milk Bones—to tame the dogs.

I grew wily as a fisherman. I worked the creek's skinny headwaters in April and May, before buttercups completely closed over the surface. I plied the Mud Lake terminus in summer heat, when the trout had gone into hiding but big warm-water fish were on the prowl. I learned to be invisible and silent to trout. I once lay so quiet on a low wooden sheep bridge that a muskrat swam almost into my hands. (Thinking myself hilarious, I lunged forward and went *BOOO!* at the muskrat, inspiring a lightning quick flip-ass escape dive that drove a quart or so of muddy water up under my eyelids.) I took pruning shears to impassable tunnels of briars, cutting my way back into secret, sunless holes from which I snaked large, nearly black cutthroat. I learned to sight-fish for warily cruising carp—and thirty years later applied the same knowledge to catch bonefish and tarpon. It all empowered me. In fact,

I bewildered my father, every Opening Day six years in a row, by refusing invitations to visit the high-desert rivers I loved best. I then dissipated his bewilderment, six years in a row, by bringing home ten-fish limits of Fairview Creek trout. The thing about the creek: I didn't have to just visit; it was home.

I did much more (however inadvertently) than fish. To spend so much time on a single body of water is to encounter every life-form that water supports. My presence in small marshes and thickets so seldom trod by humans enabled me to catch baby killdeer, baby mallard, baby cottontails in my hands. I stood face-to-face with one of the last blacktail deer ever sighted in East Multnomah County, and glimpsed perhaps the very last fox, which a teen idiot named Booth, no doubt related to John Wilkes, promptly shot. I stumbled onto wood ducks, raccoons, ringneck and lost golden pheasants, possums, turtles; I ran into horned owls and herons, Indians and winos, gregarious winter wrens, kinglets, and joyously fucking teenagers. I learned survival in the creek's two utterly different, confounded worlds—learned, for instance, via terrifying encounters and one painfully lost fight, how to spot and quickly duck hoodlums, but also learned how to build lean-tos in a rainstorm, make small, smokeless fires, create hobo meals of fare I'd find along the creek (stolen corn, green bean, onion, and catfish borscht simmered in a tossed Van Camp's bean can; filberts, apples, blackberries, raspberries collected in an old Dairy Queen cup; the entire heart of a watermelon lifted from a stack of fifty at a crowded company picnic; and of course trout, obscenely fileted with a pocket-knife, broiled on a willow spit.

In this age of rapid-fire, unconsidered change, I suppose that anyone older than five or six is the relic of some sort of lost era. For my part, I'm one of the last Americans raised close to a major city who learned what he knows not just from sitting in thirty desks crammed into eight successive classrooms, or from tough night streets, or from TV screens (though I knew these too), but from full immersion in wind, rain, forest loam, brush, briars, and clean and fouled air, water, and dirt. I gleaned my working knowledge of flora and fauna by being the Huck Finn–style confidant, lover, and terror of a five-mile-long ribbon of life, sticking my hands, feet, nose, eyeballs, tongue, ears, and body into a thousand places they did and thousand places they didn't belong. I learned by tasting and feeling things, poking at things, gathering, stealing, stalking, killing, cleaning, cooking, and eating things; learned by letting things mesmerize, dazzle, and hypnotize me, forming the million impressions that, when I'd collapse in bed at night, became an equally informative scramble of impression/nightmare/vision/prayer/ dream. I learned from Tri-Met bus exhaust and Southern Pacific locomotive smoke, from Crown Zellerbach papermill stench and Reynolds Aluminum effluent, from cottonwood fluff on May pools, tractor dust in July beanfields, October cricket songs waning and geese songs waxing, savage November storms, sudden December snows, frozen January peace.

For six years the living chaos that was Fairview Creek flowed, unmediated, through my hair, fingers, brain-halves, and heart-valves, teaching me that the world is peaceful and absolutely dangerous, wild and artificial, beautiful and wounded, healthy and sick. For six years, in other words, I studied with the most perfect teacher I can imagine for life in the America in which I've lived ever since.

Bodies of Blood and Water

Two weeks before my fourth consecutive Fairview Creek Opening Day, my eldest brother died, at seventeen, of a series of failed open-heart surgeries. The little creek's presence, its flow, its ability to keep generating life, helped me a little with this grief. The ten Opening Day trout I caught that year felt different from any I'd caught before. Their deaths especially felt different: the concept of sacrifice had begun to invade my fishing. I could articulate nothing, but big feelings swept over me as I snapped each neck—and what an eerie version of fisherman pride I felt when my family and I, we "survivors," sat down to eat the little bodies whose lives I'd taken. Men, women, and children, I had suddenly realized, were dying—and no one seemed to notice but the funeral parlors who'd turned death into an industry. But each time I bloodied my hands, killing a trout as innocent as my dead brother, I noticed. Each time I killed a trout, the pain would ease for a time inside me. Why? Christ. You tell me. I sensed a depth, in the act of killing fish, that spoke to my grief. A consciously snapped trout-neck was like a blues-string consciously bent against the day-to-day industrial harmonies. And a bent note, in the ears of the sorrow-bent, rings truer than a note clean-struck. Nothing soothes quite like the blues. A little trout stream, if played for keeps, can be a miles-long blues tune.

By my seventh Fairview Creek Opening Day, I'd grown so confident in my abilities and body of water that I bet a high-school pal five bucks

Valmiki's Palm

I'd take a seventh straight ten-fish limit. My five-mile teacher had a strange lesson for me.

At six-thirty or so on a rainy April morning, I crept up to a favorite hole, threaded a worm on a hook, prepared to cast—then noticed something impossible: there was no water in the creek. I gaped numbly at mud and exposed rock, then up at the falling rain. The sky was doing its job, had been doing it all April. How could this be? I began hiking, stunned, downstream. The aquatic insects were gone, barbershop crawdads gone, catfish, carp, perch, crappie, bass, countless sacrifical cutthroats, not just dying, but completely vanished. Feeling sick, I headed the opposite way, hiked the emptied creekbed all the way to the source, and there found the eminently rational cause of the countless killings. Development needs roads and drainfields. Roads and drainfields need gravel. Up in the gravel pits at the Glisan Street headwaters, the creek's entire flow had been diverted for months in order to fill two gigantic new settling ponds.

My favorite teacher was dead.

I was sixteen, drove a car now. I didn't know enough to rage, protest, or grieve. I felt so panic-stricken by Fairview Creek's death that I tried—as if attempting to keep a stranded fish alive in a bucket—to transfer my need for water, whole, to the other stream in easy driving distance: Johnson Creek, source of my first glimpse of a coho and an inner realm. But a decade and fifty thousand industrious new human inhabitants had been murder on this old friend, too. I encountered none of the magic of Fairview Creek, little of the wildlife, no native fish species, few of the birds. Johnson Creek's only catchable trout were drab hatchery rainbows, planted in March by Fish and Wildlife to entertain local yokels on the April Opening Day. By May, no one fished for them because the same Fish and Wildlife people pronounced them too toxic to eat.

I kept after them, though. I was old enough, now, to know a metaphor when I hooked one: I was fascinated by the trout's growing discoloration, growing scarcity, growing weakness. I entered a zone, fished Johnson Creek hard. By June it was low, warm, filmy, and the trouts' living skins had burst out in a pox of strange, clear bubbles. By midmonth the rainbows had stopped taking any kind of bait or fly, but I'd still see one drift past now and then, in a flotilla of foam, sometimes belly-up, sometimes weakly finning. One hot June day I managed to catch a few suckers near the creek's terminus with the Willamette: they were on a spawning run, hadn't been in the creek long enough to be killed by it. One July day, near the 55th Street bridge, my catch was a discarded car radio and a woman's dress (red, with small white polka dots; short; sexy; poisonously sopped). Another day it was twenty bags of rotten meat and vegetables floating along in Ziploc bags, looking like twenty disembodied stomachs still trying to digest their meals. By August, and drought, my new native teacher was an oil-scummed, fetid, foam-flecked sewer, there were warnings posted on phone poles telling kids not to swim, and even the hatchery trout of June seemed like a comparatively beautiful vision. On one of the last days I fished Johnson Creek, I waded into a nice-looking run, knelt low, cast a fly up into the riffle, noticed a more-offensive-than-usual stench coming from the creekbank behind me, turned—and started gagging at the sight of the crawling, maggot-filled head of a horse.

I pronounced Johnson Creek, too, something worse than dead.

There was a gigantic commercial nursery near my home, the whole thing full of skinny ten- to fifteen-foot trees—maples, most of them—planted by machines in perfectly straight, quarter-mile-long rows. I passed them often in my teens, late at night, after I'd been out catting around with friends. If it was past curfew and headlights approached, I'd duck into the long rows to hide. One night, after the car passed, I hung back in the skinny trees, suddenly fascinated by their situation.

In the muggy summer heat a faint, forestlike coolness could be felt amid the maples. Yet it didn't console like a forest's cool. These trees felt haunted. Trying to think why, I noticed that my feet, as I strolled the nursery, fell silent in thick, black Willamette Valley soil—soil created by consecutive millennia of thick, mossy, two-hundred-foot-tall ancient firs. To make way for our suburbs, those groves had been eradicated. These anorexic maples were now trying their best to replace the primordial giants. And though they stood in the summer dark, doing that dignified thing that even tiny trees do—which is to say, in dead earnest, *Here*, then grow—somehow it wasn't working. The endless perfect rows, the military order, undermined their earnest effort. *None of this is their fault*, I felt as I walked the night-black nursery. *But look at them. This is no forest. It's an arsenal: every tree for sale, destined to be uprooted, bound in burlap, shipped out. So all their earnestness—all the downward groping of roots, upward yearning of limbs, careful breathing of leaves—is going to be betrayed.*

Then it hit me: How could I, or any boy of those Vietnam-bound suburbs, not feel exactly as betrayed as these trees?

Valmiki's Palm

Crash-Test Dummy

My two best boyhood mentors were a brother and a creek, both now dead. My coho compass seemed to die with Johnson Creek. I still loved rivers. But rivers don't come with you to school or ball games, don't brother you when you're haunted, don't speak English, don't intellectualize. So—linguistically, socially, fraternally, intellectually—I felt alone and unguided. The fishing talk of the best anglers I knew—honest working stiffs, men I guardedly liked—was a lingo of technique, conquest, and gloat. The rivers within driving distance—the Columbia, Clackamas, Sandy—were the domain of fishermen who on their work days helped destroy rivers and on their off days plundered them. There was no one to whom I could even mention such perceptions. Love for animals, birds, wilderness, led to no A's on report cards. If Henry Thoreau or Gary Snyder had attended my giant suburban high school, they'd have dropped out if they hadn't been expelled. If they had taught, they would definitely have been fired. There would be no coho questions on my SAT exams. Free-flowing streams made no campaign contributions to senators—and look what happened to them as a result. A big trout sipping a mayfly may be a veritable hymn to the health of a watershed, but no TV or newspaper in those days covered that hymn. On TV and in the papers I watched businessmen, economists, politicians place a dollar value on everything on Earth and discount anything that lacked such a value. I knew this was wrong—knew that if everything was material, then everything was negotiable and one's body, home, friendships, honesty, honor, could all be bought or sold. I then watched American democracy itself be bought and sold; watched the TV war escalate in Asia, the campus and race riots escalate at home; watched a patriotic foster brother die almost the day he set foot in Vietnam; watched Martin Luther King and Bobby Kennedy die for expressing compassion and love of justice; watched people who define things in the crassest, most material way get what they wanted over and over; watched evil, mortality, and stupidity win and win and win.

There came a time, in adolescence, when I questioned every last thing my heart had intimated to me since childhood. All this "nature stuff" suddenly felt too hard to articulate to bosses, teachers, parents, too airy-fairy to share with red-blooded three-sport pals. My unchecked river-love suddenly struck me as a way to achieve numb-nutted poverty, cultural irrelevancy, and maybe a stint in Vietnam.

I began to want to get what *I* wanted. And what I'd begun to want, I came to believe, was not richness, not meaning, not interior truth or depth: I wanted a skin so thick this world couldn't hurt me. A skin I'd open, now and then, if the right-looking kind of girl wanted in. But only briefly.

Hoping to create such a skin, I began to crash-test everything I'd ever loved or trusted, then pick through the wreckage to see what had survived. I crash-tested my connection to creeks and rivers in the simplest way possible: I abandoned them. Quit seeking wild water. Tried my best to quit yearning for it, too.

Taking aim at nothing I couldn't eat, feel, fool, fuck, or buy, I became the most disingenuous and troublesome of high-school students, landed a series of the best-paying jobs I could find, became a cog in the purposeless box of industrial gears that had appalled me as a child, and "repaid myself" for this sense of purposelessness by granting myself every pleasure I could grasp.

I began to grow that thick skin. The sensation scared me for a bit. But life, as I was living it, thickened me so fast that I was soon unable to feel even my fear.

Valmiki's Palm

At seventeen I took a full-time summer job at a plastics factory in the industrial heart of Portland. I then began, after work, to wander the city in the company of my fine new principle of depravity, seeking whatever pleasures I could physically grasp.

One day I happened to drop into a disheveled little used bookstore: the cram-packed, cigarette-singed '69 vintage Powell's Books, as it happens. I read books as a hedonist in those days, read them to trip. Looking for the wildest but least expensive possible ride, I impulse-purchased a musty verse translation of the *Ramayana*, and headed home.

I knew, from having read Homer's *Odyssey*, that epics were a trip. I knew, from reading a remark made by Snyder or Tolkien or somebody, that the *Ramayana*—the story of the prehistoric king Rama—was India's greatest epic. But the translation I'd purchased in a post-work stupor told King Rama's story in wrenched, rhyming Victorian couplets that made even epic battles and ancient wisdom sound like the chuggity-chugging sentiments of an interminable Hallmark card. I soon threw the book away.

Before I did, though, I took one small wonder to heart:

The *Ramayana*'s author—the legendary forest poet Valmiki—states in his opening verses that he did not use his imagination while composing Rama's story. He didn't need imagination, he said, because at dawn each day he took an urn to the nearby river, filled it, carried it to his hut, sat down on an eastward-facing mat, then scooped a little river water in his palm: in this tiny body of water Valmiki saw first Rama, then Rama's wife, Sita, then every god, demon, and hero, every love dalliance and bloody battle, in his epic. Fragrances and sounds, too, rose from the water: the smoke of brahmanic sacrifices, stench of demons, cries of warriors and their victims, hissing flight of arrows, blood-burst of every wound. The poet simply sang what he saw. All 25,000 *Ramayana* verses were enacted, first, in the water in Valmiki's palm.

I was smitten by this. The notion that an epic could spring from a palmful of river gave me a jolt of the liturgical joys a garden-hose river and a three-inch fishing soldier had once given. Thanks to the insufferable Victorian prosody and my cynical teen self, this joy didn't last long. In honor of Valmiki, though, I developed a tic: I took to glancing at my own palms, dozens of times a day, as if at a pocketwatch; as if I expected them to tell me something. Just a nervous habit, I suppose. Because of it, though, I came to see that palms have skin like no other part of the body: the moisture; visible texture; almost legible-looking lines. I learned the palms' topography—those four ominous little canyons in which palm-readers claim to see secrets of the head, heart, fate, and life span. I saw that palms, compared to fists or fingers, have no agenda—that they're not a weapon, not a tool, not a talon, just a handy portable shelf. Though I tossed the *Ramayana* and wandered off in search of some more satisfyingly sensual trip, I couldn't shake my palm-reading tic.

The plastics factory that employed me produced a tough red polyurethane, dubbed Redskin, from which we made indescribable geometrical gizmos we simply called "parts." These parts were shipped to other factories to be attached to larger indescribable gizmos, which were shipped to still other factories and attached to indescribable mechanical devices, which were in turn shipped and fixed to larger machines. Five or six removes from us, rumor had it, our "Redskin" gizmos became part of something you could actually name: a raspberry-picking machine. We had no way to verify this, but our bosses told us so and we believed them. We were Americans, after all. What could be more American than manufacturing plastic crap called Redskin to produce a machine that put the real, destitute, flesh-and-blood "redskins," who in those days picked Oregon's raspberries, out of work?

I lived, at the time, next door to a raspberry farm harvested by impoverished Indians. And I liked those Indians. I didn't feel sorry for those our Redskin helped put out of work, though. The reason I didn't was this: we were being severely punished for our crime. Redskin Plant management had, it seemed, deemed the slow torture of workers an acceptable cost of the Redskin manufacturing process. What better revenge could the real Indians want?

The torture weapon was not an object, but a lack of objects. In the time I worked at Redskin I saw no blue-collar employee spend a single hour working with materials that weren't toxic, yet I never saw a respirator, an exhaust fan, a gauze mask. We spent every day stoned on fumes, and no employees expressed resentment over this. In fact, plant morale was high. I think it had to do with Vietnam, which, in turn, had to do with childhoods spent in suburbs, in arsenals, in pews, immaculate interiors, fake democracies, every thing and everyone destined to be sold, uprooted, bound in burlap, shipped out. Every Redskin worker seemed to have an AMERICA: LOVE IT OR LEAVE IT bumper sticker on his vehicle and seemed grateful to be spending his *prana,* health, and precious allotment of heartbeats making incomprehensible polyurethane gizmos. The typical Redskin Plant attitude was, "I'm nonunion, I'm underpaid, I'm making nothing I understand, I'm breathing shit, I'll be dying young. And I'm *proud of it!*"

The plant president was our inspiration. As president, he worked in an upstairs office where it was not necessary to breathe fumes. Like a good Civil War officer, though, he led the charge into death anyway— by voluntarily smoking five packs of mentholated Kent 100's per day. I'd seen chain-smokers manage four packs. The Redskin president was my first—and soon, last—five-pack-a-day guy. What gave him the edge was a big brass lighter on his desk. It looked like a set of golf clubs standing in a filthy sandtrap full of butts. When you flicked the driver, though, a flame shot rather obscenely out of the putter—a trick the president found so amusing that he did it more often than possible, so to speak, and often had two or even three cigarettes going at once.

My job, as plant lackey, was of a janitorial nature. I cleaned up spills, mostly. Redskin started out as a stew of toxic liquids that were mixed together in vats, poured into molds, placed on racks, rolled into a huge walk-in oven, baked to hardness, rolled back out, and removed as hardened "parts." There were spills at every fluid stage of this process, and spilled polyurethane quickly fuses with anything it touches. Once hardened, the only way to remove the stuff is with an acetone solvent— also toxic. I spent my Redskin career blitzed on solvent.

One of my daily tasks took place in Dumpster bins. Even after they'd been emptied into garbage trucks, the sides and bottoms of our bins remained caked with enormous slabs of waste Redskin. It was my job to climb in the Dumpster, pour solvent on the slabs, let it work awhile, then attack the now-gooey Redskin with a giant C-clamp. The clamp was hooked to a steel cable, which attached to the overhead hydraulic lift. Blinded by tears from solvent fumes, terrifically stoned by them, I'd screw my C-clamp to the biggest, meanest flap of Redskin I could find, hit the Up button on the hydraulic lift's remote, and hope the weight of the Dumpster and me would together tear the slab free while I was still fairly close to the ground. When the slab didn't tear, I'd just continue toward the ceiling, too fume-ripped to tell the Up button from the Down. It was a thirty-foot ceiling. I don't recall dropping a Dumpster from the top—management really didn't like that. But when a Redskin slab tore loose even at eight or ten feet, the Dumpster crashed to the floor with a force that brought a roar of laughter from the other workers, knowing I lay in a swamp of half-dissolved plastics inside. I laughed too, if only to show that I was tough.

Another job of mine was cleaning the walk-in oven. Every time a rack of fresh-filled molds was rolled in, liquid Redskin dripped onto the oven floor. These drips built up after each firing, creating bumps that caused more spillage. My task was to pour solvent on the bumps, then hack them free with a garden hoe. Since "time is money," though, and cooling and reheating the oven took time, the plant foreman considered 140 degrees Fahrenheit "Can-Do" cleaning conditions. At 140 degrees my solvent vaporized the instant it touched the floor, turning the oven into a blinding, brain-fogging sweat lodge. The foreman would stand by the open oven door, watching me scamper into the lodge, throw solvent on bumps, run back out, take a breath, run back in, hoe bumps, run back out, take a breath, run in, hoe, run out, till the floor was smooth. His vigilance was not a kindness. Dead workers waste time, which is money.

Most Redskin parts had thin, sloppy edges created by a skin of plastic that had overflowed its mold. We removed this skin by hand, with X-Acto knives. It was the kind of skin that I too wanted. Tough as hell.

Six weeks into my crash-test job, after yet another toxic sweat in the oven, I sat down at my work station, fetched my X-Acto, and began trimming sloppy edges from a box of parts, feeling, as I worked, as if time and space were drunk and my mind was dipped in plastic and indispensible parts of me were dying and so the fuck what. I was making eight hundred dollars a month to feel this way.

I fetched another part, trimmed away another red edge. Fetched another. Trimmed another. Then something happened: feeling a faint swirl in my left palm, I glanced down—and saw a silver fin crease the surface of my skin.

"Trout," I murmured, too oven-stoned for surprise.

A trout had risen in my left palm. Hmm. My nervous tic was finally producing the goods. The trout's dorsal lazed up into sight and stayed there; broke the surface, making no ripples, and stayed there. I'd seen a lot of fish in my day, but never one rising from inside me. Half-forgotten river thoughts began to swim through my head. *How did a trout get in me? What did it do in there all day? Did it rise to sip some kind of fly?*

Then a second set of notions slopped through me. That something as fragile as a trout could survive inside the Redskin Plant seemed even more unlikely than that one could live inside my hand. So what were my hand and I doing in the Redskin Plant? I grew aware of a throbbing that never left my body, realized it was the digestive rumbling of the whole dark building, felt it sucking at my limbs, my lungs, my life.

I grew less vaguely aware. I looked at the men with whom I worked and joked all day—the black rings beneath their eyes, lethargic movements, liquid plastics splashed on clothes and skin. Then a third wave struck: gazing once more at my palm, I suddenly began to gasp. Like a fresh-beached salmon I began gasping for life, my entire body needing clear running water, moss-trimmed cedars, clean-pebbled streambeds, the vast, preacherless church of the wild so badly that my eyes filled not with fume-tears but with real tears and my palm—*could this be happening?*—began to bleed, right from the rise. I watched blood stream down my fate-line like water down a riparian, watched it fall, then pool, on the factory floor.

It took me the longest time to realize I'd stuck the X-Acto through my hand from the opposite side and was staring at the tip of its blade in my palm. It took so long that, in the end, I reacted not to a blade but to a trout's rise—and began trying to rise myself.

Valmiki's Palm

Taking fresh aim at life and water, I told my Redskin cohorts that we were dying, quit my job, bought a box of thirty-nine-cent trout flies, an inexpensive rod kit, a bunch of wilderness maps. I built myself a glass fly rod. I then began—like a blind man with a nine-foot cane—to feel my way back toward things I had loved and trusted.

The palm of a hand is impassive. Fists and fingers have their agendas, but what rests in a palm is free to tell its silent truth. In the years since a steel dorsal rose in my fate-line I have waded the flow of hundreds of wild streams, held thousands of trout and salmon in my hands, watched a million silver rises. To this day I sometimes cup a little river in my pierced palm, cool the tiny scar, check for signs of life there. To this day I keep thanking Valmiki.

The light of the body is the eye: if therefore thine eye be single, thy whole body shall be full of light. But if thine eye be evil, thy whole body shall be full of darkness.

—Jesus, in Matthew 6:22–23

Dazzling and tremendous how quick the sunrise would kill me If I could not now and always send sunrise out of me.

—Walt Whitman

2. Birdwatching as a Blood Sport

On certain nights when I was a boy, I used to lie in bed in the dark, unable to sleep, because of eyes. Staring, glowing eyes, arrayed in a sphere all around me. The eyes seemed to be alive, though they were not visibly attached to bodies, or to faces. They were not, so to speak, attached to emotions, either: they conveyed no menace, no affection, no curiosity, no consternation. They just watched me with a vigilance as steady and beautiful as the shining of stars at night.

Because their beauty was so evident, the eyes would not have troubled me were it not for this: I couldn't escape them. They had the ability to go on staring whether my own eyes were open or shut: they could, in other words, move with me *after* I'd close my eyes, from the real into the imaginary world. I was in awe of this power. My mother and father, the moon and sun, the entire world would vanish when I closed my eyes. The eyes in the sphere did not. And I didn't even know whose eyes they were!

I told my big brother about the sphere, and asked if he'd ever seen such a thing. His reply was confident, but not too consoling: he laughed, and told me I'd flipped my lid. I tried my mother. She too laughed, and blurted, "What an imagination!" I let her know, with reluctance, that I did not consider the eyes imaginary. "If they're not imaginary," she said, laughing no longer, "you should ask Jesus to make them go away!"

I did ask Jesus. But the eyes went right on staring. And though I spoke of them no more, I was glad this was Christ's response to my prayer. The sphere of eyes had watched me many times by now. It had never threatened or damaged me. It was intense. It was beautiful. Why should I want it to go away? That no one but me seemed to see such things—this was a worry. But the sphere's sudden appearance in bed-time darkness felt like a wonder out of some old myth or fairy tale, and I *wanted* my life to feel like an ancient myth or tale. So. Much as I wanted to know more about the eyes—who they belonged to, what they wanted of me—I quit worrying and let them blaze away. I had no choice anyway.

In late winter, when I was ten, I made perhaps my first conscious connection between the mysteries of the inner life and those of the outer world. It happened on a long hike through a doomed suburban forest, when I spotted the largest nest I'd ever seen in the top of a tow-ering, unclimbable-looking cottonwood tree. Partly to dumbfound the older boys I was with, partly out of incomprehensible yearning, I began shinnying up the limbless lower trunk. A few harrowing minutes and ninety or so feet later, I was clinging to tiny branches just under the massive nest, and two magnificent great horned owls were circling the treetop within twenty feet of me. Circling, and staring—till somewhere inside I felt it: *the sense of a sphere. Vigilant, unreadable eyes, watching. Me at the center . . .*

The nest was so wide and the trunk beneath so narrow there was no way to climb, or even see, up into the nest. I therefore reached—blindly, courageously, and incredibly foolishly—into the nest with a bare hand. I learned later that had it contained owlets I would have been attacked, and possibly killed, when the adults knocked me out of my precarious perch. But though their orbit of the tree became tighter and they began to let out quiet cries, the owls did not attack; as luck would have it, my groping hand found not owlets but two large, warm eggs. Again out of mixed motives—bravado, yearning, a pagan fantasy to possess my own magnificent bird—I stuck one egg in my coat pocket, and shinnied back down the tree.

The boys below greeted me with everything a conquering hero could hope for: praise for my climbing, awe of my defiance of the adult owls, envy of my booty. "You crazy asshole!" one of them kept saying, in a way that made clear his desire to be thought the same. But seeing the mother owl return to the nest, knowing the egg beneath her was now destined to be raised alone, the word "crazy" struck me as too kind. I was just a garden-variety asshole. I'd done something stupid, knew it, and knew I lacked the strength and courage to climb the tree again and undo it.

I tried to correct my mistake in a more arcane way: leaving my friends and their embarrassing praise, I trudged home through the woods, keeping a warm hand around the egg the entire way, then fetched a shoe box, a soft towel, and a lamp with a flexible neck, wrapped the egg in the towel, bent the lamp over it, and began trying to convince myself that I had created a viable nest.

To my amazement, the egg *was* convinced: that night it began to hatch. And the next morning my mother, knowing real education when she saw it, let me stay home from school to watch. It was a surprisingly arduous process. From first crack to full emergence took twenty hours: eggs, judging by this one, are no easier to escape than wombs. The owlet was four inches long, naked, and exhausted at birth, its pink flesh blurred by an outlandish aura of slush-colored fuzz. Its eyes were enormous, but covered with bluish skin: no staring, no sense of the mysterious sphere this time. In fact I'd never seen a pair of eyes look less likely to open and see—for I was their adoptive mother.

The owlet rested briefly after breaking free, then commenced a ceaseless, open-beaked, wobbly begging. Panicked by the conviction in its body language, I phoned the zoo, reached its birdkeeper, received a scolding for my nest-robbing and a prediction of doom, but still proffered the tweezered egg, raw hamburger, and eye-droppered milk the keeper recommended. Again, to my amazement, the owlet responded. It enjoyed my cooking, it suffered my touch, it responded to my mothering precisely long enough to make me love it. Only then did it proceed to die. And even at birth, horned owls are tough. It took a full day to stop eating, two days to stop begging, another half day to stop writhing and die.

What did not die—what lives in me even now—are the circling, vigilant eyes of the parent owls.

Birdwatching as a Blood Sport

Vigilant, glowing eyes, *arrayed in a sphere all around me . . .* Even to mention such a thing puts me—both as a storyteller and as a character in my own story—in way over my head. Yet if deeper truths do indeed dwell in depths, there would seem to be no way to reach them without some risk of drowning.

There I'd lie, then, once in an unpredictable while, year after boy-hood year, surrounded by eyes. Eyes that always appeared after the room was dark, the house quiet, and I lay still, yet far from sleep. They did not appear by opening, or by moving toward me out of a distance; they just eased into visibility the way stars do at dusk. They never blinked, never retreated, never glanced to either side. They watched me, period: a mystery intelligible to me only as mystery. Yet by no other eyes have I felt so purely perceived.

In appearance they were distinctly nonhuman. They reminded me of angels, and of animal eyes suddenly lit by the headlights of cars, and of neither of these. They varied in size, or else stared at me from vary-ing distances. They varied in color, too. I recall shades of green, yellow, orange, all of which seemed dangerously wrong to my church-fed idea of angels. It also seemed angelically wrong, but beautifully so, that these colors glowed.

A final over-my-head mystery: the eyes in the sphere would array themselves not just in front of me but above, below, and behind me. What I mean to imply is a physical impossibility. The sphere of eyes was visible in *all* directions. In its thousandfold presence I became a point of pure perception suspended inside an encompassing globe. For a long time I drew no conclusions from this: I just basked in it. As I grew older, though, I deduced that I must not see the sphere through physi-cal eyes, or even through my mind's eye, but through an eye I hadn't been aware of possessing—an eye that can see in all directions at once.

Nothing else on earth had enabled me to see in this way. Nothing had ever watched me this way. So no matter how many times the sphere came, I felt awestruck by its every arrival. Awestruck, and compelled, no matter how late the hour, to stare back. But to be sur-rounded and stared at creates an air of huge expectation. In the eyes' presence, something enormously good or enormously bad always seemed about to happen. This kind of suspense is exhausting, so it was always I who lost consciousness, leaving the eyes to stare at no one. Until—one winter not long before adolescence—I realized that for weeks now, or maybe months, the vigilant sphere had ceased to visit me.

I've seen nothing like the sphere of eyes since. But I've described my recurring vision (or pathosis) for a reason: I have continued now and then to encounter actual bird eyes—like those of the circling great horned owls—that suddenly struck me as living refugees of that mysterious sphere. I've even begun, thanks to these ongoing encounters, to suspect that the sphere, though unseen, might in some way still surround me . . .

In 1968, just days after receiving my first driver's license, I am motoring through a small town in a nighttime line of commuter traffic when I see, in the headlight beams of the car ahead of me, a small brown ball rolling in the street. The car does not slow as it drives over the ball. Seeing no kids at the curb, I too chose not to slow. Then the ball rolls out from under the car in front, appears in my own headlights, and I see that it is not a ball, but a balled-up screech owl.

It's uninjured, but blown off its feet. And, having failed to slow, I now have no choice but to straddle it. It stares straight into my headlights, eyes glowing as I take aim—and I feel myself fall, once again, into a watched center, feel something very good or bad about to happen. Then it does. Just as I pass over, the owl catches its balance, gathers itself for a leap into flight, and I feel—in the soles of my feet, my legs, and all the way up my spine—the fatal thud of its head against the bottom of my car. I see, in the rearview mirror, the epileptic thrashing and cloud of feathers, see the next car, too, run it over, and the next and the next. I do not go back. I already know that I can revere a creature, mother a creature, want nothing but to love a creature, yet still kill it. I also know that what cannot be killed—what remains with me even now—is that glowing moment's contact with its eyes.

Highway 101, Tillamook County, Oregon. Again alone in a car, on the bridge over Beaver Creek, I turn toward the railing and see a solitary snipe (*Gallinago gallinago*). My field guide calls the snipe "a secretive bird of peat bogs, marshes, and sodden fields." This one is standing, as calm and incongruous as a would-be bus passenger, right on the bridge's concrete sidewalk. I immediately brake—having learned the necessity of this from a brown ball, years before. But as I pass by, the snipe doesn't fly. It doesn't even flinch. Knowing something isn't right, I pull over, walk back to the bridge, and creep up on the bird, hoping it won't flush out in front of a passing truck or car. It just watches me. I move in close, cup it in my hands. No struggle. The snipe just stares.

I stand it in my palm. Free to fly, the bird remains in my open hand, a child's dream—the wild creature you can pet—come true. I stare at it. It stares at me. Cars come and go. The bird radiates warmth. My hand returns it. The sphere closes around us. It is the peace of the sphere itself, I believe, that keeps me from seeing for so long that the entire top of the bird's skull is gone.

I carry the snipe under the bridge, sit cross-legged by the creek where no one can see me, and stand it again in my palm. I then begin trying to concoct a rite that will remove the treachery from a mercy killing. I start with simple admiration: the camouflage plumage; saber-shaped tailfeathers; earth-probe bill; black pearl eyes. I then try memory: fishing alone on the wide-open estuaries, I had come upon many a *Gallinago gallinago,* and the memorable encounters had all been the same. Silent and unseen, from high in the sky, a lone snipe drops into a dive, builds up great speed, and, as it nears the ground, veers. This veering is their magic: it turns the saber tailfeathers into drumsticks and the sky into a taut skin that explodes in an impossibly loud sound known as "winnowing." A nineteenth-century ornithologist likened the winnowing sound to "the cantering of a horse over a hard hollow road." An accurate description, as far as it goes. But the terror of these horses, when you're alone on a misty estuary, is that you've no hint of their existence till they're suddenly riding you down out of empty gray.

I congratulate my snipe, as part of our joint death rite, on its ability to terrify. I sing to it, stroke it, beg its forgiveness. It stands in my palm, pulse bubbling in the hopeless wound; watches me serenely; lets me say and do as I please. In the end, though, I feel my preparatory rite is a near-perfect failure, for in admiring and stroking and singing to such a bird, love begins. It is love, therefore, that I finally crush with a rock, and love that I entomb, still warm, in a little stone cairn. It is love whose two black pearls join my growing sphere. It is love that still watches me from in there. Never blinking. Never closing.

There is a passage in Plato that won't leave me in peace. "The natural property of a wing," Socrates says in the *Phaedrus,* "is to raise that which is heavy and carry it aloft to the region where the gods dwell." What we must understand, he adds, is "the reason why the soul's wings fall from it and are lost . . ." "All are eager to reach the heights . . . [but as most souls] travel they trample and tread upon one another, this one striving to outstrip that. Confusion ensues, and conflict and grievous sweat. Whereupon . . . many are lamed, and many have their wings all broken, and for all their toiling they are balked, every one, of the full vision of being. And departing therefrom, they feed upon the food of semblance."

In this speech, Socrates takes for granted two things I've always felt but have never heard a paid American teacher mention. One is the idea that all of us in a sense "eat" with our eyes, but that what we eat, thanks to our collective trampling and treading, are illusions: "the food of semblance." The other is the powerful link between spiritual life and bird life. The natural property of a wing is indeed to carry that which is heavy aloft, literally and spiritually. And the American relationship with the wing is characterized by the shotgun, the drained wetland, and the oblivious speeding car.

A second Platonic passage that haunts me, this one from the *Timaeus,* is an account of the origin of vision. When the gods put together the human body, Plato writes, they placed "in the vessel of the head . . . a face in which they inserted organs to minister in all things to the providence of the soul. . . . Of these organs they first contrived the eyes to give light." Not to receive light: to *give* it. As the *Timaeus* has it, the gods made "the pure fire which is within us . . . to flow through the eyes in a stream smooth and dense." When the outer light of day meets this inner light that proceeds from us and the two lights "coalesce" upon an external object, the result is "that perception which we call sight."

This passage resonates beautifully with Christ's: *"The light of the body is the eye."* And with Whitman: *"From the eyesight proceeds another eyesight."* And Rumi: *"Close both eyes to see with the other eye."* And Fernando Pessoa: *"We narrate when we see."* And Rudolph Arnheim: *"Eyesight is insight."* And Emerson: *"Perception is not whimsical, but fatal."* And Lao Tzu: *"As good sight means seeing what is very small, so strength means holding on to what is weak. He who, having used the outer light, returns to the inner light, is preserved from all harm. This is called 'Resorting to the Always-So.' "*

Yet we discussed no such theories of vision in any church, school, or science camp I ever attended.

The older I get, the more suspect this omission feels.

I was raised, like most pop science– and Kodak-educated Americans, to believe that the eye works like a camera: an external light falls on an external object, glances off that object, enters the iris (adjustable lens) through the pupil (aperture), alights upon the retina (film), is delivered by the nerves (mailed) to the brain (darkroom), processed instantly (just the way we Americans like it), then stored in the memory (photo album) as an image (snapshot). This metaphor works well enough as a mechanistic description of the eyeball. What we pop scientists and Kodak customers tend to forget is that the eye is only the instrument of sight, not the sense of it.

If we focus not on how the eyeball works but on how we experience our sense of sight in action, the camera becomes a hopelessly inept model. We all live, at all times, in the center of an extremely complex, perfectly visible sphere. There is at all times a visible ceiling or sky above us, a visible floor or ground below, and an almost infinite number of visible objects occupying a 360-degree surround. What we see of this up, down, and surround is, almost literally, nothing. Human vision is as remarkable for what it screens out, or simply fails to see, as for what it actually perceives. Our sight zooms in constantly on details, blinding us to the surround; it pans, constantly, over the surround's surface, giving us "the view" but no detail; it is sidetracked, constantly, by desire, fatigue, daydreams, moods, fantasies, during which we see outward objects yet perceive them not at all. This is hardly the performance of a Kodak product. If our eyes were intended to be cameras, we all deserve our money back.

Human vision in action reminds me of many things more than cameras. A fiberscope, for one. The various forms of fiberscope (arthroscope, proctoscope, etcetera) consist of a bundle of transparent fibers through which images can be transmitted, enabling surgeons to probe the human body, focus on minuscule bits of internal tissue, enlarge and project these bits on the monitor, and operate on this "technologically enhanced" tissue with previously impossible accuracy. Vision, as I experience my own, is a similarly abstract, selective, often surgical procedure—a procedure I perform involuntarily on the body of my world, with sometimes joyous, and sometimes deadly, results.

Another analogy between vision and fiberoptic surgery: any fiber-equipped surgical device—an arthroscope, for example—does not just transmit images of tissue. It also illuminates tissue. The interior of the body cannot be lit from outside; what a surgeon perceives through an arthroscope is therefore dependent not on external lights, but on a tiny light inside the arthroscope itself. In a similar way, our perceptions of the world depend not just on exterior lights that bounce off objects and into our eyes "camera-style," but on an internal light or energy that proceeds from within, *outward,* arthroscope-style, illuminating the few objects we choose to perceive.

If this sounds too wild or metaphysical to describe plain day-to-day seeing, it's a metaphysics we all practice constantly, in perfectly mundane ways. While writing the past paragraph, for instance, I swiveled my eyes from the page to grab a blue ceramic coffee cup from a shelf directly behind me. En route to and from this cup, my eyes moved across dozens of plainly lit objects. Yet I perceived none of them. By retracing, slowly, my eyes' route to the cup, I see that they swept across a brass banker's lamp, a Japanese painting of Ebisu playing a red carp on a cane pole, a photo of Meher Baba feeding a monkey, an old L. C. Smith & Bros. typewriter, a bunny-ears cactus, an almost life-sized figurative sculpture, two jars full of pens and pencils, fifty or so books, and a large window. Yet I saw none of this. Something in me sought an object it knew to be blue, behind me, and full of hot caffeine—sought it so decisively that I turned 180 degrees, "filming" all the way, yet made an essentially blind turn.

This "seeing blindness" is the great contradiction of human eyesight. Why, with our eyes open, don't we simply see every well-lit object? "Confusion ensues, and conflict and grievous sweat." For we *are* "balked of the full vision of being," and do indeed "feed upon semblance." Vision is a form of reception. But to an even greater extent it is a form of selection and of projection. And what concerns me, what scares me at times, is the extent to which my selections and projections are at my command.

How to see more? How to see more clearly? Light is a form of energy. Humans possess energy, and to some extent control its ebbs and flows. Can we, then, aspire to control our inner light? Can we direct the eyes' arthroscopic procedures? How sure are we, lacking such direction, of the surgeon's integrity, or even of his identity? We know so little of inner light sources, speak so little of them, sound so flaky when we do. Yet our seeing illuminates so little of our world! I want to know how to aim my inner light, how to clean its lenses, how to recharge its battery. I want access to the control panel, to the joystick, or at least to the bloody on/off switch. I want hours, *innocuous* hours, in which to fool with my light till I know just how and just when to aim it, and how far, high, and deep it can shine. Because without such control—without a reliable, directable inner light source—I frighten myself. For I have sometimes looked at a living object, even a beloved object, and have seen illusions, shadows, nothing at all.

And still I have performed the surgery . . .

I am haunted by a grebe. A grebe encountered, in the mid-1980s, at the height of the Reagan-Watt-Crowell-Bush-Luhan-Hodell-Hatfield-Packwood rape and pillage of my homeland, the Oregon Cascades and Coast Range; height of the destruction of the world I had grown up in and loved and given my writing life to; height of an eight-year spate of Pacific Northwest deforestation that outpaced the rate in Brazil; height of the war on rivers, birds, wildlife, small towns, biological diversity, tolerance, mercy, beauty; height of my personal rage; depth of my despair; height of my need for light.

Far from aware of this need, I took a long walk, on the first clear afternoon following a tremendous November storm, on a deserted Pacific beach. A beach beautifully wed, in the entire 360-degree surround, to my mood. The storm surf and swell were enormous. The air was a constant, crushing roar. Spindrift was everywhere. So were sand dollars, washed up by the storm, as if even the ocean, in that self-absorbed era, were liquidating its inventory in the name of quick currency. The hills to the east were logged bald. The sun, as it sank, grew enormous and red. The stumps and my skin turned the same angry orange. My shadow grew a hundred feet long, fell clear to the high tide-line, which, to my half-crazed King Learian satisfaction, was a grave-yard. Storm-killed murres. Oil-killed puffins. Carcasses of gulls tangled in washed-up shreds of net. The carcass of a sea lion shot, mostly likely, by a fisherman who blamed it for the salmon no longer returning from a drift-netted, trawler-raked ocean to rivers mud-choked by logging . . .

As a lifelong Oregon Coast fisherman, I had a few beautiful secrets. I could, right up until that autumn, still sneak into one stream in a virgin cedar- and hemlock-lined canyon, find big, wild steelhead and salmon in a place that felt primordial, and have them all to myself. That year, however, the elk from the surrounding clearcuts—hundreds of cuts, hence hundreds of elk—had been squeezed from their once-vast range into that last intact canyon. And, having nowhere else to go, they'd begun crossing and recrossing the stream every day, right in the gravel tail-outs where the salmon and steelhead all spawn. Till they'd obliterated the redds. Pulverized eggs and alevin. Turned my secret stream's banks into an elk-made quagmire reminiscent of the worst riparian cattle damage I'd ever seen. A quagmire that sloughed into the little river with every rain, suffocating the salmon fry that had escaped the countless hooves.

When wild elk, to remain alive, are forced to wipe out wild salmon, it is time, in my book, to get sad. I quit fishing, exercised my rights as a citizen, wrote "my" Republican senators the usual letters of distress. They answered with more rafts of four- and five-hundred-year-old logs shipped away to Japan as if they were nosegays the senators had grown in their D.C. flower boxes. Meanwhile, robbed of food and habitat by the same vast clearcuts, the black bears came down out of my home forest, moved into a marsh near town, lived by raiding garbage cans and dogfood bowls at night—a danger to humans—so the Fish and Wildlife people came in and shot them. Six in a week. And the owl that used to sing to me mornings, attracted by the lights after I'd written all night—the owl that scared me worse than winnowing snipes, actually, because it happened to be a Northern Spotted, which has an insane guffaw of a predawn cry—was now a silence, a nonexistent pawn, a hated cartoon on some poor lied-to logger's cap. And in its stead, as if even the Pentagon grieved its passing, we'd built a forest-funded graphite bomber whose stealth in flight was as perfect as an owl's . . .

So down the storm-smashed beach I strolled that bleak November, kicking at dead birds and drowned logging dreck, wondering what reason I still had to be grateful to live on the "scenic" Oregon Coast, wondering what possible definition of "democracy" I represented through my freedom to write, without persecution or incarceration, such words as

Dear Senator Packwood, I know you've got huge personal problems, but please! Our home here is dying, the only home we have, and we're bound by a political system in which none of the forces killing us can be stopped except through you, so please don't get mad, don't think this is political or personal, please know I'm only begging for our lives when I say that our last few trees are still falling and our mills have all closed and our people are so sad and broke and lied to, and our schools are in ruins, our totem owl dead, and our elk jammed in a last few canyons, pulverizing our last spawning beds with hooves they've no other place to set down, so that the salmon we cherish, salmon our whole Chain of Being needs to remain unbroken, salmon that have forever climbed these rivers like the heroes of some beautiful Sunday sermon, nailing their shining bodies to lonely beds of gravel that tiny silver offspring may live, they no longer come, no more sermon! And our bears, old honey-paws, the joy their tracks alone gave our children, them too, gone, and skinned, their bodies, so human! And our kids, our voteless kids, their large clear eyes, now squinting at stumps and at slash burns and at sunlight that shouldn't be there, squinting at Game Boys and TVs and anti-queer ads, squinting at anything rather than turn open-eyed to windows and see places so ancient and so recently loved, huge groves and holy salmon, clouds of birds and dream-sized animals, a whole green world so utterly gone that already they begin to believe that they only dreamed, they never really knew, any such blessings . . .

What I knew, there on the beach, was that I'd be writing no such letter. My politics had become raw pleas for mercy. Prayers, really. And I pray to God, thank you, not to men like Bob Packwood.

I turned, tired, back to the dunes, to my car, and to the road through the clearcuts to a cold house I'd once wept with joy to call home. But just shy of the first dune—its eyes as red as fury, as red as my feelings, as red as the fast-sinking sun—sat a solitary male western grebe.

And I was back in the mysterious sphere.

The grebe was sitting in a curl of kelp weed at the storm's high-water mark. His eyes, in the evening sunlight, were fire. In the center of each blaze, a black point. Punctuation. Hot lava spinning round a period. A stillness, deep contact, was instantaneous. A life-and-death contract should have been, too. But—sick of humans, sick of my own impotence, sick with the knowledge of how much had been destroyed—I gazed out at the grebe through my sickness. That its body was beautiful I saw as tragedy. That it seemed uninjured I saw as irony. From studying wildlife care books, visiting wildlife care centers, from firsthand experience with scaups and gulls and murres, I knew that seldom do humans make a difference once a seabird washes ashore. God knew what had brought this bird to this beach—hidden damage from a net; spilled oil; hidden disease; weakness from lack of food in a dying sea. *But it wouldn't be here at all,* I thought, *if it wasn't too late already.*

Yet, in perfect contradiction to this pessimism, I felt fear. The molten eyes, the bird's very health and size, intimidated me. Its beak was a dagger. When I'd move close, its neck would draw the dagger back, ready to stab. To even capture the grebe, I'd have to take off my coat and smother it. The beach was cold, the walk back long. Once I got it in my car, it might fight its way free. Once I got it home, then what?

Light is a form of energy that flows in waves. When a healthy wave strikes an object, we see that object in what we call its "true colors." When a lesser wave strikes the same object, we see even the truest colors as shades of gray. The sun striking that November beach was brilliant. The grebe's eyes were two brilliances. The world was doing its part. It was a wave, a light that failed to come from me, which allowed me to leave that beautiful bird where it lay.

A premonition—or maybe a criminal's desire to return to "the scene"—brought me to the same beach three days later. I found the grebe in the same curl of kelp, very recently dead, its body, wings, and plumage still perfect, its burning eyes plucked out by gulls. This was bad enough. But months later, when I dredged up my sad tale for a bird-loving friend, he hit the ceiling. When a grebe, he said, any grebe, is washed up on a beach like that, *all it needs is to be set back in the water.* Grebes require a runway of flat water to take off flying, but they don't need to fly in order to live: even in storm surf they can swim like seals and hunt like little sharks. The grebe I'd found was a fisherman, same as me. Just as I can't walk on water, he couldn't walk on land. "He was a hitchhiker," my friend told me. "Needed a lift of a hundred yards or so. And you refused to pick him up."

Years passed, storms came and went, I walked mile upon penitent mile on those same beaches. I never saw another grebe. I only added two molten eyes to my sphere.

Yet once those crimson eyes became part of me, something changed. Perception, that grebe taught me, is a blood sport. Life itself sometimes hangs by a thread made of nothing but the spirit in which we see. And with life itself at stake, I grew suspicious of my eyes' many easy, dark conclusions. Even the most warranted pessimism began to feel unwarranted. I began to see that hope, however feeble its apparent foundation, bespeaks allegiance to every unlikely beauty that remains intact on Earth. And with this inward change, outward things began to change, too.

Hurrying home in my pickup, late (as usual) from a fishing trip, I rounded a blind curve on an Oregon Coast byway, noticed a scatter of loose gravel on the asphalt in front of me, and felt an impulse. There was a steep, logged-off slope above this curve. A solitary elk could have kicked such gravel onto the road while crossing. I'm a hellbent driver when I'm late; I go barreling through mud and gravel, even dodge fallen trees without thinking twice. But this time, though I saw nothing, I had that sudden sense of something good or bad impending, slammed on the brakes, and as my truck slowed from fifty to thirty to ten I was amazed, then elated, to see the gravel turn into birds.

Pine siskins—a whole flock, parked right on the two-laned asphalt. I crept my bumper up next to them. They didn't fly. Maybe thirty siskins, refusing to budge from the road. Reminded me of late-sixties college students. I got out of my truck, walked up and joined them. I liked the late sixties. Such easy excitement! Now I too could be killed by the next vehicle to come barreling round the curve!

All but one siskin flew as I sat down next to them. The flock then circled back overhead, chirping vehemently, begging the flightless bird to join them. The siskin in the road, a little male, had been nicked by a previous car, had a small wound above his eye, was in shock. Were it not for my strange impulse, I would have massacred an entire flock of avian altruists as they huddled in sympathy around a helpless comrade. Something inside me, I realized, was wildly more aware of things than I am—two imperceptible points of molten red, perhaps. I took the wounded siskin home, kept him in my bird box overnight, drove him the following morning back to the curve where I'd found him, released him in perfect health. I was a happy man.

That was just the beginning. I remain haunted by a grebe, but it's been a wondrous haunting, for with the accompanying refusal to despair, a new energy began to flow. Not dependably. It's something to pray for, not something to be smug about. But I began, especially when driving, to feel a simple alertness, and an occasional intuition: thousands of road miles, thousands of glimpsed roadside movements, thousands of half-glimpsed roadside eyes began to work in concert to help me avoid killing, and occasionally even to save, a few animals and birds. I am not laying claim to supernatural skills. The intuitions that save lives are almost all purchased, like so many mercies, with an earlier being's innocent blood. But this is not to say that, upon descending, these visual intuitions are not a joy . . .

Exactly a year after I abandoned the grebe, I was driving home down Oregon Coast Highway 101 in torrential November rain. It was a Sunday night. A steady line of weekend storm-watchers was returning to Portland. Pitch dark. The road looked like a narrow black river topped by two endless rows of insanely speeding boats. Because of the terrible visibility, I was watching the road lit not just by my own headlights but by those of the pickup in front of me. It was in the pickup's lights that I happened to glimpse a brown ball rolling along the streaming road.

I hit my brakes instantly, certain of what I'd seen. I was also certain, because it was rolling when I glimpsed it, that it had already been run over at least once, and that the pickup would run it over again. There was time, before the truck did so, for a one-syllable prayer: I shouted, *"Please!"* terrifying my two passengers. But as I braked and pulled hard toward the highway's right shoulder, the ball rolled out, unscathed, in the pickup's tailwind and tailwater, then righted itself on the road as I shot past. It was an adult pygmy owl.

I knew by its ability to regain its feet that the owl was not hopelessly injured. Just too disoriented to escape the road. But in my rearview mirror, approaching at fifty or so miles an hour, I saw its doom in the form of at least ten cars. Though I braked as fast as I could, momentum carried me perhaps two hundred feet past the owl. I pulled on the parking brake before my truck stopped rolling, jumped out without a word to my stunned companions, and took off running.

The approaching line of headlights was maybe two hundred yards away. I couldn't see the tiny owl in the dark and distance. Ten cars doing fifty, me on foot doing maybe sixteen, a living bird somewhere between. I didn't do the math. I just ran. And how right it felt, no matter what! How good it felt to tear eyes-first into another November gale, straight down the lane in which a helpless bird huddled, straight into the headlights of ten city-bound cars—for in this running I'd found a penance that might let me again meet, without shame, the crimson gaze of a grebe.

I've played enough ball to have a ballplayer's sense of trajectories and distances. I knew, the instant I spotted the fist-sized silhouette in the lead car's high beams, that my hands would never reach it in time. I also knew that the lead car's driver wouldn't see me or the tiny owl till he or she was upon us, and so wouldn't slow for either of us. I still couldn't stop running. It still felt wonderful. To be an American, a life-long motorist and a bird and animal lover is to carry a piano's worth of guilt on your back. I was outrunning my piano.

The owl had been staring, stupefied, at the approaching cars. When it heard my pounding feet, it swiveled its gaze at me. Instant sphere. Great good or ill impending. I heard cars in the opposite lane, coming up behind me, and realized the cars in my lane, if they saw me, could be frightened into swerving. I was risking lives besides my own. I had succumbed to a kind of madness. Yet as I sprinted toward the cars I had an unaccountably calm vision of a conceivable, beautiful outcome.

The lead car saw me and hit its horn just as I reached the owl. I swung my right foot in the gentlest possible kick, chipping the bird like a soccer ball toward the road's shoulder. I followed instantly, not quite needing to dive as the lead car shot past, outraged horn blaring. All ten cars shot past. I ignored them, searching the rain gusts and night air. And at the edge of the many headlight beams I suddenly saw my tiny owl in uninjured, earnest flight, *circling straight back toward the traffic-filled highway . . .*

I don't know what my body did in that moment: whether my heart stopped or my eyes sent out energy; whether my lips and lungs actually uttered the *"Please!"* When your whole being yearns for one simple thing, it may not be necessary to add the words. All I know is that a gust of sideways rain blasted my owl, its wings twisted in response, and it rose inches over the crisscrossing headlights and car roofs, crossed both lanes, left the highway, and vanished, without looking back, into the forest and the night.

Our eyes, it has been said, are the windows of our souls. Since the soul is not a literal object but a spiritual one, eyes cannot be the soul's literal windows. But they are, literally, openings into and out of living human beings. When our eyes are open, they become not one of our many walls but one of our very few doors. The mouth is another such door. Through it we inhale air that is not ownable, air that we share with every being on Earth. And out of our mouths we send words—our personal reshaping of that same communal air.

Seeing, I have come to feel, is the same kind of process as speaking. Through our eyes we inhale light and images we cannot own—light and images shared with every being on earth. And out of our eyes we exhale a light or a darkness that is the spirit in which we perceive. This visual exhalation, this personal energizing and aiming of perception, is the eyes' speech. It is a shaping, it is something we make, as surely as words are a shaping of air. I feel responsible for my vision. My eye-speech changes the world. Seeing *is* a blood sport.

I'm still in way over my head. I believe this is my Maker's intention. I'm in so far over my head I believe I'll need wings to get out. But even over my head I sense that if all souls are one and the eyes are its windows, then those siskin, owl, snipe, and grebe eyes must all, in a realm outside of time, be my very own. So in killing or saving them, in abandoning or loving them, I kill, save, abandon, or love what is outside of time—that is, what is eternal—in myself. This is Buddhist, Christian, and Islamic platitude, Native American platitude, too, and platitudes don't make very good literature. But they make excellent aids to memory. And in a world in which one's living eyes and body must fly into split-second meetings with the eyes and bodies of others on wet night roads, storm-smashed beaches, in treetops or on blind curves, one needs all the aids to memory one can get.

The God of the Bible commences creation with an exhalation of light from spirit. The great god Shiva is capable of destroying creation by simply opening an eye that rests above his two. Through a life spent looking, or refusing to look, at an endless stream of other creatures, I've learned that by merely opening my eyes, I too partially create, and partially destroy, the world. By abandoning a grebe that entered my sphere of vision, I closed two beautiful molten windows through which I might have gazed upon a real salvation. By kicking a twice-run-over owl skyward, I opened two wondrous dark windows upon the same.

One of the terrors of being human, and one of the joys, is that for all our limitations and confusions we have been given power. The life that terrifies me and the life that I adore are one life.

3. The Non Sense of Place

A "place" is, by definition, a somewhere that isn't going anywhere. After forty-one years spent calling northwestern Oregon my "place," it became painfully clear that, according to this definition, many places—including much of northwestern Oregon—are not places at all: they're a flux; an industrial by-product; an unending sequence of rapid, man-made changes. During my four Oregon decades I witnessed the ruin of so many beloved native places that, right there in the same one place, I came to feel displaced. The culmination of this feeling was my first attempt at time travel: I tried, in the summer of 1993, to move from the Oregon of the nineties back to the Oregon of the sixties—by moving from Multnomah County, Oregon, to Missoula County, Montana.

As the literature of time travel would lead one to expect, my trip through time succeeded in some ways and backfired in others. At its worst, a big move like mine is a kind of death. At its best, though, such a move is a rebirth. I have tried to keep quiet about this second discovery, for the same reason that those of us who believe in marriage try, around strained, married friends, to keep quiet about the joy of divorce. At times, though—seeing the strained or grief-stricken or irate expressions of Montanans who know what's happening to their place from a perspective of decades or of generations—I feel as though my non sense of place is one of the most valuable things I own. As a forty-four-year-old man but only a three-year-old Montanan, my experience of Montana is as much like that of a three-year-old as it is like that of a grown man. The ignorance this implies is nothing to brag about. But I'm a long way from complaining about the freshness and blitheness and goofy joys.

Not long after arriving in Montana, I read James Galvin's *The Meadow,* a memoir/novel hybrid set in a high mountain valley in Colorado. This is a book by a man born, raised, and so deeply steeped in a single mountain meadow that when he speaks his love, you hear the place singing. *The Meadow* made me realize that, even if I live to be a hundred, I'll never know my new niche in Montana the way Galvin knows his Colorado meadow. My children may know Montana in this way, because as a child you eat, drink, and breathe a place in so deeply it becomes part of you for life. This is precisely what excludes me: as a child I ate, drank, breathed, and became part of someplace else.

Anything that fills your heart the way a loved world does doesn't leave the heart ready for a quick refill. True home places are like true loves. I imagine a lucky individual could experience three or four such places. But the usual karmic dose, per lifetime, seems to be one, maybe two. I know writers who have got clear up into their fives and sixes and still consider themselves "poets of place." That's fine if they feel it, I guess. But to me they sound a bit like Frank Sinatra or Mickey Rooney singing about his one true marriage.

I'm often asked, after three years in Montana, whether I'm "in place" and writing about Montana yet. One way of answering that question is to mention that my novel-in-progress is set in Portland, Oregon. Another answer is that my first made-in-Montana book consisted of 270 pages set in Oregon and three set in Montana. I wouldn't be surprised to see the 270-to-3 equation eventually reverse, but the key word here is "eventually." I'm in no hurry to write of Montana for the simple reason that, when writing of place, you can't *be* in a hurry. A place, I repeat, is a somewhere that isn't going anywhere. So an experience of place can befall us only when we do the same.

Anyone who's spent time in the wilds has had the experience of walking through woods, thinking those woods are empty. Then they stop to rest, sit silent for a time, and the woods slowly cease to be empty: animals, birds and insects, botanical and geological nuances, movement of cloud, sound of wind, unseen water, make themselves known. A home place is like this. "Homing" is an interaction that begins when all other action ends. We must be going nowhere in order to be somewhere. Sense of place is received, not aimed at.

For the Argentine aphorist Antonio Porchia, "place" and "home" are so dependent upon a person's degree of receptivity that travel is, essentially, an illusion. "Man goes nowhere," Porchia averred. "Everything comes to man, like the morning."

The range of experience available as we travel noplace, however, is infinite: "Heaven's closer than your sandal-straps," insists the Prophet Muhammad. "And so is hell." Jesus echoes this with, "The kingdom of heaven is within you." But the holy Prophet and Christ are the Prophet and Christ. For the unholy rest of us, with our devout but buried souls, hedonistic bodies, and agnostic minds, I like the American folk version of the same saying: "We're all being dragged, kicking and screaming, into Paradise."

I also can't help but admire the inconclusiveness of many contemporary novelists regarding "sense of place." When the French fictioneer René Daumal, for instance, applied his mentations to our topic, he came up with this: "To enquire where each of us came from, at which precise point on the globe we were, or if it were really a globe (and in any case it was not a point) and what day of what month of what year, was beyond our powers. You do not ask such questions when you are thirsty." The equally thirsty Edward Abbey, despite his renowned love of desert places, offered this dizzy sense-of-place aphorism: "The world dissolves around us, hour by hour. Whole ranges of mountains come and go, mumbling of tectonic vertigo. Nothing endures, everything changes, and all remains the same." Then—the classic Abbey afterthought that makes us miss him: "I could be wrong about this."

I twice heard an anecdote, shortly after my arrival in Missoula County, Montana, about a "Hugo reading" during which the honored writer lay across three folding chairs in front of his audience, too drunk to stand or to make out the lines of his poetry, but bellowing out melodious corrections when he didn't agree with the way the volunteer at the podium *mis*read the work. Sad though the spectacle was from a Twelve Step perspective (and it would be unfair not to mention that Hugo later defeated the demons of drink), I admired the anecdote for its portrayal of a writer destroying his body, yet still loving his native tongue, still shepherding his best moments out into the world.

On the other hand, I didn't *believe* the anecdote for a second the first time I heard it, and the reason I didn't was this: I thought the Hugo in it was Victor. Author of however the hell you pronounce *Les Misérables*. The trouble with the Hugo yarn, as I saw it, was that Victor was born in 1800 or so. I'd heard of one pretty fair writer who passed through these western Montana valleys during that Hugo's lifetime—fella by the name of Meriwether Lewis. For a while after that, though, the Missoula literary scene was a mite sparse.

A few seasons in my new place taught me that the only Hugo ever mentioned in Missoula County is Richard. The same few seasons did *not* qualify me to hold forth on my new "sense of place." What I have as a "Montana writer" could fairly be called "the non sense of place." Yet, to my surprise, I've been enjoying that. Sense of place, as "a theme in Western writing," has become a sizable sacred cow. Back in Oregon I was, I suppose, an inadvertent member of the cow's priesthood. Here in Montana, I find it refreshing to be so new to my place that I'm unable to worship its cows.

In case my "sacred cow" accusation causes the ruffling of deeply placed feathers, let me make a distinction in hopes of smoothing them back down: "sense of place" as a political force, a cultural allegiance, a way of daily life, a combative alternative to the industrial juggernaut that treats watersheds, people, soil, and forest as liquid inventory, strikes me as being as necessary to human beings as water or soil itself. Sense-of-place *writing,* on the other hand, is just an art form, like bebop. As any jazz buff will tell you, bebop is a wonderful form, full of strong traditions, strict disciplines, and wild freedoms. Yet on a bad night, or from a bad musician, bebop can really suck. Yes, James Galvin and Dick Hugo are brilliant sense-of-place musicians. But no form guarantees an artistic outcome. Kudzu, Scotch broom, spotted knapweed, and leafy spurge possess ferocious "sense of place." They're also noxious weeds that are destroying, more irreversibly than forest fires, the health and diversity of their places.

Heaven's closer than your sandal straps.

Ditto: hell.

Non sense of place, I'm also finding, has a thing or two to teach.

Consider that "Hugo story" the way I first understood it: picture *Victor* Hugo sprawled across the three chairs at his own poetry reading.

Victor the national hero; adviser of politicians; defier of Napoleon; poet laureate of France. Victor Hugo was a literary giant, no question. He was also, by many accounts, a virtually humorless man who, for all his intelligence and eloquence, never failed to agree with fawning followers who considered every word he spoke a national treasure.

So picture the great Frenchman lying, hammered, on the folding metal chairs before his audience. Didn't Missoula's Dick, if time travel were possible, have something crucial to demonstrate to Paris's Victor? Wouldn't it have done the poet laureate a kind of good he never knew to loll and whirl there, calling out corrections when the rhythms came out wrong, not caring a rat's ass which admirer, politico, literary cop, or army general was in the audience, because he suddenly *was* a great poet—that is, a man who cared for nothing but the truth and music made by words?

The truth is, I haven't managed to make it through much Victor. But way back in the seventies, when I was in still madly in love with westernmost Oregon and writing a love novel to it called *The River Why*, the Missoula Hugo had already written a poem, called "The River Now," that prophesied my future heartbreak and move to his faraway Montana town:

"Hardly a ghost left to talk with," he wrote, describing my beautiful coastal home ten years ahead down the Reagan road.

> *Runs of salmon thin*
> *and thin until a ripple in October might mean carp.*
> *Huge mills bang and smoke. Day hangs thick with commerce. . . .*
> *My favorite home, always overgrown with roses,*
> *collapsed like moral advice. . . .*
> *The blood still begs direction home. . . .*

One of the harsh but deep consolations of watching a loved home place slip away from you is that, without the loved home, you're suddenly naked enough to feel the blood, begging direction. To feel that inner begging: to me, that's *being* home.

Who hasn't noticed, in their world wanderings, the way we sometimes slip into a mysterious niche, even in the most foreign of places, and find things so suddenly familiar that we feel inexplicably yet completely at home? The cause of this *at-homeness* is a mystery. The sensation is no less certain for that:

In a fetid alley in an alien city, we squeeze up against a dirty wall as a ragged little girl leads a donkey past us. Once past, the girl turns back and smiles a smile of unguarded radiance: *home*. On a hill above a nightmare barrio, we suddenly catch, over the smell of open sewers and bad food, a whiff of distinctive woodsmoke that erases everything that's happened since we stood oceans and decades distant, burning boughs of the very same fragrance: *home*. On a crowded Third World street, among the menacing faces, religious fanatics, scam artists, thieves, an ancient woman suddenly peers in past our foreignness and greets us, eye to eye, as one of that street's very own: *home*.

I had a close friend back in Oregon, the poet Tom Crawford, who fled the state the same year I did and is now living in Kwangju, South Korea, on a street called Yong bong-dong. Tom moved to Kwangju because South Koreans are under the wonderful false impression that America's literature still matters to mainstream America. It's a bizarre but common scenario there: in order to better understand American culture, Koreans hire American authors, profs, and poets marginalized, impoverished, and ignored by American culture. So Tom—a lifelong West Coaster, fifty-nine years old now, and surely the finest backwoods poet ever to sing the praises of South Tillamook County, Oregon—sold his little house and writer's shack on tiny Farmer Creek; gave away his beloved goats and half-wild ducks and pinhead collie and guard-dog geese; gave away even the old redwood chair by the cedar-lined pool where he'd sat for hours each November, writing the best damned salmon poems you ever read while a pair of thirty-pound Chinook danced themselves to death in the gravel before him; and moved to Kwangju, Yong bong-dong.

Yet one evening last winter, in his alien cubicle, foreign culture, huge apartment building, Tom fell into one of those sudden homeless homes, picked up a pen, and wrote this account of his falling:

> *Outside it's Korea and snowing.*
> *White flakes float in under the eaves*
> *and slide sideways into my window.*
> *Inside I'm talking to this big Asian ink brush*
> *about a fish I'd like us to draw.*
> *I've loaded it with the blackest ink*
> *and now I'm holding it, poised*
> *over a clean sheet of 3-foot-long, white paper.*
> *I'm keeping my voice down*
> *though I'm pretty excited*
> *and the snow falling outside doesn't help,*

but here's what I say, "You know
already from the way I'm holding you
that I'm not an artist."
All right, that's out in the open.
It can't hurt, I figure, to own up
to what the brush knows anyway.
"I'm asking for just one terrible black fish," I say
and inch the brush closer to the white paper.
I know it's cheap of me
to imagine the brush could actually be tempted this way.
Outside snow's beginning to pile up
on the metal railing, the patio.
The bare branches of the maple below my apartment
look like tall zebras. Very beautiful.
In the distance the buildings of Kwangju
grow even bigger, darker, in the falling snow.
"This fish, I only want to look at it!" I implore.
"If not the whole fish, then at least some part of it.
Draw me an eye for god-sakes!"
I hate it when my voice gives me away
like some old man who's discovered
he's on the wrong bus.
In my hand is a long length of yellow bamboo
with a shock of horse hair black with ink.
Made in Korea, it says,
and not the Romantic Period. I let that go.
There will always be the detractors.
Outside it's growing dark, Presbyterian
as the red, neon crosses begin to come on
across the city.
I put my tongue on the glass window
to feel the cold,
to feel what snow feels.
If I could leave my body right now
where would I go more amazing than this—
this black fish for company,
alive down there somewhere in the paper
and me, up here,
happy, alone in the snow.

Heaven's closer than your sandal strap. So is hell. And outside it's growing dark. In a world in which 15 percent of the population are refugees and 70 percent are poor—a world in which almost everyone's home has at some point been blighted, hurricaned, bombed, bulldozed, burned down, clearcut, subdivided, gentrified, downsized, drought-stricken, flooded, purged, starved, or plagued—these mysterious No-place Places feel as crucial to me as anything that has come, in our literature or academies, to be called "sense of place." We may be wage-enslaved Americans forced to move, at the absurd national rate, to a new "home place" every four years. We may be old men climbing on the wrong damned bus. We may be elk at heart, forced to live like sheep, or salmon forced to live like carp. The blood still begs direction home. No matter how circumstance has dealt with us, or how disenfranchised or placeless we've become, we will never be dispossessed of the right to feel at home in *these* little blood-filled bodies, on *this* reeling planet, as often as we can, as deeply as we can, any goddamned God-blessed place we possibly can.

4. Tilt

It was easy to forget, during the mere two seasons that constitute an Oregon coast year (seven months of wet, five of dry) that like a long-ago-injured woman who's learned to walk gracefully with a cane, Earth leans ever so slightly on her axis, inclining now toward the sun, now away from it as she orbits, thereby causing the angle at which sunlight strikes her to change constantly. It is impossible to forget this in Montana: Earth's "limp"—and the resulting shift of the landscape now toward, now away from, the sun—gives us four dramatically different seasons and all the migratory compensations of wildlife, the annual growth/deaths/dormancies of plant life, and the external and internal changes in human life—that occur in response.

It's impossible to forget equinoctial tilt in the Rockies because, when ignored, it silently slides healthy creatures into environs that suddenly fail to sustain life. I watched a solitary western bluebird, last December, try for an ineffectual quarter-hour to peck bugs, woodpecker-style, from the bark of a snow-covered, rime-blasted pine. This bleak drama took place a stone's throw from the nest box in which several bluebirds had hatched and fledged and thrived a few months before, yet the lone December blue was doomed by one small mistake: it had failed to respond to Tilt. Migration is a life-preserving path that animals *must* discover and trace as Earth's limp turns their homelands and homewaters inhospitable. The circumpolar seasonal journeys of terns and phalaropes, the marathon gauntlets run by wildebeest and caribou and swum by oceangoing tuna and salmon, the six-thousand-mile swims of the Alaska fur seal and humpback whale, are famous attempts to cancel the effects of Tilt. Watching the life of the Rockies, though, has led me to discover another form of migration about which I hadn't much thought: the equinoctial ride not of those who leave a given landscape, but of those who stay behind.

In the fly-fishing classic *The Habit of Rivers*, Ted Leeson glimpses this journey when he looks up from his home river at departing Canada geese. He writes,

> *As the recognition of autumn comes suddenly, in a moment, so one day you first hear the geese. . . . Bound for the south, these birds seem to me a strange point of fixity . . . for in a sense they don't move at all. They take to altitudes to stay in one place, not migrating, but hovering, while the equinoctial tilting of the earth rocks the poles back and forth beneath them. The geese remain, an index of what used to be where, and of what will return again. Their seasonal appearance denotes your passing, not their own.*

With this upside-downing of the word "migration," the so-called stasis of sedentary things becomes the illusion it in fact is. In relation to Earth's spectacular annual ticktock upon her axis, it is the so-called "migratory" mammals and birds that travel thousands of miles north and south who maintain their true solar place, and every geological and biological form that *fails* to respond to Tilt—every mountain, for instance, and we who remain in them—that does the traveling.

That the entire sedentary landscape migrates was never more clear to me than during my first Montana winter. I'd arrived in the Rockies in July and set about learning the new landscape in the best way I know: by befriending the trout stream that flows through my backyard. This friendship seemed to grow rapidly intimate. I memorized a two-mile beat of water, and was soon catching and releasing its inhabitants at will. I met the beavers, coyotes, deer, and elk. A cow moose one day stepped from the willows forty feet upstream of me, analyzed my fly-casting for a moment, then responded with the most prolific and foamy urination I've ever seen, let alone been forced to stand in. I cleaned up the garbage and charted the flows of the creek. I made painstaking, hand-built improvements to its trout habitat, figuring I'd know these same riffles, pools, and improvements for years to come. In November, though, something unexpected happened: the entire watershed took off—mountains, trees, tributaries, animals, houses, humans, and all—on a journey into Tilt.

This migration began to grow perceptible on the day before Thanksgiving, when the temperature suddenly dropped fifty degrees and stayed there. Within a week, the fluid body I'd spent summer and fall befriending had become a motionless, silent solid. Because the skies stayed clear and there'd been no snow all fall, each subtle stage of transformation was perfectly visible:

On Day One, Thanksgiving Eve, when the air hit zero, a viscous ice that looked like fog began to slide down the creek's clear current, sheathing everything in the stream—submerged trees, water weeds, barbed wire, deer bones, car parts—in a soft cocoon of gray. On Day Two, Thanksgiving proper, at minus five, I found myself disconcertingly blessed with an ability to stand like Saint Peter on pools in which, just days before, I'd battled brown trout. Day Three, minus eight, the glides froze over thick but as clear as glass, and a prolific crop of geometric white roses sprang from that unlikely soil. I'd never seen such blossoms, or such terrain beneath: I'd stand in bright, heatless sunlight on what I still thought of as water, peering at white-petaled ice-roses sprung from clearest glass. Beneath glass and petals the fog-streams and galactic currents of the creek flowed in perfect silence, the bottom stones glowing sunlit beneath the viscous ice "fog-streams." Trout and whitefish finned above the glowing stones, dappled by geometric rose-shadows as they calmly dodged the "fog."

On Day Four, even the fastest waters closed over, the last little open rapid becoming a heap of smashed china plates. Beavers slipped in and out of the broken china through small, carefully maintained holes. Stripped willow twigs piled like fresh-hewn chopsticks at each hole. Standing by a pile of these artful sticks and china shards, I realized that, as surely as I have ever journeyed by boat, car, or plane, I had been carried into foreign country. The entire Earth had been my vessel. Though I walked the same few miles of trout stream daily, those miles and everything they contained had slid deeper and deeper into the foreign realms of Tilt.

I traded waders for skis, traversed the ever-changing glass plains, passed fresh-bloomed ice flowers, ever toothier icicles, ever-less-describable sculptures. Tiny hanging grottos of moving icicles tinkled, near each stilled rapid, like wind chimes. The wintry realm I'd entered grew so exotic my creek-skiings finally reminded me—no matter how cold the cold—of swimming through warm tropical reefs. Same complete immersion in intricacy and creativity. Same inexhaustible extravagance and style. Same inchoate gasps of thanks for all that I was seeing. Same no one listening, taking invisible bows.

Returning home from these soundings, I found that our house, too, sat differently upon the land. The log walls were no longer anchored to solid ground: they cut through the axial stream like a ship's prow. I'd step indoors with a sense of climbing aboard, make tea, sit at the window, watch the mountain world plunge, shiplike, through the slow equinoctial flow. Winter solstice became not a date on the calendar but a destination: something to sail toward, then *around,* the way schooners used to round Capes Horn and Good Hope. When my daughters climbed in my lap, I couldn't contain my wonder.

"We're moving!" I told them. "The house, the mountains, the whole world is sailing. Can you feel it?"

They gazed gravely at the mountains, then nodded with such serenity it seemed they'd always known. And on we glided, deep into winter, out around Cape Solstice, then straight on back toward spring.

5. Who Owns the West?: Seven Wrong Answers

Preface

The American West is famed for its mountains and sprawling deserts, Indian wars and surviving tribes, boom-'n'-bust mining towns, big-name national parks, and mediagenic cowboys and wildlife. In the past few decades the West has also become known for a new wave of telecommuting, entrepreneurial settlers; for its nonextractive new economies grounded in sustainable land use, outdoor sports, art, and tourism; and for strange new adjustment problems such as ranchette sprawl, noxious-weed infestations, and government-baiting, openly racist "militias" digruntled by the direction of change.

It's easy to forget that more than 50 percent of our so-called "Western states" are the property not of those states or their residents, but of all 270 million Americans. It's also easy for industries accustomed to exploiting the West to forget that public lands are not theirs. When state or federal politicians cede mountains, wilderness, rivers, and forests to "quick-return" exploitation by multinational business interests, they are offering up for destruction not a purchased and legitimately private property, but an American birthright. Millions of residents of the "New West" are fighting to end this paradigm. Millions of "Old West" residents like the old paradigm just fine. The result has been a political and rhetorical war resulting in spectacular posturing, legislative gridlock, lawsuits, and an occasional spate of violence.

The fine William Kittredge manifesto, *Who Owns the West?* (Mercury House Books, 1996), wrestles with some of these new tensions. The book also inspired a 1998 lecture series in the minor-league cities of Santa Barbara, Eugene, and Olympia. Bill led the series off. I batted second, with Charles Wilkinson, Patricia Limmerick, Terry Tempest Williams, and Gary Snyder lined up as the series' "Murderer's Row." The pay was good weighed against the three-night demand, and our talks were to be gathered in an anthology that promised larger-than-usual royalties for shared authorship. Trouble was, immediately after Bill and I shared our finest thoughts on Western ownership, the "Who Owns the West Lecture Series" went bankrupt.

After taking part in a lecture series on ownership that failed to own even itself, I became fascinated by this koan of a topic. Who *does* own the West? Given our short spans of life and attention, who really owns anything? Some unowned thoughts on the matter . . .

Who Owns the West Wrong Answer #1: Isumataq

"Who owns the West?" is a difficult question. The fiction I write is often fueled by difficult and unanswerable questions. In a fiction I feel comfortable with this, because the rules of literature allow you to leave the Difficult difficult and the Unanswerable unanswered.

The rules of rhetoric and lecturing encourage a more didactic response. The lecturer thinks: "I can't just ask questions in response to a question. I should make statements, present my credo, set straight the facts!" Yet if I'm the rhetorician, how quickly the presenting of credos and setting straight of facts becomes the grinding of personal axes. Is anyone curious about the sound of my ax grinding? With advance apologies, here's a sample:

"Who owns the West? Well, in Montana, New Mexico, Georgia, Patagonia, Ted Turner (may the gods of humility tomahawk-chop *his* Atlanta Braves cap). Then there's the transnational corporations—man, do *they* own some Western real estate, not to mention Congress, the legal system, our conditioned consumer responses, the White House, the food chain, the minds of our kids. And how about the owner of the Virtual West? You've all surely heard about Bill Gates's latest exploit. The quick divorce. Even quicker remarriage. To Janet Reno? The new business they've fired up? Along with McDonald's, Disney, General Motors, Exxon, Monsanto, Apple, and the American Psychiatric Association, all of which Bill and Janet just bought, Microsoft is opening a chain of drive-thru psychological counseling service/Western Think Tank/World Website/gas station/software swap/body shop/DVD rental/DNA-upgrader/fast-food eateries in one. *"MicroPsychoMcMacTank,"* they're calling it, *"Home of the Happy Problem."* Just pull up to the golden-arched Mickey-Mouse-eared location nearest you, and they'll troubleshoot, liposuck, counsel, rethink, retool, refuel, upgrade, entertain, and bloat you in a minute and thirty seconds. Same great plastic Disney baubles to co-opt the kids. Same great Freudian, Skinnerian, Zen-of-Snoopy, and Chicken-Soup-for-Assholes counseling menu. Same great fries that gave President Clinton those corporate-friendly love handles. Same flexible plastic *preta*-straws to let you suck at the bovine-growth/olestra shakes. Minimal anal leakage. All available starting January 1 at the MicroMcMacSoft Portal nearest you—provided you've purchased the McWindows 2010 software, and are driving the Me-Mac/McMinivan, and have installed the version 6.66 McPenis implant or, if you're Mcfemale, the encoded MicroPsycho forehead tattoo that wires your consumer and sexual urges and wallet so pleasantly into the system . . ."

That's *my* ax in full grind. And you may laugh for a minute. But after an hour, believe me, you'd have ground your molars away.

Who owns the West? I'll tell you: I'm not going tell you. I'm just a storyteller, not a pundit. I like Barry Lopez's borrowed Inuktitut definition of the storyteller as *isumataq*. The *isumataq* is "the person who creates the atmosphere in which wisdom reveals itself." The person who uses words to try to stuff you full of wisdom has confused wisdom with turkey stuffing. Wisdom must reveal itself, because wisdom lives, hidden, within the self, where only the lone reader, lone listener, the self itself, can summon and free it. With seven stories counting this one, I hope to create an atmosphere: nothing more. If "Who owns the West?" gets answered in that atmosphere, you'll have answered it for yourself.

Who Owns the West?: Seven Wrong Answers

Who Owns the West Wrong Answer #2: My Father-in-Law's Landlord

As a born West Coaster who has, for decades, been leading a fairly pared-down literary life on a series of westward-flowing trout and salmon streams, I used to feel I had an almost indigenous claim on what we call "Westernness." Then, in the late-1980s, I learned that my new father-in-law, a perfectly intelligent man named Joe Arleo, also considers himself a Westerner—because he lives on the Upper West Side of Manhattan. What's more, when I visited Joe in New York, I completely agreed with the logic of his position. To be any more western than he already was would have forced him to fall off the edge of his known world into the Hudson. We can't have that. He's my father-in-law.

Should a who-owns-the-West rumination take a West like Joe's into consideration? I can't speak for others, but *I'm* going to take it into consideration. I'm here to tell you that in addition to what we call "the American West," there's an Upper West that's just as American, and my father-in-law and his wife, Lillian, have a very nice apartment there. I can't tell you who owns that particular Western property, but I can tell you it's rent-controlled. And one more thing: the first time I entered it, first time I laid eyes on Joe Arleo, I rared back and asked him, after a few pleasantries, for his daughter Adrian's hand. And while it's possible the outcome of my request wasn't entirely up to Joe—possible, even, that he and I were just a couple of wistful European-Americans enacting an Old World rite in the New Country before getting on with what Adrian's and my hearts and the American way of doing things had already decreed—the ritual asking itself was a pleasure. And how touched I was, how New York City brightened in my eyes, when this first-generation Italian-American, this quintessential Manhattanite, this urbane, sartorially splendid, grammatically exacting Ph.D. who polishes his shoes daily and carefully pronounces the *l* in the word *salmon,* took in my wayward grooming, ne'er-polished shoes, vowel-flattenin', *g*-droppin' accent, and the fact that in all my years on salmon streams I've caught only the silent-*l* variety, and nevertheless granted me his daughter's hand.

Now, God help him, Adrian lives with me in *Lolo, Montana*—a place so alarmingly like it sounds, a place so lacking in Lala, a place so far beyond Joe's Hudsonian conception of Uttermost West that he must summon the courage of Magellan before sailing off the edge of his known world to visit his daughter and granddaughters. The least I can do in return is try to integrate Joe's "West."

Who Owns the West Wrong Answer #3: The Personal Geography

My Upper West Side "Western" father-in-law knows more about world geography than I do. So when I point out that his personal definition of utmost "West" is the Hudson, I'm obviously not talking about world geography. I'm talking about an alternative geography we all possess: the personal geography.

Joe Arleo's personal geography has many unique features: one is a distinction between what he calls "the Country" and "the City." The City, of course, is New York. The Country, it turns out, is Long Island. (And I used to think *I* lived in the country!) Lest it sound as though a Lolo, Montanan is calling a more urbane Manhattanite "provincial," though, let me confess that my personal geography is just as provincial: it is the *purpose* of the personal to be provincial.

The personal geographical truth of my existence is this: I'm so Columbia Basin–bred and Pacific saLmon–fed, so steeped in the rain, rivers, moss, and mythos of the northwesternmost corner of the lower forty-eight, that I felt I'd migrated to my uttermost East when I moved, eight years back, to Montana. Just as the Hudson is as far west as Joe can go without ceasing to be the Manhattanite he is, so the Continental Divide is as far *east* as I can go without ceasing to be me. Why? Because every creek and river I've known intimately, all my life, has ended up in the Pacific. And in crossing a nondescript spine of mountains just east of my Montana home, the watersheds trade that trajectory for the mythos of the Mississippi and Gulf of Mexico. This changes nothing, really. Yet it changes everything: no more salmon, sea lions, gooey-ducks, gray whales, or orcas waiting at the river's downstream terminus; no living connection to any known living family member; no more cedar/spruce/hemlock/alder/Doug fir temperate forests; no totem-carving, salmon-eating, Raven-worshiping tribes; none of the cities I've known since boyhood, including Portland, city of my birth, city I've moved back to and away from seven times. Those who have left every such connection behind and feel they're doing fine without them could fairly ask: *So what? Who needs all those connections?*

65

I wouldn't argue. I feel no need to present my case; the need I feel is to *represent* it. I choose to live this life under the influence of mountains that tilt their rivers into the Pacific because when I first wakened to this life I was already under that influence. I didn't ask to be born, didn't ask to be put precisely here. But I've grown to trust the mysterious indigenous wisdom that took care of all that for me. In fact, I value that wisdom so highly that, more days than not these past thirty or so years, I have reinforced my indigeny with a walk not so much along as *in* a Pacific-tilted stream or river.

At the age of twenty-five or so, I consciously chose a life of rivers, words, and contemplation over, among other things, any real possibility of a large income, instead making it my habit to walk in water as often as I could. I used to call such walks "fishing trips." For diplomatic purposes among those scared of pagans—or, worse, mystics—I still do. But I've spent thousands of days now, in the waders I call my "portable sweat lodge," simply strolling, or standing in, running water. I possess no deed to any creek or river I traipse—because I need no deed. I bring almost nothing, in the way of food or memento, home afterward—because the rivers *are* home. I possess no friend or family member, not even the closest, with whom I've spent more time than I have with rivers. And I daresay that—in their hard-to-describe, cold, wild way—rivers have befriended me in return. They're very serious and cool in their friendships, incapable of sentimentality or preferential treatment, and would always as soon drown as coddle you. Yet if you touch a river's skin with the least tip of your finger, it visibly reconfigures what it was doing in instantaneous response. Is there a better name than *friend* for something this ceaselessly vigilant, this ready to respond to your most nuanced touch?

Who owns the West? On water walks, my experience is that nothing can stop me, no matter how little I legally own, from allowing loved things, trustworthy things, beautiful things to enter the continuum of my life. I need only move slowly and be open enough to *let* them enter. This entry—the mysterious movement of natural objects and wonders from without to within—for me, *is* ownership.

Who Owns the West Wrong Answer #4: Manhole Covers

"Who owns the West?" being a difficult question, reminds me of the first truly difficult question I ever wrestled. The struggle ended when the question gave up on wrestling, unleashed a fist, and nearly broke my jaw.

I learned a lot from that blow. Before it landed, I was a typical American teen laboring under the false impression—planted in equal parts by fundamentalist Christianity and the public school system—that the only right way to handle any question is to cough up the One Correct Answer. I still remember Correct Answers of that era, long after having forgotten their corresponding questions: "Coffee, bananas, hemp, cacao." "The Bill of Rights." "Be Am Is Are Was Were Been." I now refer to this kind of thing as Answerizing—an activity that stands in relationship to truly answering a question as the ability to memorize the phone book stands in relationship to the ability to love every pre-posterous flesh-and-blood concoction whose name the phone book happens to contain.

Questions that tap into our mortality, our pain, our selfishness, our basic needs, questions that arise from the immeasurable darkness, light, or mystery of our lives, require more than Answerization. They require our suffering, steadfastness, silent yearning, and deepest faith. I learned this back in 1969, thanks to a blow to the jaw.

The same blow revealed to me an extremely valuable technique for dealing with exceptionally hard questions with irresolvably multiple answers—a technique I call the "manhole cover." It all happened like this:

In 1965, when I was thirteen, my seventeen-year-old brother died of staph infection after a number of unsuccessful heart surgeries. In the dismal years following his death, I couldn't help noticing that other young men his age were dying, too. These other sons and brothers, though, were dying of far more avoidable causes. Knowing how the loss of my brother had blasted my family and me, I began to question those other deaths—by asking myself and others whether it was right that the boys of my brothers' and my generation were waging war in Vietnam.

The family supper table was the test site where I'd detonate my questions. And, like the test sites of Nevada, it proved a dangerous place. I am the son of a good father, but a father seared, at the age of twenty-two, by the experience of liberating a Nazi concentration camp. I'll never forget Dad's description of the fat, glowingly naked, freshly murdered body of the camp's German commandant, killed by surviving Jews as the camp was being taken by Americans, lying on the ground beside the heaped, wasted bodies of hundreds of his victims.

My father loved his country and his children. He expressed those two loves by serving in World War II, then by working in the electronics industry all his life, where he helped make, among other things, components for nuclear weapons. He also expressed his two loves by embracing the idea that Ho Chi Minh and North Vietnam were a threat to America comparable to Hitler and Naziism. Dad embraced this idea, I believe, because it was passed down to him by solemn-faced American leaders in the same positions once occupied by Generals Patton, MacArthur, and Eisenhower and President Franklin D. Roosevelt. It never occurred to Dad that between 1942 and 1966 one small thing might have changed: the Americans in power might have become bald-faced liars. After my brother died, though, it occurred to me. As I began to hear increasingly disturbing accounts of the war, then looked at the faces of President Johnson and his cabinet, I believed I was seeing a liar served by liars. My father saw no such thing. We had a problem.

A sidebar: a crucial Johnson cabinet member, Robert McNamara, has since confessed to his lies in a book. But his book came out in 1995, thirty years after the lies. I found McNamara's confession sickening: for its belatedness; for the insult it gave to the veterans, false enemies, and innocents who served, suffered, and died for his lies; for the fact that McNamara, despite his avowed remorse, continued, even after his grandiose Vietnam-era lying, to inflict pain and debt on still more Third World countries with the equally grandiose, ill-conceived development projects he launched as head of the World Bank.

Another sidebar: a lesser servant of the same cabinet was a Texan with the scrubbed looks of a Baptist seminarian, who, as LBJ's press secretary, would dutifully stand in front of reporters, and lie and lie and lie. So far as I know, this man has never publicly confessed his regret; he has simply *proven* it, by leading a different life ever since he stopped lying. His name is Bill Moyers.

But my topic is not the war, its architects, or its morality. My topics are difficult questions, and a life-saving device I call the manhole cover.

In 1966, when I was fourteen, I began to question the war at our family supper table. The instant I'd speak up, my father would snap that the only reason I could criticize the war at all was that our troops in Vietnam were protecting my freedom to do so. I would argue back by saying that my freedom did not strike me as being dependent upon the clique of Saigon businessmen whom Americans were actually protecting, or on the deaths of the civilians our troops kept "accidentally" killing. Dad would then go off like a bomb, bellowing that I would never talk such rot if I'd ever seen a concentration camp.

I'd learned in school that this response, for all its emotional vitality, was a logical fallacy known as a non sequitur. Needless to say, I didn't tell my father this. What I did instead was try to *bury* his position, by Answerizing it into oblivion. I read scores of far-from-mainstream accounts of the war, studied the arguments of ex-hawks who believed the war was unwinnable, honed my rhetoric, memorized statistics and tales of American atrocities. Dad, meanwhile, spent his days obeying defense-industry bosses in order to earn the salary that supported his family, including a son now bent on making a fool of him each night at supper. In his justifiable frustration, his rhetoric became ever less cogent, more blustering, closer to a position of: "Just shuttup! North Vietnamese are Nazis and if we don't kill them fast we'll die like the Jews."

I know now that no argument I could have constructed would have changed my father's mind, any more than his "Nazi" mantra could change mine. We needed wisdom. And wisdom is not a rote dogma, not ideology, not research material, not something we stuff into one another. The inner feeling that brings light to the eyes, the humor that helps create empathy, the fresh angles of vision that can waft into a room when hearts remain light, were gone; we had stopped creating the suppertime atmosphere in which wisdom could reveal itself. To stop creating this atmosphere is to move beyond help.

For three long years we wrestled our hopeless question. Then— one night in 1969, after I had Answerized my father into foolishness with a particularly vehement and lawyerly antiwar harangue—he shoved back his chair in a fury, rose up over me, and began yelling his same counter-harangue down into my face, as if the higher elevation of his voice could give his "Ho Chi Minh/Hitler/concentration camp" sputterings the gravity they so mysteriously lacked.

I saw red. When he ended with "I was in *Germany!* I *saw!* I *know!*" I shoved back my own chair, stood six inches from his eyes, and shouted with all my might that he did *not* see, that he did *not* know, that Germany was a quarter-century gone, that napalmed Asian women and children were now the "Jews," that *we* were now the "Nazis," and that *he* was the stupidest son of a bitch I'd ever listened to in my life.

Next thing I knew, I was airborne. And, odd as it sounds, it was sheer release. That my flight was involuntary, carrying me backwards over my chair, that my father's fist had launched me, didn't matter. I've heard it said that mental suffering is worse than physical pain: this moment proved it to me. The anguish of a three-year stalemate begun in simultaneous grief for my brother, the uselessness of every word we'd hurled at each other, were so unendurable that his blow was pure relief. Even when I hit the floor and the physical damage registered, I stayed giddy with relief. Better a fist than the battle we'd been waging. *Infinitely* better a fist than an M-16 in my hands. I bounced up in an adrenaline rush, as if we'd been playing tackle football, left the room and house without speaking, and didn't call or return home for three days.

When I did return, Dad was waiting. And I saw at once that he'd been feeling nothing but fear for my safety. I hadn't been feeling so great myself—about the name-calling, about staying away so long just to make him sweat. We ended up in a race to see who could apologize first. In relation to the question "Who owns the West?"—in relation to any of life's hard questions—it is these apologies of which I would speak:

Both Dad's apology, and mine, were clumsy, ponderous, heavy things. They created no agreement between us whatsoever. *Manhole covers.* That's what our clunky apologies felt like: two almost unliftably heavy lids placed down over grief and rage, over the truths of a heroic war skewed by the lies of a shameful one, over the deaths of young men made unbearable by the same lies. The causes of our grief and rage remained exactly as they had been. Nothing had healed. We were laughably clumsy with each other. Yet how necessary our apologies felt! Two chasms of hurt were covered despite the awkwardness. Realizing we would *never* close the gulf between us with words, realizing the other was somehow helpless to cross to our position, we had each, at the same moment, lifted a heavy lid and placed it voluntarily down over the hatred, the helplessness, our positions, the gulf.

We then continued with our lives. Dad stayed in the defense trade, rooting for the troops, voting for war hawks and war chests. I went on opposing the war, evading the draft, advising every young man I knew to do likewise. Yet by continuing to honor our manhole covers, we began, once again, to be friends. We drove over the covers daily: drove over them so often we forgot to worry about whether they'd hold. Of *course* they held. Who ever falls through a manhole cover? The problems occur when people remove the covers from their places.

Who owns the West? Anyone who can hear this obnoxious question and *not* hear the unforgivable, irreparable betrayal of Indian nations and of African tribes has forgotten that we all walk daily over two of the most tragic manhole covers on earth. These United States are founded, let's face it, upon the enslavement of innocent Africans, the extermination and robbery of innocent Indians, and a revered piece of paper that lies in the face of both that "all men [*sic*] are created equal." These States are founded, in other words, on hope, faith, idealism, sacrifice, ingenuity, courage, and some of the most staggering hypocrisies and injustices in the history of humankind.

Without manhole covers, the founding hypocrisies that gave us an America and a West will never be bearable, let alone discussable, let alone capable of being healed. The need for big, ponderous apologies is endless.

Who Owns the West Wrong Answer #5: The National Water Situation

Personal geographies can be wet or dry, hot or cold, crowded or solitary, urban or rural, microscopic or vast. I believe we all possess them, and that they're all quirky, provincial, limited, and that it's a more serious blunder to think you're *not* quirky, provincial, and limited than to admit that you are.

I believe in the effort to broaden the mind, but still more in the effort to deepen it. I seek ways to go about this, daily—and often find broadness and depth to be at odds. Aren't one's mental energies a bit like a knife-scoop of mustard and one's geography a bit like a piece of bread? Isn't it true that if your bread is thousands of miles across, you'll be spreading your mustard mighty thin? The world, it seems to me, is awfully big, a human is awfully small, life is awfully short, and most of our plates are mighty full for our personal geographies to approximate the international or national geographies. When humans go global with their geographies, bad things happen to their thinking. I could point a finger, here, at Mobil, Coca-Cola, carbon dioxide, CFCs, the WTO. But keeping to the personal geographical point, let me point a finger at me:

My friendships with a few rivers have resulted in three books. As an author of rivery prose I've been asked, more times than I deserve, to speak to gatherings of river-lovers. Twice those gatherings were "national." In preparing those talks I initially felt I should say something about "the nation's rivers." But my mind, in the presence of such a concept, simply wilted. I'm seventy-two inches long. At a full shout, my voice carries a quarter-mile or so. I can walk maybe twenty miles at a go without quite dying. I've lived my whole life on a few small Oregon and Montana streams. How does a creature like me address a national anything? I tried. In the name of Democracy, Rhetorical Grandiosity, or some damn thing, I once tried to compose remarks that would be found equally interesting by every member of a fifty-state audience. What emerged from my exoskeleton were sentences of such fiberless banality and gross generality that they could have served as an any-ol'-party presidential campaign speech:

"Good evening, National River People. Powerful wet stuff, our national water. As a thing to float your boat on, you can't beat it. Oil. Gas. Beer. They'll float 'er, too. But not as cost-effective.

"We had water back home. Powerful wet stuff, as I recall, though of course we stayed out of it, unless we had on the swim trunks. We were the heartland, not Hollywood. Swam clothed, if at all. You had to love the water, though. So wet, as I remember it. On the reservoirs of wet water, we had our boaters. Fishin' in it, we had our fisherfolk. And our farmers would, uh, squirt the crops with it when the, uh, sky water—'rain' as we called it there in the heartland—wasn't gettin' the job done. *Not gettin' the job done.* Remind you of anybody we know hopin' to move into a big white house in Washington? Don't let 'em! It's time America squirted *me* on the crops.

"One thing I'll say about our national water situation. The two hydrogens, but only the one oxygen. Is this democratic? I smell hydrogen soft money here! Should the nation choose to squirt me on the crops, you can bet your heartland-big swim trunks I'll fight to give our oxygens the same opportunities as our hydrogens.

"That's the national water situation as I see it. Thank you."

The great Irish poet W. B. Yeats once explained his approach to life and art in these words: "If I had written to convince others, I would have asked myself not, 'Is that exactly what I think and feel?' but 'How would that strike so-and-so? How will *they* think and feel when they read it?' And all would be oratorical and insincere. If we understand our own minds, and the things that are striving to utter themselves through our minds, we move others—not because we have understood or thought about those others, but because *all life* has the *same root.*"

For all my love of rivers, "our nation's rivers" have not moved me once. The rivers that move me are those I've fished, canoed, slept beside, lived on, nearly drowned in, dreamed about, sipped tea and wine by, taught my kids to swim in, pulled a thousand fish from, fought and fought to defend. I've come to suspect, for this reason, that it is *only* the personal geography—the one experienced in daily depth—that can in fact be *in*-habited, and only the personal geography that has that Yeatsian ability to connect us, root to root, to people or places we've never met. I have never laid eyes on the Ohio River except from jets flying 30,000 feet above it. But I have been so moved and haunted by my own Columbia and Snake and Clark Fork rivers' struggle for life that, when I first read the poet James Wright's words on his dying Ohio, I was moved to tears. Before I ever laid eyes on Montana's Big Blackfoot River, I was so enthralled by the wild fish and flow of Oregon's Deschutes, and so crushed by the loss of a brother, that when I read Norman Maclean on the Blackfoot and the loss of his brother, I was enthralled and crushed all over again. These are not geographical overlaps, shared landscapes, or firsthand linkages: deeper within us than we can see, these are *roots touching roots*. The personal geographies conveyed via the arts converge in our interiors, create resonance, expand knowing through mysterious soul-to-soul empathy. Whereas "the national water situation," I have come to suspect, will never create anything more artful than bureacrats.

No matter how many times I forget this is the Way of it, the *particular* keeps circling back, gathering me up into the universal—a paradox I find so sweet that, a hundred and fifty or so times a year, I keep walking, with boundless gratitude, my particular, provincial, Pacific-bound waters.

Who Owns the West Wrong Answer #6: The Heron and the Moon

Isn't it possible that what we call "legal ownership" is impossible? Which part of ourselves do we own with? Our hands? Our minds? Our file cabinets full of legal documents? How do documents, minds, or hands *own* a thing? By gripping it? Thinking about it? Typing a description of a thing, affixing a notary public's stamp to it, and filing it at city hall? How long can minds, filed documents, and hands keep owning in this way before they cease to remember what they think, experience what they've filed, remember what they hold?

The questions I'm now asking have little legal meaning. But how profound is legal meaning? A name, a picture ID, and a dinnertime call from a telemarketer will bequeath us a piece of plastic that lets us legally own quite a bit—till the credit card is canceled. But isn't such ownership, when you get down to it, mere purchasing? Isn't *ownership* something entirely different? Isn't it possible to purchase a thousand products and still own nothing—and to own a thousand wonderful things yet purchase nothing?

Most of us have purchased so many things that we have forgotten many of them for years at a time. Though the forgotten things are legally ours, in what sense do we own them? Or: say we own a thing and love it well, but are going to die before we get around to touching, seeing, or using this thing again? Do we own it? The quarter-million or so acres in Montana, three-quarters of a million in New Mexico, and gazillion or so acres in Patagonia owned by Ted Turner are acres that have never been and never will be touched, comprehended, or inhabited, in any physical sense, by a fellow named Ted Turner. In what sense does Turner own any of it?

The Japanese hermit monk Ryokan owned a bowl, a robe, a handmade hut, a pen, a little ink, and some paper. But even this was often too much for him. Picking violets by the side of the road in an attempt to add, so to speak, a few wildflowers to his portfolio, Ryokan got the violets home all right, but forgot his begging bowl. A begging bowl, to a Buddhist monk, is what a fly rod is to a fly fisher, a piano to a pianist, the airplane to the pilot: it defines his relationship with the things of this world. Back home at his hut, Ryokan wrote a poem about his loss. It ended:

> *How sad you must be, my poor little bowl!*

Fourteen years ago I made a bowl of clay, fired it in an anagama kiln, and gave it to my wife-to-be on the day I knew I wanted to live with her for keeps. I don't know just how Adrian feels about it, but I feel this bowl is the most accurate gift I've managed to give her. I loved giving her a bowl because bowls are beautiful but also as humble, utilitarian, handmade, and breakable as a marriage. I loved giving her a bowl because now both of us, our two daughters, and even our dog eat out of it, as if out of the marriage. I loved giving her a bowl because my mind seems at times about the size of a bowl, if not smaller. I loved giving her a bowl because, once you've wandered your house looking for reading glasses or car keys only to find the latter in your pocket, or even in your hand, the former atop your head, or even on your nose, you can't help but wonder in what sense they're "your" glasses or keys even after you find them—which in turn makes you wonder whether it's really "your" house, "your" life, "your" marriage, and whether even *you* are "yours." I loved giving Adrian a bowl because my life, home, marriage, and self are gifts I must beg daily—must place in the moment as if in a bowl, and bend down over as if over a mound of begged rice—lest I forget to consider them, forget to be grateful for them, and so lose them, though they rest on my very head, in my hand, on my nose.

A sho, in Japanese, is the amount of rice needed to sustain a man for a day.

A *gogo* is half a *sho.*

An *an* is a hermitage.

Ryokan named his handmade wilderness hut *Gogo-an.*

In America we have the "Home of the Whopper," "Home of the Big Boy," "Home of the 72-Ounce Steak." Ryokan lived in *Gogo-an*: "Home of Half the Amount of Rice Necessary to Sustain a Man for a Day."

One day Ryokan, fresh home from begging a bowlful of rice, noticed that a bamboo plant had sent up three sprouts beneath *Gogo-an*'s floor. Watching the futile way the shoots poked at the impenetrable floorboards, Ryokan took a tool, cut three holes in his floor, coaxed the shoots into them, welcomed bamboo into his home. Spring moved into summer. The sprouts made their way toward the ceiling. "Don't worry," Ryokan kept reassuring them. "I'll cut holes in the roof when it's time."

Who owned *Gogo-an*? Ryokan? Or three bamboo shoots, plus whatever might sprout up next?

Ryokan set off one night to get sake for himself and a visitor to his hut. He told his friend the wine was a short walk away. Four hours later, Ryokan hadn't returned. The friend, worried to a frazzle, went out in search. He found Ryokan ten steps from *Gogo-an*, so smitten by the sight of a full autumn moon that he'd been standing there all that time, unable to remember his errand, his hut, his friend.

With this story, I feel we're getting somewhere. Because who owns what here? Does Ryokan own the moon? Or the moon Ryokan?

Who Owns the West?: Seven Wrong Answers

In the mangroves of southern Florida a few years ago, I took the novelist/naturalist/Zen Buddhist and supposed fly fisherman Peter Matthiessen bonefishing, a pursuit that would seem to have something to do with trying to procure bonefish. Yet on a particularly good flat, as Peter was gazing at a rare white heron in a treetop, a very large specimen of the quarry we were seeking began to chew on Peter's shrimp fly, and kept chewing on it, while the guide and I, being real fishermen, began to go nuts. *"STRIKE! STRIKE!"* we hollered. *"YO! PETER MATTHIESSEN! AUTHOR OF* BONE BY BONE! *THE VERY THING IS AT YOUR FLY! JUDAS PRIEST BUDDHIST PRIEST! WILL YOU SET THE FUCKIN' HOOK?"*

But that white heron . . .

Peter had found his autumn moon.

I've never seen a longer strike by a more eager fish. But after ten or so seconds, even bonefish brains are informed by bonefish lips that a faux-shrimp is not the real deal. Spitting Peter's fiction, the fish escaped unscathed. But the heron—gazing all that while at Peter while Peter gazed at it—did not. Nor did Peter. Each, I believe, was owned. True ownership, as I see it, occurs the instant consciousness is usurped by one of these "Ryokan Meets Full Moon" or "Peter Meets White Heron" appreciations. And while true ownership lasts, nothing but the usurping wonder exists: not sake, not Ryokan's worry-frazzled visitor, not begging bowls, not bonefish, not Peter's roaring and cursing friends. Not Ryokan or Peter, either. The absentee "Huh?" Peter finally gave the guide and me was priceless. The belatedness and feebleness with which he then yanked on his rod was even better: he looked just *like* a damned heron, trying to set a hook by slowly flapping a big wing.

Who owns "the West," or anything else? He or she, I would venture to say, who enjoys the most frequent usurpations by manageably small, beloved pieces of it—such as moons and herons.

Thesis: *To forget oneself and enter the thing is to own the thing.*

(Echo: *He that loseth his life shall save it.*)

Corollaries, capillaries, tributaries: any lesser form of "ownership" than full, self-forgetful entry into a thing seems, in comparison, like a fleeting legal fiction, a mask placed over the face of our helplessness and our mortality. I believe we're all, at bottom, mere renters; mere campers; mere beggars with bowls. I believe what we seek, ultimately, is not to possess but to be possessed by what we love. I don't believe this can happen, don't believe things become ours, unless we too become theirs; love is reciprocal. I own a log home on seven streamside Montana acres. It's well built. Barring fire, it'll outlast me by centuries. What do I own, then? A camp, is my feeling. A borrowed piece of West. A loved but fleeting sleeping/eating/gathering place from which to wander, encountering the moments that define me by erasing me: moments that *become* the stream and its trout and its broken barbed-wire fences, the sunlight and snowfall, the heron and the moon.

Who Owns the West Wrong Answer #7: A Foolish Old Monk

Ryokan was a Zen master, but chose not to teach. Instead he remained at Home-of-Half-the-Amount-of-Rice-Necessary-to-Sustain-a-Man-for-a-Day, deep in the mountains, passing the seasons by visiting villages, playing with children, drinking sake with farmers, begging his rice, writing his poems. These poems, drat the luck, made Ryokan famous. His response to that? "Who says my poems are poems!" he roared. "My poems are not poems! After you know my poems are not poems, we can begin to discuss poetry!"

Who owned Ryokan's poems? No one, it seems, since the poet insisted they weren't poems at all.

One of the nonpoet's nonpoems shows his awareness of what Americans call "estate planning." This nonpoem is Ryokan's last will and testament, or last testament to the advantages of a nonexistent will:

> *What will remain as my legacy?*
> *Flowers in the spring,*
> *The cuckoo's song in summer,*
> *The crimson leaves of autumn.*

I find it hard to stop quoting Ryokan once I start, perhaps because the nothing Ryokan owns, owns me. As for "who owns the West," I spend more and more of the heartbeats that are my only true fortune living with the old monk's answers. "*I want this, I want that,* is nothing but foolishness," says Ryokan. "I'll tell you a secret: all things are impermanent!"

Who owns the West?

*In fields where frogs sing
I pick wild roses, float them on wine—
have all the fun you can!*

Who owns the West?

*Last year, a foolish old monk.
This year, no change!*

Who owns the West?

*Even in a light snow, we can see
the three thousand worlds.
Again a light snow falls.*

Who owns the West, with no help from Ryokan? If we mean the land and waters beneath our feet; the moon, sun, stars, and gravity that cast their spells upon land and water; the light before our eyes; if we mean this millions-of-years-old realm created by celestial hydrogen explosions, ages of inconceivable heat, molten rock, ages of cooling, slow congealing, ages of ice and of ocean and of oceans breaking apart, upheaving, throwing their floors skyward to become what we now call "mountains"; if we mean these endlessly rearranging carbon compounds, these cycles of condensation/cloud/snow/rain/river, these daily and yearly anglings of sunlight and the responding migrations, photosyntheses, dormancies, hibernations, and transformations that give us our lives—if we are honestly asking who *owns* this fugue of flux, harmony, humanity, inhumanity, trout streams, terror, peace, and change, then, great God Almighty, what a ridiculous question! This stupendous work we so ineptly call "the West" owns itself. Is itself. Possesses itself completely, and us with it. Humans discussing ownership of wonders this vast are like bird-lice discussing ownership of their host heron in flight. "Who owns the right wing? Who the left?"

The heron just soars on.

When I ponder "the West," I see Buddhism's chief warning (*impermanence*) and Earth's chief gift (*beauty*) in full conspiracy, slowly wicking the life from our bodies as they wick the ignorance from our souls. This impermanent beauty, this "West," designs to host us, sometimes kills us, and ceaselessly blesses us. But allow Itself to be *owned* by us? Never! No matter how we define it, no matter what the fleetingly enthroned do to it, this abused but inconceivably great blessing will go on blessing inconceivably.

These are today's seven suspicions. Since even the West's bedrock is in flux, tomorrow's could be slightly different. With fear, trembling, and the good company of Pacific-bound rivers, I'm still working it out.

The world does not become less "unknown" in proportion to the increase of our knowledge about it. . . . Our experience of the world involves us in a mystery which can be intelligible to us only as mystery. The more we experience things in depth, the more we participate in a mystery intelligible to us only as such. . . . Our true home is wilderness, even the world of every day.

—Henry Bugbee (1915–1999)

6. Six Henry Stories

1. Language has vertical limits. Not just any speaker can pack up his speech and tote it at will to a higher elevation. Where there is a will, there is as often a major embarrassment as there is a way. Like a gymnast on parallel bars, the speaker or writer who successfully conveys exaltation must possess sufficient mental muscle to hoist himself above the level of everyday verbiage without appearing to strain. Again like the gymnast, he must be able to lift all of himself, all *by* himself. It is not speech coaches and writers, height of pulpit, number of advanced degrees, thickness of thesaurus, histrionic techniques, or any such contrivance that truly lifts language: it is personal integrity. It's the ability to imbue one's words with the physical momentum, intellectual clarity, and psychic depth that only the actual deeds of a life can provide. If Martin Luther King Jr., in his Lincoln Memorial speech of 1963, had said "In my heart I know I'm right," and if Richard Nixon, in his resignation speech a decade later, had said "I have a dream," the world would have remembered King's heart and forgotten Nixon's dream. It is not just the words that make words memorable.

This principle, I believe, is one reason why so many people, often decades after the fact, still remember certain statements the philosopher Henry Bugbee made to them. I, too, remember in unusual detail the first time I heard Henry speak. It happened like this:

In July 1993, a few weeks into my first summer in Montana, I listened to a program on the local NPR affiliate devoted to Norman Maclean's famed novel, *A River Runs Through It.* I normally take pains to avoid "literary educational opportunities," my entire working life being one relentless such opportunity. I tuned in this show not for literary reasons, but out of fly-fishermanly regard for my esteemed new neighbor, the Big Blackfoot River. I was pleasantly surprised, though. Two of the Maclean experts turned out to be astute. And, to keep things tense and interesting, the third was a crackpot. My apologies to this fellow for calling him a crackpot. Special apologies if he's reading this and turns out to be handy with his fists. All a crackpot is, by definition, is a vessel that won't hold water. I often don't. What brought the word to mind in this case was the fellow's claim that Maclean's novel was just a slick literary "cover-up attempt." He loved this term, "cover-up." He said that Norman was "covering up"—with useless love, useless hindsight, and treacherously beautiful prose—the fact that the Macleans were a dysfunctional mess of a family. He said that Norman and his father oppressed every woman they knew, denied every complex thing that happened to them, and failed to own up to the brother Paul's need for psychotherapy and an alcohol treatment center. As several call-in contributors pointed out, in Paul Maclean's day there *were* no therapies or treatments besides the whiskey bottles and gambling halls he so faithfully patronized. The cover-up expert never budged from his position. He was finally simply buried by articulate disagreement from callers who loved Norman's book.

The radio show changed gears: two local fishing guides and a retired fly-fishing philosophy professor came on the air, not to philosophize, but just to chat about the sudden national mystique of fly fishing. No sooner had the host and guides launched their discussion, though, than the old professor veered off topic to make some of the most insightful comments I've ever heard on *A River Runs Through It.* The show ended with the prof's comments, as it should have; they were authoritative and climactic. Then, a couple of weeks later, as happens in small towns, friends invited me to dinner—and there the old professor sat.

It was Henry, of course. And after we were introduced, I told him how much I'd enjoyed the show—especially his contribution to it. Henry thanked me, said that he, too, enjoyed the broadcast, but confessed to a very inexact recollection of what his contribution had been. I should point out that this was before Henry's stroke or his brain disease; the inability to remember his own animated words has been a lifelong attribute. Henry is one of these people who zeroes in on the direction of a conversation, then so loses himself in its flow that, though he's left with a profound sense of what we might call the "hydraulics" of the situation, he retains little memory of the specific and often wonderful things that he himself so often says.

This is a fine way of maintaining one's humility. But since I happen to be the sort who remembers *lots* of the clever things that *I* say, I decided, there at the dinner party, to try to mess with Henry's humility by showing him how bloody insightful he'd been about *A River Runs Through It,* and see whether I couldn't puff him up a bit.

I told Henry that he had evoked the novel's famous oatmeal scene: little Paul Maclean, aged five or so, sitting at the table before a heaped bowl of oatmeal, silently refusing to even taste this food that, as Papa Maclean puts it, "we Scots have been happily consuming for thousands of years." Paul is not swayed. Nor will his father excuse him. A classic battle of wills. The rest of the family finishes eating and leaves the table. The boy remains, looking small and vulnerable. He doesn't complain, doesn't squirm, doesn't display emotion; he just sits before the ever-more-monolithic-looking oatmeal, refusing to touch it, till we realize, as does his father, that young Paul Maclean will sit there forever before he submits.

It was a scene, in the Robert Redford movie, that one could easily describe as "cute." But on the radio as Henry Bugbee conjured it, the scene felt darkly prophetic. There was tacit violence in the father-son impasse, a frightening intractability on both sides. And Henry, on the air, summarized this intractability thus: "For all the love and admirable qualities of the father, it was, one felt, his dogmatic stance that prevented grace from flowing in the son."

This sentence rang in me like a bell. It underscored everything I love about *A River Runs Through It*: why the story feels so tragically inevitable; why the book speaks to so many of the pious parents and renegade daughters and sons who've read it; why Paul's death is so shattering to his father especially, for in that death we see how the father's greatest strength—his rock-solid faith—somehow became a mere rock, a dead weight, when he tried to will it to his son. Above all, Henry's statement helped me see why Paul's fly fishing is so central to this story, and so hauntingly beautiful: in this willful young man in whom the flow of grace is blocked, fly fishing is the one pursuit, the only pursuit, in which we literally do see "grace flowing in the son."

Well, back at the dinner party, I said more or less what I've just written. And Henry's reaction amazed me. His eyes filled; he seemed half-overcome. With a radiant smile and in a voice close to a gasp, he said, "You did that very well!"

I quickly pointed out that all I'd done was parrot him to himself, but Henry refused all credit. And the more I thought his refusal over, the more impressed I was with it. The trout we catch in these hard-fished Montana rivers have often been caught by some previous woman or man; the day we catch one ourselves, we are no less alone on the river, and the trout is no less beautiful for its previous capture. In Henry I'd met a man with no sense of proprietorship in the presence of true words. In one sense I was, as I'd said, a mere parrot, but in another sense I'd plucked Henry's insight off the radio and taken it to heart. Henry honored this second capture as the solo philosophical event it was. He was loving a neighbor's insight as one loves one's own. He was being a father whose nondogmatic stance let grace flow in an adoptive son.

2. I walked around Missoula with Henry a few times after his stroke and his brain disease struck. "Walk," in fact, is an exaggeration. A life-long athlete and mountain climber, Henry now tottered along while I held his arm, struggling to find a gear that allowed my longish legs and restless nature to mesh with his knee brace and cane. Henry was a physically beautiful old man, his shock of white hair visible from a good distance, his piercing eyes and weathered face more appealing the closer he drew. He was a legend in Missoula. During our walks he attracted curious glances and warm greetings, like a magnet. Henry's part in the exchanges was always the same: he smiled beatifically at a known face, then extended a firm grip and a good word. He squeezed your hand hard, and shook it around as if you'd won a race. He had a way of clenching his teeth as he greeted a friend, as if he were biting, with pleasure, into the encounter.

The reactions to his greetings were more varied. News of a great man's disintegration travels fast in a university town. Some spoke to Henry as if he had transcended the physical and become some kind of holy man; others spoke with an exaggeratedly loud and simplified friendliness, as if he'd become a toddler, or a tragic but likable village idiot; a few others whom Henry clearly recognized as we approached pretended not to see him and ducked away before close proximity forced them to witness Henry's "tragic condition."

For my part, I never stopped cherishing Henry's company, regardless of his condition. My feeling was, what better end than the one we were seeing for a man who believed as Henry had believed? He hadn't lost anything we wouldn't all be losing. According to our mutual hero, Meister Eckhart, Henry hadn't lost anything that was ever truly his; he was just returning some things that, as he'd always insisted, were only his on loan in the first place. What struck me about Henry to the end was what wonderful tools he'd been loaned, and how lovingly he continued to marshal the few tools he hadn't been forced to return.

I don't wish to seem wiser or more detached than I am. In the five years of our friendship, I grew exceedingly fond of Henry's unexpected phone calls, his warm, high-pitched voice, his sometimes fumbling, sometimes gorgeously chosen words, his raunchily reverent fishing stories; I loved the way he looked at his wife, Sally, when she'd enter a room; I loved the solar smile he would turn on his friends at times— and on me—nonplussing us when he simply left it on us, full-beam, for such a long, long moment that we'd finally have no choice but to realize this was no social smile, no rote kind of friendliness: this was what it felt like to be completely seen and loved for a moment.

Henry had, as it turned out, to return every borrowed gift but his inert body and heartbeat before he left us completely, and his harsh losses made me, and all who knew him, intensely sad at times. Yet almost everything about him continues, even in his absence, to be an antidote to sadness. Henry lived the kind of life that made it impossible to mourn his losses without betraying the life. Because of this, you saw a beautiful struggle in his family and friends the last few years. Our awareness that Henry was leaving us, and our urge to grieve, was cut by a simultaneous wish to honor the fact that Henry had stood, lifelong, by traditions holding that the loss of a loved one is not so much an occasion to mourn as an occasion to be true to love. "To give thanks lyingly," said Jalal al-Din Rumi, "is to seek the love of God." In the eyes of those who greeted Henry as his mind and body failed, I was touched again and again by this "lying thanks," this seeking of love.

I saw panic in some eyes, too. When those who live the life of the mind see an anchor of a friend taking leave of the mind, there is bound to be terror. But, while I still have a mind with which to be afraid, I embrace Rumi's "lying thanks," Eckhart's "emptiness," Zen's "no-mindedness," Christ's "poverty of spirit." This mind of mine was never mine to start with; in sleep and in dreams I lose it every night. Henry, in his final state of mind, reminded me of that Chinese, or maybe Japanese, roshi, his name now lost to me, who, when asked, "What is my real self, O master?" answered, "Mountains and rivers and the great earth." Henry reminded me of that Japanese, or maybe Chinese, poet who, when asked, "What is self?" answered, "Rambling in the mountains, enjoying the waters." He reminded me of Jim Harrison (finally a name I remember!), who, in "Cabin Poem," says, "I've decided to make up my mind / about nothing, to assume the water mask, / to finish my life disguised as a creek, / an eddy, joining at night the full / sweet flow, to absorb the sky, / to swallow the heat and cold, the moon / and the stars, to swallow myself / in ceaseless flow."

Henry's condition reminded me, finally, that though I once knew the names of the makers of all the above statements, what difference do names make if the statements are true? A man once given to speak sentences such as "There is a stream of limitless meaning flowing into the life of a man if he can but patiently entrust himself to it" drew slowly toward the end of a life of patient trust. The few people we approached on the street, the ones who ducked away, made me want to shout, "Come back! Don't be pathetic! There's nothing scary or sad here! A wonderful old man is falling slowly to pieces. Come say hi to him and his pieces while you've got the chance!"

One of the last times I saw Henry, a circuit crossed and he greeted me as "Mike." I say, close enough. I say Henry finished his life disguised ever more perfectly as a creek. I say, call me David, call me Mike, call me Ishmael, and give me, please God, the courage and grace to embrace the same disguise. The courage to become mountains and rivers and the great Earth. The courage (to steal it straight from Henry) to make wilderness my true home.

3. Some teachers never retire, despite their retirement. Henry, for instance. Almost every philosophical poker hand the old sharp plays in his legendary book of reflections, *The Inward Morning*, will still win the pot. The reason Henry couldn't and can't retire is this: When you align yourself with emptiness and no-mindedness, then spend your life teaching that alignment, what you've taught goes on teaching itself whether or not you're even alive, let alone whether or not you've retired.

My Story as Told by Water

I experienced the nonretirement of Henry one recent December when I was invited to spend three days, in my capacity as a novelist, with forty students at a small college in Oregon. This was a *Christian* institution, mind you, with a Christian plan for my visit. What the students wanted me to talk about, it turned out, was my "personal faith" and "personal experiences as a churchgoer."

This plan presented two problems. One: the phrase "personal faith" is impossibly paradoxical. As soon as you talk publicly about personal life, personal finances, personal anything, it's no longer personal. Two: upon attaining religious autonomy more than thirty years ago, I began to worship at Henry's church: the church of "wilderness, our true home." As a result, I have since enjoyed a grand total of zero personal experiences as a churchgoer.

Bivouacked among the forty young Christians, then, with a single night to prepare remarks on "personal faith" and "personal churchgoing" in order to earn my personal honorarium, I felt disturbingly cognizant, for the first time in my life, of a slight vocational resemblance between me and Pat Robertson. Must I, too, feign piety to get paid? Or should I take things in a more Swaggartish direction and speak forthrightly about how sitting in church pews, shortly before I fled them, used to give me such uncontrollable sexual fantasies that I'd pretend to be reading the hymnal in order to cover my erections—and in gratitude for said coverage at last grew vaguely fond of hymns? The options looked dark. The hour grew late. There was no booze, on that accursedly clean-cut campus, to fuel even a madcap nightcapped musing. No hymnal either. What a relief, suddenly, to recall a deft card hand played by Henry in *The Inward Morning,* aimed at the word "wonder."

I didn't have Henry's book with me, but did recall him saying something like "The tenets of religious belief are not intended to be the termination of wonder: they're intended to be *occasions* for it." This felt like a desirable entry point into my thoughts on "personal faith," in that it would at least put an end to any resemblance between me and Pat Robertson. I then realized I could answer the "personal faith" question by simply ignoring its Christian connotation, speaking instead of something in which I *do* have faith—namely, this state so beloved by the never-retiring Henry, the state called "wonder."

I grabbed my pen and legal pad and set to work, finding it incredibly helpful not to have *The Inward Morning* with me, since this freed me to crib Henry's thought with shameless abandon. The next day I gave my forty Christian charges a talk that began like this:

My earliest conception of the meaning of the word *wonder* was a feeling that would come over me as a little kid, when I'd picture the shepherds on the night hills above Bethlehem. Even when those shepherds were made of illuminated plastic, standing around in Christmas dioramas on my neighbors' lawns, their slack-jawed expressions of wonder appealed to me. Years later, having become literate enough to read, I learned that those shepherds were also "sore afraid." But—a personal prejudice—I didn't believe in their afraidness. I believed the star in the east smote them with wonder, and that once wonder smites you, you're smitten by wonder alone. Fear can't penetrate till wonder subsides.

Wonder is my second favorite condition to be in, after love, and I sometimes wonder whether there's a difference; maybe love is just wonder aimed at a beloved.

Wonder is like grace, in that it's not a condition we grasp; it grasps us.

Wonder is not an obligatory element in the search for truth. We can seek truth without wonder's assistance. But seek is all we'll do; there will be no finding. Unless wonder descends, unlocks us, turns us as slack-jawed as plastic shepherds, truth is unable to enter. Wonder may be the aura of truth, the halo of it. Or something even closer. Wonder may be the caress of truth, touching our very skin.

Philosophically speaking, wonder is crucial to the discovery of knowledge, yet has everything to do with ignorance. By this I mean that only an admission of our ignorance can open us to fresh knowings. Wonder is the experience of that admission: wonder is unknowing, experienced as pleasure.

Punctuationally speaking, wonder is a period at the end of a statement we've long taken for granted, suddenly looking up and seeing the sinuous curve of a tall black hat on its head, and realizing it was a question mark all along.

As a facial expression, wonder is the letter *O* our eyes and mouths make when the state itself descends. *O*: God's middle initial. *O*: because wonder *O*pens us.

Wonder is anything taken for granted—the old neighborhood, old job, old life, old spouse—suddenly filling with mystery. Wonder is anything closed, suddenly opening: anything at all opening—which, alas, includes Pandora's Box, and brings me to the dark side of the thing. Grateful as I am for this condition, wonder has—like everything on Earth—a dark side. Heartbreak, grief, and suffering rend openings in us through which the dark kind of wonder pours. I have so far found it impossible to feel spontaneously grateful for these violent openings.

But when, after struggle, I've been able to turn a corner and at least *accept* the opening, the dark form of wonder has invariably helped me endure the heartbreak, the suffering, the grief.

Wonder is not curiosity. Wonder is to curiosity what ecstasy is to mere pleasure. Wonder is not astonishment, either. Astonishment is too brief. The only limit to the duration of wonder is the limit of our ability to remain open.

I believe some people live in a state of constant wonder. I believe they're the best people on Earth. I believe it is wonder, even more than fidelity, that keeps marriages alive. I believe it's wonder, even more than courage, that conquers fear of death. I believe it is wonder, not D.A.R.E. bumper stickers, that keeps kids off drugs. I believe, speaking of bumper stickers, that it's wonder, even more than me, who I want to "HUG MY KIDS YET TODAY," because wonder can keep on hugging them, long after I'm gone.

4. One warm May evening a couple of years before he died, Henry and I sat in lawn chairs on a rocky point, overlooking the runoff-swollen trout stream that runs through my backyard. This evening marked the first time I'd seen Henry since he'd suffered his stroke. The hundred-yard walk from my house to the rocky point was a slow, serious undertaking. The stroke had clearly returned a few pieces of my friend back to the "mountains, rivers, and great earth" from whence they'd come.

As we sat above the fast green water, I told Henry of spectacular seasonal changes I'd witnessed on the creek over the past year, of encounters with local wildlife, of fish I'd hooked in the flow right before our eyes. Henry listened calmly, but seemed more interested in the unaccompanied sound of the stream.

I stopped my babbling and let the creek's take over. The evening was beautiful, the sun warm, and I was relieved at once by the cessation of my own voice. I was sinking into things, giving myself to the day, and to the curious tension that rises and falls when we sit long, without speaking, with a friend—when I suddenly noticed something odd going on with Henry.

He was seated directly to my right. And he'd begun to slump way over on the right side of his chair. The ground beneath our chairs was rough and rocky. He kept slumping farther. Fearing he'd fall—fearing some strange symptom of his stroke had set in—I surreptitiously placed my foot on the base of his chair and held it firmly down.

Six Henry Stories

Henry lowered his right arm clear to the ground. I looked away, feeling embarrassed somehow, but could hear his fingers fumbling in the rocks, feel his chair writhing as I steadied it with my foot. I was just beginning to think he was having another full-on stroke when he suddenly straightened, and the chair came back into balance.

Henry did not look at me. Instead he leaned slightly forward, briefly studying the surface of the swollen creek.

Then his right arm flashed. A large flat stone I hadn't even known he was holding sailed down over the green eddy, hit the water, bounced up in a sunlit crown of spray, hit the water, bounced again, hit the water, bounced again. A triple skip! From a bad angle, out of a lawn chair, over rough water (a rough *eddy,* no less), by an eighty-one-year-old who'd just had a major stroke. On the authority of a life spent skipping skippers, I tell you: this throw was an *ecstasis.*

I turned. Henry was still studying the creek, but his "innocence" was a sham now. The slow turn of his head, toward me, then away again, was eagle-regal. He was painstakingly careful to wear no trace of a smile. But the look in his eyes as they met mine, then turned back to the creek! I tell you . . . I tell you . . . It was even better than the lines "The readiness to receive is all. Without that, what can be given?" Better than "This above all, then: be ready at all times for the gifts of God, and always for new ones." Maybe even better than "To love is to understand what is perceived as eternal."

5. The last time I saw Henry, I don't know how to describe his presence except to say that he seemed no longer home in any sense but the anatomical. Though his body was being well cared for, his consciousness had returned to the mysterious place consciousness goes after, as Tom Waits puts it, "the wheels come off." Henry's wheels came off in this order: he lost the ability to take care of himself, then the ability to walk, then the ability to recognize his friends, children, and finally even Sally. Meanwhile he lost the ability to convey a thought. Then the ability to speak. And finally the ability to recognize food or water in his own mouth. With this loss came the loss of the ability to eat and drink. So loss of life followed. But not nearly so soon as one would think or hope or pray. Henry's long, slow loss of everything was a mystery intelligible to me only as mystery. It was a dark, dark wonder. It was wilderness.

Sally had to take me to the Home for Those Whose Wheels Have Come Off, get me inside, show me to Henry's room. In the room next door was a frail old woman who, Sally had learned, was the poet Dylan Thomas's last extramarital lover. To give me time alone with Henry, Sally went in to read Thomas poems to this woman. I watched the reading begin. The woman's eyes, when we first saw her, were staring straight ahead at a white curtain. When Sally greeted her, then introduced me, her face never changed expression and her gaze never swerved. The Dylan Thomas poems commenced. The gaze didn't change. So much for poetry in the face of mysteries intelligible only as mystery.

I went to try my luck with Henry. How did it feel, being with such a man after his wheels had come off? I'm still pondering that. I'll ponder it till my own wheels go. I took the chair by his bed, said hello, and when Henry turned slowly to me I took his hand, held it, and vowed not to let him have it back unless he absolutely seemed to want it. He didn't. He stared at me a long while, said nothing, but struggled, I felt, to figure out just who the hell I was. We still had that in common.

There was no creek to turn to, and Henry had been silent for days. I had a monopoly, now, on the babbling. I took advantage of it. I first told Henry, despite some embarrassment about how kiss-ass it sounded, a couple of recent anecdotes about how much he'd meant to a variety of wonderful people. Henry stared at me the same way Dylan Thomas's last lover was staring at the sound of Dylan Thomas's poems.

I told Henry stories about the changing of the year—how the Indian summer of '99 was the most adamant I'd ever seen, the slowest to pass into autumn. He stared at space in response, he breathed, he lived on, while the resemblance between his state and the summer of '99 reverberated in the air.

I played my sorry trump card. I told Henry I'd been having the best trout fishing of my life, thanks to this summer that refused to die. I then launched a fish story. Henry still just stared. But so do trout and water. I was in my element now. Telling fish stories felt almost like an exchange between us, since when you start telling fish stories it makes sense that people just stare.

I told Henry of a spring-fed pond I'd discovered in a huge grassy field in the middle of nowhere: a pond that looked and felt like something in a dream. I told him, truthfully, of lying behind a log on a sandbank, four feet from this pond, while twenty-inch rainbows ate live grasshoppers I tossed to them with my hands. I told Henry, truthfully, of a twenty-seven-inch brown trout I'd caught in this dreamlike pond, how it flashed at but refused an artificial grasshopper, flashed at but refused even real grasshoppers kicking along on the surface with no hook attached. It then rose to an artificial blue damselfly, though no such insects had been in the air for weeks—rose, perhaps, out of yearning for this blue harbinger of high summer. I told how the brown threw my fly on its first hysterical leap, but was spinning so violently that the leader lassoed its snout and the thrown hook drove itself, a second time, into the trout's nostril. I told how the pain of a hooked inner nose made the big fish leap more relentlessly than any brown I'd ever seen, leap itself to early exhaustion, leap itself, weakly, right into my waiting hands. I told how I sat for the longest time, cross-legged in twelve inches of clear-as-air springwater, with this twenty-seven-inch, yellow-and-gold-bodied, crimson-spotted animal resting in the shade of me, allowing me to admire it, allowing me the pleasure of watching it fin and breathe.

Henry just stared. And it had, I felt, been a pretty good story. So I let one of my own wheels come off: my truth wheel. I told Henry of the forty-two-inch brown trout I hooked, on the very next cast, in the same dreamlike pond, then watched for his reaction. He just stared. So I rared back and told him of the ninety-inch brown. The largest ever seen, anywhere. Forget Loch Leven browns, Henry, this was a Loch Ness fish. Lived on geese, ducks, and spring calves that fell in the pond. He didn't object. His stare was not eagle-regal. But now it at least felt like a statement—felt like the response my nonsense deserved. This made me a bit happier.

I called off the last two browns with a "not really." Henry stared. I said, "Not only do your friends and family and Sally miss you. I bet *you* miss you, too." He said nothing. The man before me had once written, "As we take things, so we have them; if we take them in faith, we have them in earnest; if wishfully—then fantastically; if willfully, then stubbornly; if merely objectively, with the trimmings of subjectivity—then emptily; and if in faith, though it be in suffering, yet we have them in earnest, and it is really them that we have."

And now he and I had this.

I looked at my friend carefully, knowing suddenly that it was for the last time. It seemed helpful, as I looked—at least in terms of controlling emotion—that our visit had felt so one-sided. Henry seemed beyond visiting. He was no longer Henry exactly; his body had become a temple, closed seven days a week, with the Henry I loved locked inside. But when that old temple suddenly, competently, cleared its throat, and I heard in the clearing the tone of Henry's beautiful, vanished voice— Henry the unexpected, Henry our *anam ċara*—all kinds of things rose in my chest and throat and eyes, and I had no more words for either of us that weren't silent and weren't prayer.

Not till December did Sally call to say that Henry's heart had stopped.

At the sound of her breaking voice after so many months of "patient trust," "the readiness to receive," and "taking in faith," I felt waters rise behind my face, felt a fresh crack in my heart, felt mind, mouth, and heart fall open, and knew—via raw ignorance and dark wonder—that these are the waters of life; that grasses, trees, and flowers grow from such cracks.

Henry's slow departure, hard as it was, is "the world of every day." *"Our true home is wilderness."*

6. Indian Summer '99:

The sky a blue so outright it falls like snow to the ground. The air a beam-prone gold that pierces the blue, and me, each time I breathe it. The days, dawn to dusk, lit by a low, long-shadow-making sun that brings little warmth but finds the integrity in everything: pine bark, alluvial stones, tansy stalks, the spent garden, nine cords of fresh-split firewood, the browned backs of my wood-battered hands.

No wind. No breeze. Stasis. A lone fox barks somewhere, just once. After forty-seven years I realize it's gravity, more than anything, that tilts me, come evening, to the nearest river. Today the flow slides by in silence, a quavering, less convincing world splayed upside-down across its surface. Cricket songs slow in the gathering chill. The grasshoppers' hops grow shorter. I watch sudden silver rises on the thick, refractive water. Watch turned aspens shoot false fire through each rise. The cliff swallow colony's been vacant for weeks. Three days ago the ospreys set out for Mexico. A dull red water-birch leaf taps its blind way down through branches, softly daps the river, finds sunlight, turns crimson, slides blazingly away. Fifty winter crows and a single trailing magpie pass, without comment, into the mountain's growing shadow.

More silent rises. More false fire. More breath,
more blue, more gold. "The sky is vast
straight into the heavens. A bird flies
just like a bird." Even in
Montana, how I long
for Montana.

75.29-8 *Ebisu Catching a Carp* (detail) by Kawahabe Gyosai (1831-1889). Japan, Edo period, Ukiyo-e school. Album leaf: ink and color on paper; 15.5 x 22.8 cm (6⅛ x 9 in). FREER GALLERY OF ART, Smithsonian Institution, Washington, D.C. 20560.

Here we go, David!

Henry

Ebisu Catching a Carp, KAWAHABE GYOSAL

A c t i v i s m

We live in an occupied country,
misunderstood; justice will take us
millions of intricate moves.

      —William Stafford

7. Native

I would like to think aloud about a single English word: the word *native*. If that sounds like thin entertainment, let me lay that worry to rest: I *am* thin entertainment. I'm native entertainment, though. Maybe that's the trouble: my native land is the Columbia River Basin. Looking at my Basin's native salmon count, native big game and bird counts, native tree counts, Native American count, I see a thin native world growing thinner. That's why I want to think about the word fast; if I wait much longer, the noun *native* could become a verb meaning "to vanish."

....

AUTHOR'S NOTE: This essay was originally a talk, given on board a sternwheel riverboat moored at the upper end of tidewater on the Columbia River system, to an Oregon fly fisher's club. As I spoke, the salmon and steelhead born of the waters beneath us were joining the Endangered Species List, losing their world, fighting for their lives. Their plight fueled a desperate act on my part: my a capella singing debut. The fly fishers joined in—in tentative disbelief at first. But after a couple of verses we were rocking the river, and the "repaired song" herein has since become a standby at river-watchdog gatherings all over the Northwest. I pray the salmon people heard.

A problematic use of the word *native* appeared on the bumpers of Columbia River Basin cars about a decade ago. Following the World Series Earthquake in San Francisco, a lot of San Andreas Fault–fried Californians came chugging up Interstate 5 into Oregon like, I don't know, a horde of U-Haul drivin', BMW-towin' Okies was how they struck me, all hoping the Global Environmental Apocalypse wouldn't be so advanced up in Oregon, with its lovely state bird, the meadowlark, and long-lasting state flower, the tree stump. When these masses arrived, thousands of old Oregon-license-plated rustbuckets began to greet them with a bumpersticker: OREGON NATIVE, it read.

I was intrigued. The stickers' owners obviously felt that being born on the same clearcut soil their vehicles were now polluting was a thing worth gloating over to the nouveau-Okies in the U-Hauls. Judging, however, by the hundreds of Oregon natives I'd known all my life, the only real difference between born-heres and newcomers was that the born-heres had spent more time turning the native landscape into an alien, nonnative place. "Cascade Mountain native," my Uncle Don could brag as he almost singlehandedly wiped out that Range's cougar population. "Montana native," Grandpa Duncan could gloat as he helped convert his native Rockies into open-pit copper mines, drove alien cattle up to overgraze the native hills, then rode off into wilderness to exterminate the native grizzlies for the Cattlemen's Association. Mere nativeness, for most of us, is nothing much to brag about.

Even the best intentioned of us techno-industrial humans are mired in cash-driven, car-propelled lives. Those lives render us so nonindigenous that the word *native* is an honor we must earn afresh, every day. Our individual words, actions, and purchases either do or do not contribute to the health of what Aldo Leopold calls "the biotic community." For now it is those words, actions, and purchases that seem to make us, Indians included, most truly "native." I have longed all my life to go this definition one better—longed to become some kind of reborn Highland *bhakti* tribesman; to join a valid spiritual community; to live, in daily detail, a sustainable, grateful, impiously reverent life. So far I manage to clean up the trash in the backyard trout stream, feed and house native birds, scare off housecats with a BB gun, annoy and occasionally scare off corporate industrialists with a livid pen, and write some stories that attest to certain native truths. But those stories are published by a global media conglomerate; I own a car, a TV, and a computer; my garden pretty much sucks; and my tribe is scattered to the winds. To call this a "native life" just diminishes the word.

I believe we'll all, eventually, become natives of our places—we'll have to, in order to remain alive. But it's going to take time. I daresay *lifetimes.* In the meantime I want the word *native* to mean as much as it can. So it frequently cannot mean me.

Another way to sneak up on a word's meaning is to find its antonym.

For the "Average American"—those bland creatures Gallup and Harris always manage to locate before conducting their opinion polls— the opposite of *native* is probably a word such as *foreigner, alien,* or *immigrant.* If Gallup interviewed a bunch of Western fly-fishing freaks, though, they'd learn to their amazement that the opposite of the word *native* is a hatchery trout! Surprises like this are among the things I love about nativeness: our homes, our loves, our obsessions refract and color everything, region by region, human by human, like light when it enters a prism. Gallup thinks a scud is something Iraqis fire at Israelis. My fish-nut friends know it's a fly we fire into surface film to deceive trout. Gallup thinks a sage is either a smart Oriental fella or David Carradine dressed as one. We fishing dweebs know it as a fragrant desert bush and an overpriced, overstiff line of fly rods.

Who's right about scuds and sage? Who's wrong? Is it a question of right or wrong? It just may be: because Gallup Think governs the impulses of the nation. Yet Gallup Think—the sort of generalized knowledge gained from public-opinion polls and PR firms—is the precise and often killing opposite of the detailed, hands-on knowledge that involves us in native life.

Gallup Think strikes me as wrong in spirit even when it's mathematically correct. Gallup Think, for instance, assumes that public opinion has value and ought to pack a wallop. But Native Knowledge has shown me that I've never caught a fish, cut and stacked a cord of firewood, or grown a garden on opinion yet. Gallup Think assumes that our samenesses define us in some crucial way. Native Knowledge demonstrates, on the other hand, that our samenesses are largely uninformative, and that it's our peculiarities that define us. When my father played baseball, for instance, he pitched three-quarter arm, and had an odd motion that gave his pitches weirder stuff. He casts trout flies with the same three-quarter-arm motion now. I threw overhand in baseball, and cast flies that way now. According to Gallup Think, the two of us fishing a mountain lake are two guys fishing a lake. But Native Knowledge, zooming in for detail, reveals that Dad, with his loopy delivery, puts a casting-knot in his leader on every cast, hence weakens it, hence snaps off every sizable fish that hits his fly, while my knot-free leader and I bring home the dinner. That's the defining importance of a native detail with regard to fly fishing. It is also, with regard to baseball, why my father struck out ten times more batters than I did.

Another Gallup Think flaw: if 68 percent of Americans, with a 4 percent margin of error, say that a scud is a missile, is it any less a trout fly? And if 24 percent of the Columbia/Snake River Basin's residents say they prefer cheap electricity to the existence of native salmon, are our salmon any less worth saving for that? In my particular overhand-castin', hatchery-trout-hatin' scud of a native opinion, any such 24 percent can go sit on the pencils they filled out their poll with. If we're talking about the survival of native species, so can the 99 percent. Fishermen and fisherwomen are, first and foremost, catchers and connoisseurs of *fish*. Hell, we're named after 'em. A native fisher's physical, mental, and spiritual connection to his native fish comprises what the ancient Hindus call a *dharma*—a way of life. It's absurd, it's an insult, to think one's dharma should change the day the majority of a Gallup-polled populace decides to save a nickel on their kilowatts.

We people of the fish have our own poles, thank you. We have learned via bamboo, fiberglass, and graphite that our native species are interdependent and all worth saving, and that if a mere human majority states a polled preference that would exterminate a species, all it means is that the chuckleheads conducting the poll ought to have asked better questions.

Think about it. To ask some overworked cluck, point-blank, whether he wants to spend more of his inadequate paycheck on electricity in order to help a few salmon over a dam shows about as much tact, on the part of the pollster, as a drunk asking for spare change while he pisses on your shoes. The Columbia/Snake River Salmon Poll I'd like to see might begin by asking the populace whether they love animals and birds, including their pets, and other humans, including their children; it might then ask whether they'd be willing to pay a doctor or vet to keep those children and pets alive; next it would ask whether they realize that the Columbia/Snake system is the great doctor and vet to the life of our entire region; then it would ask if they realize that our generation is presiding over a biological holocaust—a third of the native plant and animal species on the planet annihilated in our brief lifetimes; it would ask if they knew that *nothing like this has ever happened,* that even the end of the dinosaurs did not compare; it would ask how long they think they can live with the food chain, the atmosphere, the Web of Life in tatters; it would ask how long people are living now in tattered places like industrialized China; Honduras and Haiti; lowland Brazil; the Pentagon-enhanced portions of Utah; and when it finally reached the money question, my Salmon Poll might phrase it thus: "Would you be willing to sacrifice a few annual dollars in order to protect your life, your children's lives, your entire biotic community, the very Web of Life, beginning with the Columbia and Snake Rivers and their vanishing wild salmon?"

But that's too wordy for a poll. That's the trouble with the Web of Life. Even in tatters it has an unpollably large number of beautiful living parts. You can't invoke those parts with numbers, or even with words, really. Yet mere numbers, evoking nothing but dollars on a rigged gaming table, can make the choice of lifelessness over Life sound like sound economic strategy.

So there's my gripe with Gallup. The pollsters' lowest-common-denominator conclusions pretend to be the "voice of democracy." But even in the age of polls we remain living, breathing, eating, defecating parts of the Web of Life. Our utter dependence upon that web remains *the* basic economic, political, scientific, and poetic fact. The voice of *every species* in the web remains the one truly democratic voice. Most of these voices—wild salmon and ancient tree voices, for instance—speak no louder as they're being annihilated than they do in health. But my favorite political argument, all my life, has been that we must remain native enough to speak for and represent salmon and trees—which is to say, *our greater physical selves*—as powerfully as we speak for our financial selves.

How to speak for other life-forms effectively: there's a crucial native question. I once heard the CNN newscaster David Goodnow speak of our native river system's salmon. "Some strains of Columbia River salmon appear to be in trouble," he announced to the nation, and my heart skipped a hopeful beat. "Only one sockeye salmon made it back to Idaho's Snake River this year," he added disapprovingly (though it was a full six months after that particular sockeye, having found no mate, had become cat food). I quickly turned up the volume, anxious to see how CNN would play this crucial story. *But the story was already over!* "*Dollars and Sense* is up next," said Goodnow with a wan smile, then out popped a Nissan ad. Every half hour for the rest of the night, CNN repeated the very same salmon sound bite, followed by the same ad, leaving even me, a raving native fish fanatic, with the feeling that the solution to the Columbia/Snake River mess might be to kiss off the salmon, paint the car red, and rename it the Nissan Sockeye.

On a single TV station, not long ago, I watched the bloated bodies of hundreds of civilians murdered by machetes float down an African river and wash over a postcard-pretty waterfall, and the very next instant, no warning, a range of North American mountains framed a $29,900 SUV I was expected to feel in a mood to buy. It's a fascinating assumption. When real hacked bodies in beautiful rivers flow into lust for cars, when a real woman's slashed throat leads to hunger for a taco, when the opening of a salmon-killing aluminum beer can causes greased babes in bikinis to writhe before us, who knows, the extinction of crucial native species might lead to multiple orgasms.

What can any would-be native make of the TV news team, shooting its orthodontically flawless cathode smile into us as it says:

"Good evening. America's greatest scientists adjourned a week-long meeting at the Miami Convention Center last night and concluded that the entire Eastern Seaboard is an impending ecological dead zone. Over to you, Tammy."

"Thanks, Ralph. Well, the reptiles are happy in Iowa today. They just found out that, thanks to erosion, petrochemical farming, and the merciless plundering of the aquifer, the whole state will be a desert by the year 2020. Move over, Las Vegas! Now, here's Bob with the weather."

"Okay, Tammy. Thank you. Well, it's warming up in Iowa . . ."

What can anyone do with such disembodied, nonspecific, no-hands, no-experience knowledge? TV has made Ted Turner rich enough to hoard some incredibly nice acreage in Montana, New Mexico, and Patagonia. But can it help the rest of us save anything, anywhere, ever? And if it can't, what kind of knowledge can?

In researching my latest novel, I read of a contemporary band of natives, down in South America's Colombia, who spoke to me on my river of the same name:

Colombia's Makuna tribe are a Neolithic people—grass-and-tree-bark clothing; handmade hunting and fishing tools. That makes me nervous in searching for cultural models, since I don't believe we'll be surrendering what technology has given us anytime soon. I do believe, however, that compassion will, of necessity, become the basis of every technological decision we make. And the Makuna live in a way that dissolves the Industrial World's usual compassionless split between nature and culture, between product and conscience, between animals and people, between deadly daily work and life-loving daily beliefs.

The Makuna maintain that humans, animals, plants, all of nature, are part of a great oneness. Our ancestors, they say, were magical fish who came ashore along the rivers and turned two-legged. As these first land beings began to conduct their lives, and to sing about it, everything in the world began to be created from their songs: hills and forests; animal and bird people; insect and fish people.

But—the twist I love—*this creation process is ongoing.* The making of the world is no past-tense event, as Christian fundamentalists would have it. The world, say the Makuna, is *still* being created: our words, actions, and songs still determine the nature of the hills and forests, and still help create, sustain, or destroy the animal, fish, and bird people.

We share a spiritual essence, the Makuna say, with the swimming, flying, and four-legged peoples. They live in communities, just as we do, with their own chiefs (picture a bull elk) and shamans (picture an old coyote, a raven, a great horned owl). They have dance houses and birth houses, songs and rites, and material possessions, just as we do. (We think easily of feathers and fur in this context, but remember, too, the nests and dens, and the carefully defended territories; remember the salmon's virtual ownership of the herring, the seal's of the salmon, the trout's of the mayfly, the osprey's of the trout.) Fish, according to the Makuna, even have ceremonial paints and ritual ornaments, which they don, as we do, for certain crucial occasions. (Consider the endangered coho, justly named "silver" during its life in the ocean, but donning greens and crimsons for the sex-driven return to its birth house.)

I'll cut to the chase: according to the Makuna, our essential oneness with other species is not just a source of vague mystical pleasure, or of cool, ripped-off Indian images for hip writers and artists. Our oneness is the source of an enormous obligation. We depend on fish, animal, and bird people to eat and live. In return, the fish, animal, and bird people depend on us to spiritually enact, *daily,* the hidden oneness of all life. Anytime humans eat, anytime we gather, anytime we make merry or celebrate in our world, we have a dire obligation to offer "spirit food" to the winged, fish, and animal people, that they may celebrate in their worlds. And if we fail to make such offerings—if we do not spiritually share with the other species—they quickly die. So say the Makuna.

I confess my modern bias: the words "spirit food" make me think of peyote and coca cults, hallucinogenic jungle brews, hopelessly Neolithic people, "primitives." But what does the word *primitive* mean? A shaman of my own coast, Gary Snyder, reminds us that the root of the word *primitive* is *primary.* "Primitive" things are, then, the most basic and essential things there are: water, earth, fire, air, food, shelter, nurture; things we die without.

What about "primitive beliefs," then? Are they equally primary and indispensible? Fish, say the Makuna, consume spirit food, and need us two-leggeds to offer them such food. What on earth does this notion mean?

Trying on the idea in my own watershed, I thought of the huge chinook salmon of the Columbia—June hogs, we used to call them: sixty-, eighty-, even hundred-pound salmon that swam the entire river from the Pacific clear up into eastern British Columbia, fighting the pre-dam runoff, mightiest currents of the year. And those chinook ate nothing—or nothing physical—the whole thousand-mile way. Non-food. Ghost food. *Spirit food.* Is there a better name for what sustained them? And the humans of their day, the native tribes, did indeed offer elaborate gifts, dances, and feasts to honor their coming.

Were these rites the ingredient that sustained those magnificent salmon? This is a stretch for us Visa-carded, jet-propelled Info-Agers, I know. But maybe there's a falls or dam we need to leap here in order to enter our native place. The Makuna insist that we must offer "spirit food" to keep the bird, fish, and animal people healthy. We squirm at the archaic flavor of the idea. Yet what industrial man offered the June chinooks, instead of spirit food, was Grand Coulee Dam. And now those unparalleled, irreplaceable creatures are extinct. Is there some *primitive,* i.e., *primary,* i.e., *essential* wisdom we're overlooking that could prevent the extirpation of what remains?

I sense two things here. Both sound silly to the rationalistic half of my brain. But I feel in my native heart and bones, first of all, that most of us drastically underestimate—with tragic results for our fish, forests, rivers, wildlife, and greater selves—just how primitive we still are: how basic we are, despite our modernity; how dependent we are on the company of native plants, animals, earth, water, air. And the second thing I feel we underestimate—again with tragic results—is how spiritually alive and capable we are.

It's a prickly topic, spirituality. Sloppy and pedantic talk about God is obnoxious and dangerous, and those who parade such talk have knocked the religion clean out of a lot of us, with no sense of loss. But reverence for life is not religion. Reverence for life is the basis of compassion, and of biological health. This is why, much as it may embarrass those of us trained in the agnostic sciences, I believe every life-loving human on Earth carries a far-from-agnostic obligation to remain primitive enough, and reverent enough, to stand up and say to any kind of political power or poll or public: *Trees and mountains are holy. Rain and rivers are holy. Salmon are holy. For this reason alone I will fight with all my might to keep them alive.*

This is not an argument, not a number, not a polled opinion. It is more than mere words. It's naked native belief. And if we put our full conviction in such belief, if we feel no embarrassment over it, if we stand up and stand by it again and again, we might begin to discover a spirit-power in ourselves that moves from there out into our friends or kids, or into our scientific research, our art, our music or writing, and from there on out into beautiful but threatened laws such as the Clean Air, Clean Water, and Endangered Species Acts, and thence into our homelands, watersheds, native country, native co-inhabitants, making Grand Coulee and Snake River dam-style species holocausts illegal and impossible from now till doomsday. Economic, political, and scientific arguments just aren't cutting it. Our salmon people are leaving us. And so many other natives—finned, furred, winged, and two-legged—have already gone.

So. What is "spirit food" for us industrial/indigenous half-breeds? What is a modern-day spirit offering? I'd say that now, as ever, it is anything we truly value. Our energy, our focus, the hours of our days. Anything we respect so much that, as we pour it out on the finned, feathered, and four-legged peoples' behalf, we kind of hate to see it go. Maybe single-malt scotches from the literalists among us. Prayers and mantras from the mystics. Money, time, and trouble from the capitalists and activists. Unflinching accuracy, no matter the political climate, from the scientists. Stories from people like me. The big blockade to change is lack of passion. And the birth-house of passion is the heart. A spirit offering, then, is anything we can offer with a whole heart—any song, dance, phone call, plea, letter, insight, gift, or prayer that helps determine the way we, and other humans, continue to create our world, rivers, hills, and forests.

It feels awkward, I know, to just stand up and do a "spirit thing." But so does the Web of Life find our lethal industry and greed awkward. Even a hokey spirit offering expresses a dream, a hope, a moment's love for another life-form. If we don't get to work with the tools at hand, we may never get to work.

On that note, I'd like to try my own hokey hand at a spirit offering.

Ever get a song stuck in your head when you're out fishing?

Sure. It's a fishing universal.

And did you ever hate the song that got stuck?

Sure. That's universal, too.

But did you ever get a song you hate stuck in your head for *thirty years?*

I did. So that's the raw material of my spirit offering. Industrial Man has fucked up so bad that a lot of the native work to be done over the next few centuries is going to be *repair* work. My spirit offering today is a repaired song.

That this song got riveted to my brain was hardly an accident. The Army Corps of Engineers and all manner of other Industrial Gladiators have bronzed its lyrics to the concrete walls of dams, tourist centers, factories, and parks all over the Columbia River Basin, and Northwest public school kids, including me in the fourth grade, get its irresistible melody and idiotic words implanted in their brains like hatchery-fish DNA a full decade before they know what terms like "brainwash" and "co-optation" even mean. The worst reason the song sticks in my head, though, is that I love the guy who wrote it. He had a Judas of an off day, is all. Working on commission from the federal Bonneville Power Administration, a wonderful songwriter—the writer of "This Land Is Your Land," for Christ's sake!—whipped off an evil spirit offering after admiring a spanking new species-extincting, culture-destroying, Indian-impoverishing dam: Grand Coulee, as a matter of fact.

Poor Woody Guthrie. I can just picture him, arrived fresh from Oklahoma and the Dust Bowl, not yet able to sort the Pacific Northwest's shit from its Shinola, hunched on an unmade bed in some cheap motel, picking at his guitar while his kids play with the gravel in the parking lot, dutifully whipping off a few industrial river ditties to keep body, soul, and family together, never once suspecting the rash of Manifest Destinarian bronzes and Tourist Brainwashing kiosks that would one day immortalize his sweet face and no-brainer lyrics—bronzes and kiosks that might as well proclaim:

LOVABLE AMERICAN FOLK HERO SINGS WHOLE-HEARTED APPROVAL OF RACIST, TREATY-BETRAYING, SPECIES-

EXTIRPATING, FISHERMAN-BANKRUPTING, RIGHT-WING-FAT-CAT-ENRICHING INDUSTRIALIZATION OF ENTIRE COLUMBIA/SNAKE RIVER BASIN!

I have therefore made a few alterations to Woody's song.

I doubt we'll see my version bronzed on any new dams, though when the old dams start coming down we may see a few lines spray-painted on the rubble. I can't sing worth a *dam*, either. But there's no copyright on this thing. Feel free to steal it, sing it, quote it, photocopy it, de-program co-opted kids with it, graffiti it on public-school walls, fish ladders, wheat barges.

I'm the crassest kind of neophyte in the shaman department, but I do offer this musical repair job, with all the reverence that's in me, to the surviving salmon people of the Columbia and Snake Rivers' high mountain birth-houses. Are you with me, Idaho sockeyes? Here goes, then:

I got skunked on the Dee-schutes with one o' my pals,
Drank too much Glenfiddich in downtown The Dalles,
Then failed to conceal it when we phoned up our gals.
Mine said, "Better not drive, you morons."

So we checked in at a motel to avoid the state cops
An' our beds had machines that for two bits a pop
Produced cute little earthquakes as to sleep we did drop
While outside the Columbia rolled on.

I had just drifted off when my spirit awoke
To the sound of a git-tar an' a sad voice that spoke
In a sweet Okie twang tailor-made to sing folk,
While outside the Columbia rolled on.

"Dave," the voice said, "this idn't no joke.
I been shanghaied to Limbo for a song I once wrote.
The BPA paid for it. Shit. I was broke.
It's called 'Roll On, Columbia, Roll On.'

"The song brags up the river an' that part deserves fame.
It's the braggin' 'bout factories an' dams that was lame.
Can you take down dictation so I can salvage my name?"
I said, "You betcha, Woody. Go on."

Native

Then he sang:

"Roll on, Columbia, roll on. Roll on, Columbia, roll on,
Once a free-flowin' river, now a big poison pond,
But roll on, Columbia, roll on.

"When I fled from the Dust Bowl an' first saw your dams
I was stunned by the power an' blind to the scams
That'd steal the life pulse from an entire land,
But roll on, Columbia, roll on.

"Those same mighty dams killed the great salmon runs
Turned the planet's best fishery into barge routes an' lawns.
Now your June hogs 'n' sockeyes 'n' coho are gone.
But roll on, Columbia, roll on."

Everybody:

Roll on, Columbia, roll on. Roll on, Columbia, roll on.
Once a free-flowin' river, now a big poison pond,
But roll on, Columbia, roll on.

Big Douglas fir stumps where your channel cuts through
Remind us of forests our grandfolks once knew,
But if you want to find wildlife, better look in a zoo,
Roll on, Columbia, roll on.

Your water-use laws are a huge public con
So in summer you become a huge public john
Windsurfers grow tumors while trash fish grow brawn,
But roll on, Columbia, roll on.

Roll on, Columbia, roll on. Roll on, Columbia, roll on.
Once a free-flowin' river, now a big poison pond,
But roll on, Columbia, roll on.

The Yakima, Snake, an' the Willamette too
Add toxins, dioxins, an' cowshit to you,
E. coli *an' pesticides, human doo-doo,*
But roll on, Columbia, roll on.

Meanwhile upriver on the great Hanford Reach,
They're growin' the brains to plug nuclear leaks
By mutatin' kids into three-headed freaks,
But roll on, Columbia, roll on."

Now the salmon's-eye-view:
Dam! Dam! Dam DamDamDamDam!
Dam! Dam! Dam DamDamDamDam!
Dam DamdaDam, DamdaDam, Dam Dam Dam Dam!
But roll on, Columbia, roll on.

When Jefferson sent Lewis 'n' Clark to the West
An empire of small farmers was the dream he loved best,
Not a plague of industrialists shittin' our nest,
But roll on, Columbia, roll on.

Your factories grind Mama Earth into hash
Creatin' extinctions to line pockets with cash
An' if we shout, "It's a crime!" they say, "Let's not be rash.
Let's sing, 'Roll On, Columbia, Roll On.' "

So we fixed it:
Roll on, Columbia, roll on. Roll on, Columbia, roll on.
Once a free-flowin' river, now a big poison pond,
But roll on, Columbia, roll on.

Rain on Mountain makes River—that's the Law on this Earth.
The wild waters'll keep comin' till that law is reversed,
An' dams can be unbuilt to show folks the worth
Of a land where free rivers flow on.

The sunlight, the winds, the great waters shall last.
It's Industrial Madness that one day shall pass.
Sweet Columbia's just waitin' for the day we all ask
Where our beautiful river has gone.

I admit it feels a bit crazy, especially with a voice like mine, to stand up and sing for the disappearance of something as inarguable-looking as a dam. But there's a primitive, i.e., *primary,* honor in certain forms of craziness. Spirit offerings are not so much logical as geological. Appearances are deceiving: the Columbia and her salmon are as ancient and God-given as mountains and seas. Whereas the average dam's life span is about the same as yours or mine. As I slide toward my half-century mark and feel the currents of time lapping at my knees, my memory, my libido, *I* sure feel removable as hell. Welcome to the club, dams!

What keeps me from fearing mortality? Lots of things (most of them not even *things,* really): glimpses of eternity; the whole tapestry of wild nature, including wild human nature; every least act of love; every moment of wonder, yearning, ardor; the thought of my kids learning fearlessness from the same unerring primordial teachers.

I feel fearless, for instance, every time I conjure a day in October 1968 that took a sudden unexpected turn toward the primordial. I was sixteen at the time, my big brother was recently dead, and the Vietnam War was raging, scaring me shitless; fear made me wild and unschoolable; my grades grew too crappy for college; the draft was a year and a half away. Something in the autumn air pierced my worry, though, and moved me to drive, without purpose, up the Columbia Gorge in my old '55 Buick.

The big river was at its Indian Summer low, leaving it broken, downstream of the dams, by hundreds of long, beautifully sculptural sandbars. Picking the longest such bar in sight, I begin walking the finger of it toward the tip to try to see what it was pointing at. In the center of a two-mile-wide stretch of river, I ran out of finger. No one in sight. No wind. No sound but the river's near-silent slide. No waders with me, but I eased in up to my pockets, the better to feel the big seaward sliding. Sopped my wallet, though I didn't know it yet.

Junkie that I am, I'd brought a rod, and started throwing one of those big spinners of the day with the fluorescent orange golf tees on 'em—a ridiculous means of seeking salmon. I hooked the nothing I deserved. But who cares when it's just you and two miles of empty river, even measuring sideways: you and two *thousand* miles, measuring lengthwise. Seeing a fish or two roll, I kept casting for a time. But as the air turned eveningward, turned magic, my lure started looking to me like a shot-up bomber going deservedly down over North Vietnam. I stopped casting. I just stood there. What an incredible good fortune it's been to have learned, so early in life, that rivers *always* reward the man, woman, or child who just stands there.

The gift came this time, just shy of dusk, when all across that vast plain of water, beneath a still vaster dome of orange and blue, every salmon I couldn't catch, in accord with some invisible signal, began to jump and roll. And there were thousands! The entire face of Chewana, the Great River, became a miles-wide cauldron: great chinooks and bright coho; sockeyes and huge Idaho steelhead too, in those days; all but two of the dams in place; the extinctions coming fast; yet *still* the river put on her ancient show. And the sound! The body language. Salmon dance and salmon drumming. Coho slashing the surface so close by they made me yell, then laugh at myself. Huge chinook leaping so far off, their bodies had long since vanished when the cymbal crash arrived across the orange and blue. Ocean energy, mountain-born, boiling and flying, roiling and spiraling, both directions, as far as the eye could see.

For those who've never seen them in their rightfully vast numbers, my words, all these years later, might sound like one more bitter elegy to wonders glimpsed, then lost forever. But this is not elegy. This is invocation. The gifts Nature keeps trying to bequeath us are astounding, if we simply greet those gifts with a world that enables them to be.

To see a magnificent ocean fish, in fresh water, is always like a dream. And in a dream, everything is inside you. A piece of my interior will never leave that sand fingertip amid the salmon-shattered flow. And this piece of me, I swear, is not afraid to die. Salmon are a light darting not just through water, but through the human mind and heart. Salmon help shield us from fear of death by showing us how to follow our course without fear, and how to give ourselves for the sake of things greater than ourselves. Their mass passage, from the sea's free invisible into the river's sacrificial and seen, is not just every American's, but every Earth-born man, woman, and child's birthright. Their bodies remain the needle, their migration the thread, that sews this vast, broken region into a whole. No kilowatt can replace this, no barge can transport it. The Columbia that Industrial Man has given us is dying. The rivers least touched by man thrive. The finned, winged, and four-leggeds watch, waiting to join us, or not, in the world we do or do not create.

Make your offerings, *compadres*. Columbia, Cowlitz, Grand Ronde, Deschutes, John Day, Clearwater, Bitterroot, Boise, Salmon, Skagit, Soleduck, Snake, Spokane, Metolius, McKenzie, Yakima, Umatilla, Humptulips, Klickitat, Klamath, Kalama, Clackamas, Malheur, Minam, Blackfoot, Nestucca, Wallowa, Owyhee, Payette, Powder, Boise, Flathead, Okanagan, Coeur d'Alene, Elwha, Quinalt, Clark Fork, White Salmon, Willamette, Washougal, Wind. Roll on.

8. Lake of the Stone Mother

Three Thousand Wagons, Nine Hundred Graves

On January 14, 1844, Captain John C. Frémont and twenty-four other white men were searching the deserts of western Nevada for a river said to flow east to west from the Rocky Mountains to San Francisco Bay—a river reputedly large enough to be navigable, at least by large canoes. What Frémont found instead, at the terminus of the unnavigably small, swift river now known as the Truckee, was a huge, landlocked, saline lake. On this lake's eastern shore, miles away across the water, Frémont spotted a four-hundred-foot triangular rock that reminded him of an Egyptian pyramid. In his journal he wrote:

> *We've encamped on the shore, opposite a very remarkable rock in the lake, which had attracted our attention for many miles. This striking feature suggested a name for the lake, and I called it Pyramid Lake.*

There is just one problem with Frémont's journal entry: the lake already possessed a name. Resident Paiutes had long ago named it after a little tufa-rock formation just behind Frémont's grand pyramid, a formation called *Tupepeaha*, which translates as "Stone Mother." Unprepossessing though she was, the Stone Mother's legend was the Paiute people's origin myth—their three-dimensional Book of Genesis, if you will—and for centuries the tribe had told stories and sung songs that gave her real presence in their lives. It was her tears that had created the lake and its life-giving bounty (and when you taste the water, sure enough, it's salty). According to Joe Ely, the tribe's ex-chairman, the Stone Mother and her legend "sets our identity, and forever fixes the components that make up our way of life." In the tradition of Great White Explorers the world over, however, Captain Frémont was not interested in indigenous tongues, mythic names, or mysterious presences. Frémont desired a navigable east-to-west river, not a navigable inner life. And most of our forebears have inherited, by choice or by force, the tongue and mind-set of Frémont, not of the Paiutes. So the Stone Mother continues to be an ignored matriarch of knowledge lost or forgotten. And the lake continues to bear a trivial name.

How important is this loss of meaning? Does it matter who names a lake, or any other body of water? Does it matter *what* they name it?

I believe that it may. It rains an average of five inches a year in west-central Nevada. The wettest year on record here is nine inches. The dry year's record is *no measurable rain at all*. In a land this arid, H_2O ought to be measured in karats, not acre-feet. Water here is the essence of life, the only possibility of it. And to be careless in the way one handles life's essence can be fatal.

Four years after Captain Frémont "discovered," de-named, and renamed Pyramid Lake, gold was discovered in California. In the ensuing cross-continental rush of "Forty-niners," an estimated 45,000 would-be millionaires crossed, or attempted to cross, the nameless, forty-mile-wide, soft-sand desert just south and east of Pyramid Lake. By the end of the year, that little no-name desert contained 9,771 dead domestic animals, 3,000 abandoned wagons, and 963 fresh human graves. Yes, there were precious metals in California. But on the trail through Nevada, water proved even more precious.

Nevada is a strange state for many reasons. High on the list is the fact that 88 percent of the state isn't even the possession of the state: it's public land owned by every citizen of the United States. Equally high on the strange list is the legal gambling, which has created a multibillion-dollar tourist business, which has in turn created Las Vegas, Reno, Tahoe, and other casino cities, which have in turn created dire water shortages, extinct species, traffic gridlocks, foul air, high crime, mafia corruption, environmental devastation, and all the other urban amenities. But stranger and more crucial than either of these things—especially juxtaposed to these things—is that five annual inches of rain.

A "Fun Nevada Fact": there are twice as many people employed full-time by the Mirage Casino in Las Vegas as by every farm and ranch in the entire state.

Another Fun Nevada Fact: there are only eighty-six fewer security guards working for the Mirage than highway patrolmen working the entire state.

An Un-Fun Nevada Fact: the Mirage Casino, the 1.2 million residents of greater Las Vegas, and the city's 20 million annual casino-bound visitors are dependent not on Nevada's own rivers, rainfall, or mountain runoff, but on the state's entire portion of Colorado River water, *and* on the eons-old, nonreplenishable underground reserves the city is sucking at a No-Tomorrow pace.

In "Living Dry"—his definitive essay on the American understanding and misunderstanding of the arid inland West—Wallace Stegner pointed out that the syllable *pah*, in the Great Basin's Shoshonean tongues, means "water," or "water hole." This is why so many Shoshone place names (Tonopah, Ivanpah, Pahrump, Paria) contain this syllable. It's also why the region's prevalent tribe are called Paiutes: Pah-Ute means, literally, "Water Ute."

The Paiutes of Nevada, accordingly, lived in small, highly specialized, lake-dwelling, marsh-dwelling, or river-dwelling bands, most of which were named after the prevalent food of their small ecosystems. The Paiute word for cattails, for instance, is *toi*, and the word for eating is *dokado*, so the band that lived on Stillwater Marsh was known as the Toidokado—the cattail eaters. Trout, similarly, are *agai*, so the trout eaters of the Walker River region were the Agaidokado. And the endemic (and now endangered) food fish of Pyramid Lake were the cui-ui (pronounced "kwee-wee"), so the band that lived here were the Kuyuidokado—cui-ui eaters. Cattails, trout, cui-ui—pah foods, water gifts, all.

"The West is defined," Stegner wrote, "by inadequate rainfall (and) a general deficiency of water. . . . We can't create water or increase the supply. We can only hold back and redistribute what there is. . . . Aridity first brought settlement to a halt at the edge of the dry country and then forced changes in the patterns of settlement. . . . It altered farming methods, weapons, and tools (and) bent water law and the structure of land ownership. . . . In the view of some, it also helped to create a large, spacious, independent, sunburned, self-reliant western character. . . . Of that, despite a wistful desire to believe, I am less than confident."

Sipping scotch on the rocks in an air-conditioned casino while pumping one's paycheck into a one-armed bandit, a person might feel infinitely removed from the natural laws of the desert. But the fact remains—sorry, gamblers—that the rocks in those scotches come to us compliments of a *pah,* a place of water. This is why, minor as the point may seem, I'm serious in my refusal to accept Frémont's offhanded renaming of the Kuyuidokados' desert lake. Five inches of rain per annum is not a viable climate, it's a perennial crisis. As 963 graves just south of the Stone Mother demonstrate, to be careless in the face of this crisis is fatal. And a cavalier naming of a desert body of water is a form of carelessness.

There was a culture that lived with quiet grace beside these waters for tens of centuries. There is another culture that's left devastation, dreck, and dead bodies strewn all along the path of its half-cocked arrival. The Kuyuidokado, the Agaidokado, the culture that considered water to be the Stone Mother's tears, has nearly vanished. The culture of the gold rush and the Mirage has begun to feel the desert heat. In this land of constant critical aridity, whom can we trust to properly name and care for the precious springs, hidden seeps, and rare bodies of water? What should the inland sea known as Pyramid really be called? I don't pretend to know. But I do know that we must soon find out; that we must ask the water questions unselfishly; that we must dig deep, and listen to the Earth, and each other, very closely.

Where, exactly, to begin?

Fly-fishing Atlantis

One fine day in April, a century and a half after the arrival and departure of Captain John C. Frémont, a battered American pickup empties an expedition of four white guys—me; a sculptor friend, Frank Boyden; the Nature Conservancy's Graham Chisholm, and the Paiute tribe's fisheries biologist, Paul Wagner—onto the shore of a large saline lake at the terminus of the Truckee River. Maps, road signs, countless books, and the local populace all refer to this body of water as Pyramid Lake. But scattered along the beach upon which we've parked are fishermen—fly fishermen, most of them; eighteen, at a quick count. And each of them has carried an aluminum stepladder out into the lake, and is now using it as a casting platform as he plies the wide waters for trout. Watching them cast—and still obsessing on John Frémont's taste in names—I pop open a beer, reach for my pen, and make a journal entry of my own. I write:

We've encamped on the shore, opposite a very remarkable row of men in the lake, which row had attracted our attention for many miles. This striking feature suggested a name for the lake. I have therefore decided to hell with the maps, road signs, books, and native populace, and have renamed the whole shit-a-ree "Aluminum Step-ladder Lake."

This beach also has a moniker. It was named "The Nets" by the local Paiutes, after a failed attempt to raise Lahontan cutthroat trout in net-pens right off the shoreline here.

Graham has fixed us chips and salsa. He's watching birds now—and points out two kinds of warblers I've never seen in my life. We've watched five or six hundred white pelicans on the lake—plus mallards, great blue herons, coots, grebes. The hills above us are pale pink, the sagebrush pale green, the lichen on the rocks brilliant yellow. The white snow patches high up on the Pah Rah Mountains seem precious in this clime: next month's water. If we stayed on this beach and kept eating chips for a couple of decades, perhaps we'd become known to the Paiutes as the *Chipsandsalsadokado.*

In digging out my notebook, I find a tourist brochure about the lake. Not the sort of thing I normally read, but it's amusing to compare the purple brochural rhetoric to the bright blue evidence right before my eyes. Pyramid, the brochure assures me, is "a magnificent lake; a lake remarkably different from any you've ever seen. It's enchanting, a primeval lake where the weathering forces of wind and water have carved one of nature's bold statements: timelessness."

Something about this timeless prose makes me want to glance at my watch and note that it is 5:30 P.M. Pacific Standard. But I do agree that the lake is a "bold statement" of some kind. It's twenty-six miles long, four to ten miles wide, up to 350 feet deep, and its waters range, as the brochure promises, from turquoise to copper green to deepest blue. The wide beach upon which we've parked is one of "more than seventy miles of sandy beaches that make picnicking and camping ideal." A beach feature the brochure neglects to mention, though, is cow pies. We had to displace an entire herd of impending hamburger in order to park our trucks, and there are cow calling cards everywhere. Not that I'm complaining. It's an occasion for added sport, actually: the desert air dries the pies so fast that I find (after my second beer) that I can take a little run, hop onto the dried top of a pie, and "skimboard" three or four feet along the beach, leaving a fragrant green streak (another "one of nature's bold statements") on the sand behind me.

Swallows dip low over the pelican-tracked and tire-tracked sand. Sound of waves, sound of gulls, sound of fly reels cranking. But the predominant sound here at The Nets is the human voice: deep male voices, most of them; calm for the most part, and conversational; but now and then broken by the weird grunts, hoots, and laughter of men hooking and playing trout.

Pyramid is famous for its Lahontan cutthroat; "world-famous," the brochure optimistically proclaims; certainly famous enough to create a boom in local stepladder sales. In 1925 a world record forty-one-pound Lahontan was caught in the lake. During that same era, commercial fishermen were netting fifteen tons of trout from the lake *each week*. Broken down into Fly-fishing Fantasy terms, this means the lake was producing an average of *six thousand individual five-pound trout per week*. These enormous cutthroat, on their annual Truckee River spawning runs, looked more like salmon than trout. They traveled like salmon, too, up rapids and over falls, all the way up the Truckee to Lake Tahoe and its tributaries. The ranger station at Pyramid, where I stopped to buy a fishing permit, has a nice framed photo of Clark Gable holding up two big trout he'd just caught in the lake. There's a photo of Ronald Reagan's favorite president, Calvin Coolidge, giving the big cutts a try as well. But—no political innuendo intended—Coolidge got his wide ass skunked.

Four buffleheads land on the water just out of casting range. A twenty-four-inch fish (by his estimate) follows Frank's fly right into his rod tip. Then Paul hooks one. I wade over, once it starts losing the war, to give it a look. It's sixteen inches long, very silver, and healthy: it gives him a good fight. But I can see that Paul's no predator. His life's work, after all, is the breeding and rearing of these fish. As he lets the cutthroat go, he wears the haunted look of a kindergarten teacher who's just paddled one of his pupils for no reason.

I wish I could keep this story simple and just go catch a fish, but Paul's profession raises a question. In a lake and river system so prolific that it naturally produced fifteen tons of trout per week, why does the Paiute tribe feel compelled to contribute hatchery-reared or net-pen-reared trout at all? The depressing answer is that if the tribe did not contribute hatchery fish, there would be no trout living in the lake.

The fish-killing culprit here—as in so many Post-Western Blues sagas—is the federal Bureau of Reclamation ("Bureau of Wreck the Nation," as it's known regionally). It was the Bureau that took it into their heads, in 1906, to erect a dam on the lower Truckee River, the purpose of which was to divert the river into a canal, over a ridge, and down into the neighboring Carson River Valley, where it would turn desert into farmland, coyotes into dairy cows, dust into agricultural dollars, and the sleepy town of Fallon into a wide-awake fast-food strip.

To an extent, that's what happened. But there were unpredicted costs. In keeping with its reputation, the Bureau did no soil surveys, no environmental studies, no study of possible impacts on the Pyramid trout, no study of impacts on the Paiute people, resident flora or fauna, or the nearby Stillwater Marsh. According to a *Reno Gazette-Journal* account, "When the Truckee River was abruptly diverted during the dam's inaugural celebration, thousands of cutthroat trouts were left flopping in the mud. Cheering spectators, rolling up pantaloons and pant legs, wallowed in the slime and clubbed the fish to death."

By 1938 the Truckee-dependent Winnemucca Lake National Wildlife Refuge had become uninhabitable hardpan desert. Its refuge status was hastily removed. By the same year, Pyramid Lake had dropped forty feet, the Truckee River delta had become permanently impassable to spawning cutthroat, and the Lahontan trout remaining in the lake were forced to live out their life spans unable to reproduce. Sometime in the late 1940s or 1950s, the last of these lunkers sank unseen to the lake's bottom, and the primordial Pyramid Cutthroat strain was extinct. All that has kept the endangered cui-ui from extinction is their unusual longevity. But—Fun Nevada Fact—they're growing canteloupes and other water-sucking crops that already exist in surplus, just over the hill in Fallon.

The cutthroat we're now fishing for are actually a Summit Lake strain, raised in hatcheries here at Pyramid by the Paiutes, then released into the lake once they're big enough to survive. Though they can't spawn, these trout thrive in the desert lake. The largest cutthroat Pyramid has produced since their reintroduction was a thirty-six-inch, twenty-three-pound monster. Ten-pounders are common. The word is out: the sport fishery generates between 5 and 9 million dollars a year for the city of Reno and the Paiute tribe. And every spawning season the lake's cutthroat try—futilely—to break past the dam that keeps them trapped in this "magnificent . . . primeval" twenty-six-mile long holding tank.

Paul Wagner's cautious words on the Pyramid sport fishery are worth remembering. He told us, "One generation took something wonderful and turned it into nothing. We've turned it back into something. If we're careful—and lucky—maybe one day it'll grow back into something wonderful again."

We've left The Nets behind, driven to a quieter, much more beautiful beach, and as the sun drops behind the Pah Rahs, I'm wading out, rod in hand, intent on experiencing the "something."

Paul's name for this quiet cove is "Atlantis." Back in the eighties, his explanatory story goes, the boosters of Reno and Washoe County decided to sink money into a campground in hopes of luring spendthrift fishermen to the lake. They built eight concrete picnic tables with permanent (hideous) metal sunshades, several deluxe outhouses, and an all-weather concession building to purvey hot food and drink. Demonstrating the booster's unwavering fondness for tin-eared anachronism, they dubbed the place Warrior Point. But almost the day the job was finished, the record rains of the mid-eighties began. The lake rose twenty feet. The concession, outhouses, and tables were flooded. Thus did Warrior Point, for Paul anyhow, become "Atlantis."

In the drought of the past seven years, the waters dropped and the campground reappeared. But the risen Atlantis has so far been discovered by no one but the ubiquitous cows, who, judging by the ample evidence, are experiencing serious confusion about the respective functions of picnic areas and outhouses. Graham's begun making barbecued veggies and chicken while the rest of us fish. I'm happy to note that he's cooking on the beach, not in the picnic area.

Lahontan cutts are famous for feeding on the bottom, so I'm a little surprised, after a few fruitless, bottom-dredging casts, to see a fish rise nearby. I point out the rise-form. "Tui chub," Paul speculates. A trash fish.

I cast to it anyway—with a no-name, subsurface nymph a friend sent in the mail. The nymph's covered with peacock feathers, like a dancer in an MGM floor show—feathers that imitate no insect known to man, but do sometimes generate the same iridescent confusions in trout that dancers do in humans. The fly hits the water while the rise-form rings are still expanding. I send it strutting and kicking through the still-expanding rise-form. The mystery fish takes. I set the hook. But as the rod bends hard, I know before I see it that this is no chub: this is one of Paul's Lahontan pets. It's not a leaping fish, but makes several strong runs. Its speed and dogged endurance remind me of a brown trout. The thought of its birth (in a plastic tray laced with antibiotics) and its youth (in a concrete tank) are saddening. But the feel of its now lake-dwelling, electric body is, like every good fish I've caught, brief contact with the inhabitant of a beautiful alien world.

All through the long dusk and into the darkness the cutts keep rising. Aiming at rise-forms that Paul continues to think are chubs, I hook, and further educate, eight of his bright pupils. Fourteen to nineteen inches, if anyone's wondering. Rock-hard, moon-silver swimmers reluctant to let me touch them in order to let them go. No trout I take compares to the two bloodied lunkers Clark Gable was hefting in the photo. But I didn't get my ass Coolidged. And every trout with whom I danced at Atlantis is still swimming this once-ruined lake, slowly growing—if we're careful, and lucky—back into something wonderful.

I am, however, a fly fisher. And "It is not fly fishing," wrote my neighbor, Norman Maclean, "if you are not looking for answers to questions." So let me ask: *how wonderful?* How wonderful can a manufactured lake fishery ever really be? Isn't this lake, divorced by dam from its river, like a head divorced from its body and limbs? I come from the Pacific Northwest—land of migrating salmon—and have felt the wonder that passes, at the salmon's annual coming, between the fish-people and the two-leggeds. So I can't help remembering the Lahontan trout's ancient spawning runs. Will the big cutts ever again climb the Truckee to Lake Tahoe and beyond? Am I absurdly Neolithic to consider such a journey worthwhile? Or is there something to yearn for here? I have lived half my life on the shores of little rivers where, each fall, enormous, ocean-fattened, exotic-colored creatures suddenly appear on beds of gravel to circle, dig, and dance their species to life even as they batter their own bodies to death. That's the biological truth of the salmon's life cycle— but also a spiritual example that changes the way a lot of Northwest salmon-lovers live. So what about the Great Basin's cutthroat people? The potential *Agai?* Will the human friends of this inland sea one day allow its trout to set the same beautiful example as wild salmon?

I don't pretend to know. In the climate of our time, it's just a dream to me, or prayer. Were I to require an answer, though, you'd find me on the vast salty lake some windless evening, listening for the world inside this world, close by the Stone Mother.

Patching the Pacific Flyway

Five percent of the rivers in North America empty not into an ocean, but into inland deserts and lakes. Nearly all of these "closed drainages" are in the Great Basin region of the West. The Truckee and its Pyramid Lake terminus are one such drainage. The Carson and its Stillwater Marsh terminus are another. Yet whenever a Nature Conservancy staff member here refers to these two drainages, they take a deep breath and rattle off both names: "The Pyramid Lake/Stillwater Marsh project," they call it. The reason for the deep breath and the compound name is the same reason the cutthroat were wiped out in the Truckee and Pyramid Lake: the Bureau of Reclamation's Derby Dam. I just had to fortify myself with the tale of an evening's fishing before going on to describe more of the havoc this idiot dam has created.

The Nature Conservancy's principal claim to fame has been land acquisition. They're an organization whose reputation was built by identifying crucial habitat, buying it, and protecting it forever. The world's most altruistic real-estate firm. But here on the Carson and Truckee Rivers, they've been playing a difficult, volatile new game—and it's here that my admiration for them jumped a level. What they're doing on these rivers is buying water rights from farmers, then retiring those rights and letting marginal farmland return to desert, in order to pass the water downstream into the troubled lake and marsh. *Genuine* reclamation, in other words: that is, genuine restoration of critical wetlands, after the so-called Bureau of Reclamation has done its sorry work.

It's an unprecedented conservation tactic, and the unconventionality has caused the Conservancy some problems. Admirers of their traditional land acquisitions have voiced concern over the water purchases. Water rights on desert rivers don't come cheap, and some Conservancy backers feel there's something less satisfying, or less substantial, about purchasing a substance that eventually evaporates in the dessicated air.

I don't want to sound as though I'm stumping for the Conservancy, but in their defense it's crucial to remember that the mere acquisition of land has never been the motivating factor in any Conservancy land purchase: *preservation of life* and of biodiversity has been the motivating factor. And in the desert, water *is* life. In the desert, vast tracts of land can be purchased for virtually nothing—for the simple reason that waterless real estate can do little but kill you.

Nevada land without water offers virtually no nature for the Conservancy to conserve. And Stillwater Marsh, sans water, is not a marsh. With water, the Stillwater supports fully 50 percent of Nevada's waterfowl in season, including half a million ducks, 50,000 geese, 50,000 avocets, 25,000 black-necked stilts, 10,000 Wilson's phalaropes, 800 rare snowy plovers, and many more species. It supports the largest white-faced ibis colony in North America. It is a major staging area for millions of shorebirds, including as many as 275,000 long-billed dowitchers alone. It has been designated as one of just fourteen Western Hemispheric Shore Bird Reserves in North and South America.

But these are just statistics. Let me stress the Stillwater's importance in a storyteller's way:

Imagine running in one of the great American marathons. Or, if you're in the kind of shape I'm in, imagine jogging, then walking, and in the end possibly crawling to the finish of an American marathon. Whatever your condition, by the time you reached the finish line you'd be in dire need of fluids, food, and rest. Stillwater Marsh—for waterfowl and shorebirds enduring the marathon we call migration—is one such finish line. But now imagine that, after giving your all for twenty-six miles, you're greeted at the finish by a sign that reads:

SORRY. WE'RE FRESH OUT OF FLUIDS, FOOD, AND REST
AREAS HERE. YOU'RE GOING TO HAVE TO RUN ANOTHER
TWENTY-SIX MILES TO ANOTHER FINISH LINE. MAYBE
THEY CAN HELP YOU THERE.

If this happened to me, I have no doubt of the result: a short distance into the second marathon I'd lie down and die. Norman Saake—the State Department of Wildlife's resident expert on birdlife in the Stillwater—told me that migrating birds are little different from me. Norm has seen large flocks of migrating ducks, geese, and shorebirds fly into the Stillwater at dusk during the low-water and no-water years; has watched them circle, circle, and circle the marsh again, finding no place to land, no edible vegetation, no predator-safe place of rest. The sun is setting. They've been flying all day. Where is the next place of refuge? Hundreds of miles north, in the Klamath or Harney or Malheur lake basins. Hundreds of miles east, in the troubled marshes around Salt Lake. Seven hundred miles south, in the heavily hunted wetlands of Mexico. Or due west, in the Sacramento Valley—not such a vast distance, but to reach it, the birds have got to climb clear over the Sierras.

Norm believes that this is exactly what they attempt to do. He's seen them set out in near-darkness. And he's certain that any bird even slightly injured or weakened—any bird too old or too young—drops from the sky in the mountains and is never seen or heard again.

Nevada, in this century, has lost 85 percent of its wetlands. The Stillwater Marsh, in the recent drought years, shrank by 82 percent. Four and a half decades in this bewildering time and country have made me a pretty thick-skinned campaigner. But the thought of even one famished little curve-billed avocet falling out of the night sky high in the alien Sierras still brings a Stone Mother tear to my eyes. The purchase of desert water is buying these beautiful marathoners the food and safe haven they need to remain among us. To the birds, the Conservancy, the marsh, I send an ancient blessing from my own lost Celtic language, land, and tribe:

Go mbeannai Dia thu. God keep you forever.

Afterword

The preceding essay was written in 1993. In February 2000, I wrote to our tour guide and "Atlantis" chef, Graham Chisholm, now head of the Nevada Nature Conservancy, asking for an update on the (take a deep breath!) "Truckee River/Pyramid Lake/Stillwater Marsh complex." Despite his one- and five-year-old kids, Graham somehow wrote back immediately. And seldom, if ever, have I received an environmental update more crammed with good news. Some of the best of it:

In the years following my visit, the dry weather pattern changed, Pyramid Lake and Stillwater Marsh recovered from the '87-to-'93 drought, and endangered cui-ui spawned so successfully five years in a row that Graham got to eat some at a Paiute Pow-wow. The Conservancy is now primed to acquire a twenty-mile stretch of river from the Mustang Ranch down to Derby Dam. ("Unfortunately," says Graham, "the dam is not for sale.") The water-rights purchase program continues to put more flow in the river, the Bureau of Reclamation is planning a meander channel around Derby Dam, and—in a real switch from the past—the federal government has agreed to let the Paiute tribe control the releases of water from the dam to benefit downstream fish, riparian vegetation, and water quality (details still to be worked out).

The cities of Reno-Sparks and Washoe County have also settled their long fight over Truckee River water quality with the Pyramid Lake Tribe, with both sides agreeing to put up $12 million apiece ($24 million total) to buy water rights and increase instream flow. "Reno," says Graham, "has finally recognized that the Truckee River is the best thing about downtown." And though the city of Fallon and Churchill County continue to try to derail the water acquisition program, the Stillwater Marsh and all area wetlands have benefited enormously from the wet years and the Conservancy/U.S. Department of Fish and Wildlife water purchases (30,000 acre-feet to date, with a goal of 75,000 acre-feet). Hence, "Waterbird populations are up!" the normally circumspect Graham enthuses, with over a million ibis, egrets, ducks, and shorebirds in the valley in October 1999, according to aerial survey. ("P.S.," Graham concluded, "Threatened by the rising lake, those 'hideous' sunshades, concrete picnic tables, et al. at Warrior Point were moved out, permanently, last year.")

As for my 1993 "dream or prayer" question—*Will the big cutts ever again climb the Truckee to Lake Tahoe and beyond?*—the tribe has begun planting Lahontans in the lower Truckee, the fish are doing well—and there is fresh talk, this time backed by the United States Department of Fish and Wildlife, of reintroducing Lahontan cutthroat to the entire watershed.

Though it's not why I do it, sometimes it pays to dream and pray.

9. The War for Norman's River

1. *What we eventually come to mean by life are those moments when life, instead of going sideways, backwards, forward, or nowhere at all, lines out straight, tense and inevitable, with a complication, climax, and, given some luck, a purgation.*

—Norman Maclean, *A River Runs Through It*

In the late 1970s I wrote a novel—a sort of backwoods *Great Expectations* in which the Pip character, a far-gone fly-fisherman, tried to express my lifelong love for the salmon- and steelhead-filled rivers of the Oregon Coast. I wrote it in Portland, dubbed it *The River Why,* sold it, then used the advance—all three thousand dollars—to move to a cabin on a beautiful Oregon Coast river laughably like the one my imagination had bequeathed the protagonist of my book. Like a grown child, *The River Why* moved simultaneously out into the world, occasionally dropping me some breathy note such as "Jimmy Carter liked me!" or "I'm being translated into French!"

Publishers whose computers supposedly know this stuff have called my book "the second-best-selling fly-fishing novel after Norman Maclean's *A River Runs Through It.*" Judging by my bank account, it's a distant second. But from an old man's and a young man's opposite-end-of-life perspectives, Maclean's tragedy and my comedy are related: both speak in long, idiosyncratic sentences of rivers, fly fishing, and beloved but inscrutable younger brothers; both were rejected by every big publisher in the land before being taken by small presses; both were then read by hundreds of thousands, bringing their authors many satisfactions, in my case including a thousand fish-story-filled fan letters; an urban carp fly that imitates a soggy Marlboro butt; metal "trout flies" made from Budweiser cans (which really catch trout); gift fly rods, gift river trips, river-inspired CDs.

Given so much cause for gratitude, I have a grim confession to make: I would gladly give up *The River Why* and all it's given me if I could get back the waters that inspired the book in the first place. The irony of my love novel to rivers is that it bought me the freedom to live smack amid the betrayal of the very watersheds, wildlife, and rural rustics I'd just celebrated. I watched a political/corporate juggernaut steal the most beautiful temperate forests on Earth from their 260 million rightful owners and convert them, at a huge financial loss, into muddy-rivered corporate welfare tree farms. I watched the five-species cathedral groves, green-eyed streams, and tidewater towns that gave me my body, my life's work, my favorite form of worship, reduced to an unsustainable monoculture.

Toward the end of this betrayal, I became plagued by a nightmare in which Congress finally proposed to clearcut even my ability to write, with legislation that eliminated the letters *a, e, i,* and *u* from the alphabet as they'd eliminated spruce, cedar, hemlock, and salmon from my home. Their argument was that monoculture was the wave of the future, that a language with one vowel would be easier to learn as English became the lingo of global corporate conquest, and that the letter **O** was the shape of the globe. To demonstrate the efficacy of this notion, Oregon's renowned tree-hating senators, Packwood and Hatfield, invited a mixed-nationality choir of children onto the congressional floor, where the kids began to sing in the new global alphabet. Their song went,

O Boootofol for spocooos skoos, for ombor wovos of groon,
For porplo moontoons mojostoos obovo tho frootod ploon,
Omoroco! Omoroco! God shod Hos groco on thoo,
Ond crownod tho good woth brothorhood
From soo to shonong soo . . .

Spotted owls are a species that achieved national fame, and grew to be hated, for their simple inability to survive under industrial assault. As the coho joined the owls in the Land of the Annihilated and I was left on a "salmon stream" without salmon, I realized my heart was another such species. Unwilling to let despair turn me caustic, unable to shake my daily grief, I packed my family, said good-bye to forty years in Oregon, and moved to Montana not in hopes of a "better world," but at least in hopes of raising my little girls amid some inviolable wilderness and streams, that their childhood world might bear some resemblance to itself to the end of their days.

2.
I saw a strange thing with a neck and head being washed downstream while trying to swim across.

—*A River Runs Through It*

I knew when we arrived in Missoula that my plan for my daughters had flaws. Our move gave us three great rivers just minutes from our door: the Bitterroot, in whose valley we live; the Lower Clark Fork, home of steelhead-sized rainbow trout; and the Big Blackfoot—scene of Norman Maclean's masterpiece. Our move also gave us the Upper Clark Fork—a hundred-mile-long, billion-dollar-damaged, multiple Superfund site.

Strange to say, I was first drawn to the Superfund river. Though born and raised in Oregon, on my father's side I'm a fourth-generation Montanan, and my father's father—once a family man, fine singer, legendary hunter and fisherman—lived for a time in the headwaters of the Clark Fork, when he worked in the Anaconda Company's open-pit copper mines. Granddad emerged from the mines a binge-drinker and deadbeat father who abandoned my dad and his brother when they were small boys. I sought a grasp on his world. And for me the best way to begin to grasp a new world has always been to stand in its lowest point—the river valleys—with a fly rod in hand. Knowing the Upper Clark Fork was cursed by the very forces that cursed my father's father, I set out to explore it.

I'd heard surprising rumors from a few local fly fishers. They said that despite the flash-flood-caused fish kills from the Superfund ruins, a surprising number of brown trout slipped down into the Upper Clark Fork from healthy tributaries. Driving along the river one August day, I saw not a soul, though it was the height of tourist and fishing season.

But when I parked above a stunning canyon and began rigging my rod, I spotted two bald eagles circling the glide below me. And by the time I'd geared up, each eagle had hit the water and emerged with a sizable fish. In that brackish glide they could have been whitefish, but they looked, in the distance, like trout. My pulse sped up. Eagles are not great fishers. By choice they'll let ospreys do the catching, then scream down and rob the ospreys. What was going on down there?

I hurried to the glide, tried to decide on a fly, saw no aquatic insects or rising fish, and so tied on an artificial grasshopper. On the second cast the fly quietly vanished, and I was fast to a big brown. That's when my grandfather's fate caught up with me:

When you hook and play a big fish on a fly rod, its entire life-force—what the Hindus would call its *prana*—comes pulsing up the rod into your hands. An eighteen-inch brown in the nearby Bitterroot will fight your hands with its *prana* for five or more frantic minutes. The same-sized brown in the Upper Clark Fork, in August, is gasping the instant you hook it, and slides onto the bank in seconds. To make contact with a trout that big and beautiful and find its life, from the first instant, so nearly gone, is a waking nightmare. Though fifty miles upstream and long defunct, the Anaconda mine still rules this river.

I fell into a daze, kept fishing, kept catching and releasing big, gasping browns. Every trout I touched was an emissary of death—river death; food-chain death; our death. Yet every trout I touched filled me with weird bursts of empathy for a man who'd abandoned my father at age four.

The bald eagles returned, instantly caught fish, and now I knew why. Heavy metal poisoning, algae growth, and low oxygen levels made these browns easy pickings. The eagles wheeled away to a cottonwood and perched, pretty as a postcard, above the water. The trouts' tainted flesh then began killing our national symbol as it fed.

The sun was still high, the river, eagles, and trout still spectacular to the eye, when I took down my rod, hiked back to my truck, turned upriver, and said to a grandfather thirty years dead, *"You hurt us all. You were hurt yourself. I forgive you."*

I am haunted by waters.

3.   I don't like to pray and not have my prayers come true.

—*A River Runs Through It*

I learned four new rivers and twice as many streams over my first few Montana summers. I did not so much as drive past the Blackfoot. I'd heard from friends that Norman's river was still a joy to fish. But I also knew that the same blend of corporate power and political collusion that drove the trees, owls, coho, and me from the rivers of Oregon was bivouacked on the Blackfoot—and as Huck Finn remarks at the end of his river adventure, "I been there before." Powerful corporations have proposed a riverside mine that will make the Blackfoot "the most threatened river in the nation," according to the national watchdog group, American Rivers. Montana's Wise Use legislators, Republican governor (Marc Racicot), and mine-loving Department of Environmental Quality cannot open their arms wider to welcome this disaster. Having arrived here fresh from a futile struggle against a similar juggernaut—and knowing how it feels to plead mercy to a Packwood or a Weyerhaeuser—I felt I lacked the strength to befriend the Blackfoot and start pleading again. For three years I plied other waters, avoiding Norman Maclean's Death-Row-Inmate river like the plague it may soon become.

The Blackfoot began to haunt me anyway. It came for me, first, in the unapologetic love and river rhythms in old Norman's prose. Here—to cite a merely average example—is the seventy-some-year-old author's recollection of his brother, Paul, fly-fishing the Blackfoot three-quarters of a century ago:

> *Below him was the multitudinous river, and, where the rock had parted it around him, big-grained vapor rose. The mini-molecules of water left in the wake of his line made momentary loops of gossamer, disappearing so rapidly in the rising big-grained vapor that they had to be retained in memory to be visualized as loops. The spray emanating from him was finer-grained still and enclosed him in a halo of himself. The halo of himself was always there and always disappearing, as if he were candlelight flickering about three inches from himself. The images of himself and his line kept disappearing into the rising vapors of the river, which continually circled to the tops of the cliffs where, after becoming a wreath in the wind, they became rays of the sun. . . .*

The Blackfoot then began to haunt me, strange to say, in my own earlier, more innocent river prose. When *The River Why*'s hero hooks a huge chinook salmon at nightfall on an inadequate light line, he has a choice: he can try to defeat the fish, which will simply snap his line, or he can erase all tension from the line and follow helplessly upriver as the hooked but untroubled fish continues its midnight migration. I've shared this mind-bending experience with salmon and steelhead. Trying to describe the wonderful reversal of the angler's usual role, a twenty-some-year-old me wrote:

> *It had always been my way to approach the river like a wanded magician out to work deception. This night I came as a blind man led by a seeing-eye salmon—and it showed me a world I'd believed was destroyed, a world where a man could still walk unfeared beside an animal we call "wild." Moved and shamed by the salmon's trust, feeling hour after hour the faithful pulse of its tail beating like the river's silver heart, I felt the fisherman in me being unmade. . . .*

In the nights of my fourth Montana summer, I began to lie awake hour after hour, remembering a thousand days on now-blighted rivers—recalling how it felt to be not an "I" but a halo of myself, lost in heartbeat, bloodflow, tail-beat, and riverflow, feeling in my hands the pulse of wild ocean creatures whose inland migration is the very image of self-sacrifice. Night after night I'd then begin to weep, silently so as not to wake my wife, and to ask any Power that cared to answer what good Norman's or my or anyone's love songs to rivers will be, once the life-giving flows that inspire the love are corporatized, plundered, and trashed. I chose not to serve in Vietnam because I never believed that war was in defense of my country. I believe no such thing about the war for the Blackfoot. Rivers don't die, exactly, but they're easily rendered incapable of supporting life. The entire flow in which salmon tails once beat for me like the river's heart is now an industrial sluice.

I knew that if I explored Norman's river, I'd fall in love, and that if I loved, I'd soon be at war with a corporate Goliath while my family scrambled for groceries and my novel-in-progress collected dust. But what's the alternative? *Spocooos skoos! Omoroco tho Boootofol!* I reread *Mocloon's* masterpiece while its vowels remained intact, drove up the Blackfoot while God was still shedding grace on its various thees, and fell—as feared, and secretly desired—heart over head over heels for the same river that smote the brothers Maclean.

4.

I loved and did not understand.

—*A River Runs Through It*

It began, the way it often does on these rivers, when the August sun left the water, the last of the day's bowwowing, beer-and-solar-powered rafters passed out of sight, and the all-day breeze inexplicably died. The countless pines ceased their ceaseless *huuuu*ing. Deer, seemingly from nowhere, suddenly grazed in the center of every meadow. The sky slipped out of its workaday blue and began trying on the entire evening wardrobe—the lavender, the pink, the pumpkin, even the teal. The river matched it gown for gown, adding warps, wefts, and sheens the sky could only dream of. The herons who'd flapped upriver that morning coasted even more slowly back down. The bald eagles who'd coasted downriver labored back up. The air—not the sky, but the air itself—turned blue. The day's darting cliff swallows turned into darting nighthawks and bats. The Blackfoot's became the one voice in the world. Then the voice, silent pines, blue air, and nighthawks, as Norman promised, "merged into one," a river ran through it, and I began to devour that oneness in full-bodied, full-hearted gulps.

The day's long, slow coition of sun and water gave birth to delicate winged insects—clouds of pale evening duns and delicate mayflies, supervening clouds of caddis. Every trout in the river intercepted the clouds at the now-lavender, now-pumpkin surface, and began to sup audibly. Let me point out to possible bug-haters that not one of these sun-fathered, river-mothered insects bites, stings, pinches, whines, or in any way harrasses. Come evening they just swim, for the first time ever, to the Blackfoot's shining surface, shed the wet suits they've spent their lives in, open translucent wings they hadn't known they owned, and flutter silently up into evening light, where they hover like angels—in order to mate like rabbits. I know it's dangerous to profess bug-love to city denizens whose best-known bug is the cockroach. But if the mine goes in, these fragile species will be the first to die; industrial dust alone can kill them. So I've got to say it now: the river-born insects I'm praising in that blue light are the publicly owned foundation of a Chain of Life that leads from ocean to cloud to snow to river to water-born organisms to nymphs to flies to evening rises, trout, joy, famous Norman Maclean novellas, and thence to the hearts of you and me. This land is *your* land; these bugs are *your* bugs; this river is *our* river; its intact and entire Chain of Life was made for you and me. And when you stand in the Blackfoot during a rising of fish and falling of joy like this, I don't care how urban you are, you feel it: immersed in the muscles of the wild river's flow, you feel in your 78-percent liquid body and steadfast heart how even you, even now, are part of the same wildness and flow.

I'd come to fly-fish, and trout were taking flies everywhere. But as the air turned blue, I was first distracted by a dinky trout, not ten feet behind me, that began jumping over and over, ludicrously high in the air. This little guy leapt so high, so often, that I began to laugh. I mean, we earthly creatures are all supposedly opportunists—fish, humans, and transnational corporations alike. By nature we slurp the maximum number of bugs or flows of profit via the minimal expenditure of energy, thus aggrandizing our bulk, be it bodily or financial. But this troutlet was *defying* its nature. There were flies all over the river, any of which it could have sipped effortlessly. It ignored them all to leap effortfully high in the blue, catch nothing, then fall back with a splash that made the same tidy sound every time: *Doip!* This trout child was jumping not as a career move but in random celebration (*Doip!*), jumping the way my four-year-old or a good comedian sometimes jumps (*Doip!*); jumping in spontaneous, reasonless defiance of the whole tragic idea that every effort on Earth must have a bottom line, profit margin, or edible bug at the end of it (*Doip!*).

Edified, I turned upstream—and spotted an exceedingly large trout troubling the sunset-colored surface, not fifty feet away. I readied my rod. I studied the strand of now-apricot current upstream of its lie, studied the pragmatic rhythm of its feeding, and tried *not* to study the width of its head or to imagine the correspondingly sumptuous body, knowing that desire for such bodies is the enemy of artistic skill. But—hell, I'm no saint. The trout's head was as thick as my *Collected Shakespeare*: its body was surely an arm's-length compendium of every color in river and sky.

Great size implies age, which in trout, far more than in humans, implies intelligence. My cast would have to be perfect. I'd get one chance. I've watched even fine casters go spastic in the presence of big fish at which they'll get one crack. I've gone spastic myself. This night, though, I'd learned a new word I believed might keep lust from interfering with art. I began waving my wand. Hard-to-describe laws of motion were enacted. Energy gathered and dispersed. Line looped and flew. I noticed, first on the river, then in the sky, that the evening star had shown. Letting fly my one chance, I spoke my magic word into the blue: *"Doip!"*

A tiny work of fiction—a pale evening dun that was not an evening dun—alit on the apricot strand a few feet upstream of my sincerest guess at the trout's position. I stood immersed in the Blackfoot, gulped another chestful of joy, and watched my fragile fiction drift toward the invisible, broad-browed trout . . .

5.
Definition of a gold mine: hole in the ground, owned by a liar.

—Mark Twain

The proposed Blackfoot mine is called the McDonald Gold Project. Its ownership has changed twice since I cast at that trout, but I'm going to tell this story the way I've lived it.

From the day I cast to the Shakespeare-shouldered trout I was yearning to do something for the Blackfoot. One day, after giving a talk to the local river watchdog group, I met a tall, dark, and handsome stranger, named Gus, who shared my yearning. Gus doesn't want his last name in print, because he was in Missoula on the lam, it seems, from the expectations created by a recent degree from Harvard. When I set eyes on him, he was being presented a cheesy T-shirt as "payment" for the invaluable pro bono work he'd been doing for the river watchdog group. When I learned that Gus had the same name as the protagonist of my first novel, was an avowed "huge fan" of my second, was outraged about the proposed Blackfoot gold mine, and was delighted with the T-shirt, I realized I had a gifted, altruistic sucker primed for the kill, so I pounced, hiring Gus to do the interviews, fact-chasing, and legwork for a Blackfoot op-ed piece I hoped to publish in *The New York Times*. (By "hire," incidentally, I mean that Gus went to work for the same wages I was making: jack squat.)

When we began investigating the proposed mine late in 1996, its dual owners were Arizona's mighty Phelps Dodge Corporation and a small Colorado mining company, Canyon Resources. With the help of Gus's phone calls, field trips, and mounting piles of notes, we began deciphering the McDonald Project's daunting "plan of operations." We had hopes, as we began, that the proposed mine might be as "cutting edge" and safe as the mining companies and Governor Marc Racicot kept claiming.

We were shockingly disappointed. Here are just six McDonald Project features that the companies swear will not harm the Blackfoot in the least:

1. Between the Landers Fork and the main stem of the upper Blackfoot, on a pine-covered butte where, as I write, elk are calving and sandhill cranes are nesting, the miners propose to use trainloads (literally trainloads) of ammonium nitrate explosives (of Oklahoma City fame) and an armada of 200-ton earth-moving machines, twenty-four hours

a day for the twelve-to-twenty-year life of the mine, to replace butte, elk, sandhills, and pines with a hole in the ground more than a mile in diameter and as deep as the World Trade Center is tall. This hole will bottom out 700 feet *below* the adjacent Blackfoot. The most comparable hole in America is the Anaconda Copper Company's nearby Berkeley Pit, one of the least fixable industrial disasters on the planet, the source of four separate Superfund projects, and, on a personal note, the psychological bane of my paternal grandfather. In the spring of 1996, 342 snow geese landed on the abandoned and flooded Berkeley Pit and began to drink its waters. The Pit's waters killed them all, within hours. The McDonald Project partners propose, after pocketing their gold profits, to flood their Blackfoot pit with water and abandon it (perhaps dubbing it "Lake Snow Goose"). The estimated 570 million tons of "waste rock" excavated to create the pit will be sculpted into a coffin-shaped riverside mountain—larger than New York's Central Park, taller than the Washington Monument—from which heavy metals, sulfuric acid, and nitrates will leach into the Blackfoot watershed forever.

2. The corporations propose to explode, move, or process *245 tons of rock* to obtain *a single ounce* of gold. The McDonald Meadows deposit is the lowest grade of ore anyone has ever attempted to mine on this vast scale. To extract the tiny gold flecks from the crushed rock "heaps," the miners will pour literally *hundreds of millions* of gallons of cyanide-contaminated groundwater over a *second, separate* Central Park–sized area, upon which "heaps" of crushed ore will eventually be stacked to twice the height of the Statue of Liberty. The gold flecks will adhere to the cyanide, and be purified, and sold. The used heaps will be abandoned, and will contain metals deadly to all forms of life—lead, mercury, arsenic, zinc, and cadmium, to name a few. To protect the Blackfoot from this second "Central Park of death," the companies propose to line the bases of the cyanide heaps with plastic sheets the thickness of a nickel, and abandon them forever. According to the EPA, *all liners leak.* And every cyanide gold mine in Montana—Basin Creek, Beal Mountain, Golden Sunlight, Montana Tunnels, TVX Mineral Hill, Zortman-Landusky, and Kendall—has leaked.

3. The cyanide gold mines of Nevada are *the largest dewatering projects in the history of humankind.* (Sorry about the italics, but the more you learn about cyanide mining, the more *it all feels italicized.*) Just one of

the gargantuan Nevada mines creates what is called, with no intended irony, a "cone of depression" that removes every drop of groundwater from areas as wide as a hundred square miles, indiscriminately sucking creeks, wells, ponds, and wetlands dry, dehydrating the aquifer to depths of a thousand feet or more. In place of lost natural springs, marshes, and creeks, the corporate gold miners construct, and later abandon, desert reservoirs of poisonous "water" so deadly that a few sips kill any animal or bird. To prevent wildlife from drinking, they cover the reservoirs with plastic nets or black plastic balls. UV light and harsh weather destroy the nets; strong winds blow aside the balls; desert-parched animals and birds break through the token barriers anyway. The result has been predictable: vast biological dead zones; a jeopardized Great Basin flyway; thousands of bird and animal carcasses strewn around the reservoirs; aquifers too deep for ranchers to reach cost-effectively; toxic or poisoned water when they do reach it.

On the upper Blackfoot, the McDonald Project will follow the Nevada model. To dewater their vast pit, the Project plans, by its own estimate, to pump groundwater at a rate of 10,000 to 15,000 gallons a minute, around the clock, for the twelve-to-fifteen-year life of the mine. By its own estimate, *it will lower the entire upper Blackfoot valley's water table by 1,300 feet.* This will lead to two results: First, within the mine's vast "cone of depression," wells, wetlands, springs, ponds, and creeks will dry up. Second, the billions of gallons of water pumped from the pit will be tainted with lead, mercury, arsenic, zinc, cadmium, and other poisons, and returned to the Blackfoot.

4. The Blackfoot headwaters—including the Landers Fork, the North Fork, Copper Creek, Monture Creek, and others—form the most important spawning area for one of the last populations of threatened river-dwelling bull trout left in the U.S. The McDonald Project plan of operations states that these hypersensitive fish will be unharmed by the mine, because no bull trout spawn in water directly adjacent to the mine site. The ignorance implied by this claim is shocking: the Landers Fork is the sole migratory corridor to Copper Creek, where, in the fall of 1996, at least one hundred bull trout successfully spawned, leaving thirty-five redds (fertilized nests of thousands of eggs). These fish and their young must be able to return down past the mine site to the deep pools of the Blackfoot, which serve as a kind of "mother ship" in which to survive the winter. The McDonald mine's "cone of depression" would make safe migration impossible.

5. In the brutal winters of the northern Rockies, trout survive in small streams only when they contain what are called "upwellings"—flows of water surging right up out of the porous gravel creekbeds, created by powerful in-stream springs. Without upwellings, high-elevation creeks like those in the Blackfoot headwaters become so frozen that they support no fish at all. Phelps Dodge and Canyon Resources claim not to know what lowering the water table by 1,300 feet will do to in-stream upwellings throughout the mine's "cone of depression." It will, of course, destroy them. "There will be no change to the beneficial use or stream classification of the Blackfoot River and its tributaries," states the plan of operations. This is not just obfuscation; it's an outrageous lie. Salmonids without water, salmonids frozen into solid ice, salmonids that can't migrate, spawn, or breathe, are salmonids that don't survive. There is no precedent, anywhere, for this mine: no example, in terms of climate or geology, for this gargantuan cold-weather water-pumping and water-poisoning experiment. In mere preliminary tests of the project's pumping system, pipes have burst, pumps have broken, fatal levels of zinc have been dumped into the Blackfoot. No mine yet, and fish have *already* died.

6. Winters on the Upper Blackfoot are harsh. Sub-zero temperatures glacierize streams annually. The −69°F recorded at nearby Roger's Pass did not even factor in wind chill and is the coldest temperature ever recorded in the Lower Forty-eight. The McDonald Project's plan of operations calls this climate "moderate." The lie is purposeful. Cyanide technology was developed in desert climates because it is dependent on huge quantities of running water, and at subzero temperatures *water isn't water at all*: it's a rock-hard, greatly expanded solid. The same Blackfoot winters that break household pipes, crack engine blocks, and stop up septic systems will slam into the countless pumps, pipes, drains, filters, cyanide reservoirs, and plastic liner systems of the mine. Responsible miners fear this. A recent article in the industry's leading technical magazine, *Mining Engineering,* admits: "Each year the mining industry pushes the envelope a little further—higher [cyanide] heaps, higher elevations, higher rainfalls and colder climates. . . ." The same article admits that plastic liners that contain the cyanide reservoirs and heap-leach pads "begin brittle cracking at temperatures as warm as 23°F, despite laboratory results to the contrary."

The belief that one can safely pump thousands of gallons of water a minute, or safely spray thousands of gallons of cyanide, round the clock in sub-zero weather is not credible. The belief that one can create cyanide reservoirs, toxic heaps, and toxic mountains, line them with plastics that crack in the cold, and declare the adjacent river safe in perpetuity is not credible. Montana's Zortman-Landusky cyanide mine was recently fined a record $37 million for poisoning an aquifer, animals, and children they promised would be unaffected; it then declared bankruptcy and bequeathed the state a disaster site. Phelps Dodge's own Chino, New Mexico, mine has had twenty-five major poison spills since 1987; one spill (which dumped 180 million gallons of toxic waste into ground and surface water) was deliberate and went unreported for thirty-five days; thirteen of Phelps Dodge's properties are being considered for Superfund listing.

Who but a gold-crazed investor could trust such a history? The sole American precedent for the McDonald Project is the high-altitude mine at Summitville, Colorado, which froze in winter, burst its plastic containment system, killed the entire Alamosa River, maimed the Rio Grande, and has so far cost U.S. taxpayers $150 million in cleanup, since its Canadian owner declared bankruptcy and fled. A woman named Laura Riddell worked at Summitville. In an E-mail to Montana Governor Racicot, she wrote,

> I own a water-bed . . . about the same thickness [as] the pad liner. Imagine taking this liner, laying it on the ground and dumping a couple hundred tons of jagged rock on it. . . . PLEASE, check this out. I don't want you to think I'm horror story telling. . . . After the breach of the cyanide holding pad occurred, the cyanide laced water seeped into the ground water. After a short amount of time the RIO GRANDE WAS DEAD, and I mean even the trees on the bank of the river . . . along with all the water-life. There was also a jump in the number of miscarriages and birth defects of people that live along the river. I feel a responsibility for this HUGE MISTAKE.

The cyanide-doused ore heaps of the proposed McDonald Project would be fifty-two times larger than those at Summitville.

6.
> The world . . . (is) full of bastards, the number increasing rapidly the farther one gets from Missoula, Montana.
>
> —*A River Runs Through It*

Norman's old hometown, and my new one, straddles a constant resurrection: when the living waters of the Blackfoot join the Upper Clark

Fork in Missoula, the dead river springs back to life. The reborn Lower Clark Fork has a marvelous effect on our city. Of a warm summer's evening Missoula families step down to the river, Dad to quaff a beer, Mom to cast a fly, the kids to splash in fingerling-filled shallows; from riverside cafés we watch ospreys catch trout and eagles steal them; the cottonwoods in town are scarred not just with the initials of lovers but by beaver teeth; at night, lovers and paddle-tails sometimes have to negotiate, like rival ad agencies, for the best bark space. Our best walks, best art, best romances, worst suicides, and finest poetry are woven into the life of the resurrected river. Our patron poet, Richard Hugo, expressed the essence of Missoula when he wrote, "I forget the names of towns without rivers. / A town needs a river to forgive the town."

And as the first town downstream of the proposed Blackfoot mine, we are frantic. With *two* dead rivers merging in our midst, who will remember or forgive us?

Corporate spokespeople and right-wing politicians depict the war for Norman's river as a struggle between responsible capitalists and "environmental extremists." It is no such thing. This fight is between responsible residents and nonresident corporate extremists. The Blackfoot has united conservatives and preservationists, taxidermists and women's groups, priests and gonzo snowboarders, ranchers and vegans, fly fishers and bait-plunkers, cowboys and Indians, Republicans, radicals, realtors, and almost every other category of person living downstream of the mine. What power can unite such antithetical people? The Big Blackfoot itself is the overwhelming answer. The beauty of *A River Runs Through It* has helped. But another place to look is at the word *jobs*:

The McDonald Project promises 390 full-time, short-lived jobs for demolitions experts, heavy equipment operators, and others willing to help rip 245 tons of rock and 2.6 million gallons of water from the earth to produce an ounce of gold. The companies admit that almost none of their workers will come from this region, and that almost none of their profits will stay in the region. They fail to mention an even more crucial fact: the Blackfoot, the Lower Clark Fork into which it flows, the Pend Oreille into which the Clark Fork flows, and the Columbia into which the Pend Oreille flows, already give livelihood not to 390 but to tens of thousands, and those existing jobs do not threaten each other, the region's wildlife, or the hundreds of thousands who use the rivers for work, daily reverence, and fun. The McDonald Project, in other words, is a case not of creating "new jobs," but of pitting 390 *bad jobs* against thousands of existing *good* ones.

Recognition of the Bad Job has been slow to dawn on the national consciousness, but the concept is crucial to the health of regions, nations, and the planet. Building Love Canal, Hanford, Chernobyl, and Bhopal were jobs. Clearcutting the Amazon, strip-mining Kentucky, nuking Nevada, exterminating Indians, stealing Africans from their homes and selling them at auction, were jobs. Unconscionable jobs. In no century soon will we undo the damage wrought by three centuries of unconscionable jobs. Why create 390 more?

There is no way to weave an international mining corporation into the life, work, or pleasure of our beautiful river valleys, no way to invite them to coexist with us rather than prey upon us, because mining corporations are nothing like the people who make up the life of a river valley. Mining corporations descend like predatory gods from outside the life of a region, force all residents, human and nonhuman, to live by their law of short-term supply and demand, and depart the instant profit margins wane. It's we residents, human and non-, who must live with the post-profit result.

There are people in this region who have fallen in love on the Blackfoot, lost their virginity in it, lost their lives or loved ones in it, placed their wives', fathers', children's ashes in it. Doesn't matter to the corporation. The Blackfoot watershed is sacred to the Salish, Kootenai, and Blackfoot tribes, its fish and game promised to them in perpetuity by a treaty that cost them all that they once owned. Doesn't matter to the corporation. Tourism and agriculture are the economic heart and lungs of Montana. Gold mining constitutes just .07 percent of Montana's economy and hurts tourism and agriculture in the process. Economic studies predict the McDonald Project will be a boom-bust disaster for local towns, a devastating blow to real-estate values, and a huge health and financial risk to every person living and working downstream. None of this matters to the corporation. Cyanide miners are eager to maim us for the simple reason that they have no intention of inhabiting our region, and our long-term suffering would be their short-term profit. What the corporations must therefore do to sway a region like ours is create mass amnesia, not evidence of the mine's safety, for by the dictum "by their fruits ye shall know them" we have educated ourselves against them.

We have learned, for instance, that cyanide gold mining is a peace-time act of aggression that devastates like war, that it has ruined aquifers, land, and watersheds from New Guinea to Brazil to Africa to eastern Europe, but that—thanks to federal mining rules signed into law by President Ulysses S. Grant *the same year Napoleon III returned from invading Prussia*—we the people are forced to subsidize the destruction of our own land and water for the benefit of international corporations. We've learned that hard-rock mining has killed 12,000 miles of American rivers and 180,000 acres of lakes; that it has abandoned 50 billion tons of waste; that it annually creates more toxic waste than all other U.S. industries combined. Yet, under 1872 law, corporate miners still pay Americans *no royalties* on the billions of dollars' worth of minerals they mine. We've learned that Canada's euphemistically named American Barrick Corporation is now pocketing $10 billion of noneuphemistic American gold for the $9,765 price tag U. S. Grant placed on our public land—all for the benefit of such hard-strapped Barrick "miners" as ex–prime minister of Canada Brian Mulrooney and ex-President George Bush. We've learned that cyanide heap-leach devastation is now global, and has killed rivers and livelihoods on every continent where it is practiced. We've learned that a 1994 cyanide heap-leach disaster in Guyana killed an entire river and threw 40,000 farmers and fishermen out of work not for life but for generations; that 1997's so-called "peasant revolt" in Turkey was in fact the protest of a bunch of panic-stricken farmers whose water and lives were slated for ruin by their own government and a Canadian mining corporation; that Phelps Dodge alone owns, and hopes to coax Americans into investing in, fifty-six open-pit cyanide-mining claims in Costa Rica's La Amistad Biosphere Reserve, a World Heritage rain forest and home to four-fifths of the country's surviving indigenous people. We've learned that the corporation that promises its Blackfoot mine will be the first in history to cause no negative downstream impact is the owner of an environmental rap sheet the thickness of Dostoevsky's life works.

We've learned, in short, that cyanide gold mining is a colossal corporate welfare program that devastates land, water, wildlife, and regional economies, pockets its profits, thanks Congress, and saddles citizens, unborn children, wildlife, and Earth itself with the true long-term costs.

So why, an outsider must wonder, haven't we voted the bums out? The truth is, we've tried. But when companies worth billions of dollars "prospect" for cyanide gold sites, they don't send some sourdough named Snuffy up into the hills on a mule. Corporate prospecting is a process in which the staking of claims is blithely incidental compared against the work of purchasing politicians, smothering and bullying opposition, gutting environmental safeguards, dominating the media, burying past travesties, and reinvesting gold profits in lawyers' fees, lobbyists' salaries, and the huge slush funds required to handle the catastrophes that inevitably accompany this technology.

A painful example: In 1995, Montana's governor and Republican-ruled legislature took the best water-quality standards in the Rockies and turned them, against the will of the people, into the worst. Their aim: to open the state up to cyanide heap-leach and other forms of mining. Forty thousand citizen volunteers fought back at once, placing a Clean Water Initiative on the '96 ballot that would have required new mines to remove 80 percent of the pollutants from their wastewater before discharging into Montana's rivers. (Sewage-treatment plants remove 85 percent.)

Clean Water was supported by 67 percent of the populace; not bad for "the Treasure State." Then the corporations struck back. In the weeks before the vote, they unleashed a newspaper, radio, and TV disinformation campaign so prodigiously funded that, as one observer said, it could have defeated the Bill of Rights. The average donation in support of Clean Water was $178.50—a lot of money for some river-loving schoolteacher, rancher, or fishing guide. The average anti-donation was forty-four times greater. Phelps Dodge and two Canadian companies kicked in $500,000 apiece. And the lies! A daily prime-time TV barrage of ads showing people drinking glasses of "clean, safe mine effluent"; ads claiming that if Clean Water passed, we wouldn't be able to pour a glass of water down our sinks without risking arrest; ads declaring that Clean Water would "wipe out the state's economy."

While journalists beat the Militia, Unabomber, and Freeman stories to death, Montana's publicly-owned rivers received next to no national mention, and international mining money beat grassroots democracy to death. Clean Water lost 56 to 44 percent.

> The river was cut by the world's great flood and runs
> over rocks from the basement of time. . . . Under the
> rocks are the words, and some of the words are theirs.
>
> —*A River Runs Through It*

On the day Clean Water lost, tens of thousands of acts of self-giving were negated by nothing more artful than money and lies. In the dark winter months that followed, the defenders of Norman's river went right on giving themselves anyway. That's when I began, for no reason my mind could come up with, to feel crazy waves of hope. The flow of courage, perseverance, and self-giving this river has inspired in its human admirers has been as beautiful to watch as the river itself. A comprehensive list is impossible, but here is one brief paragraph of things people have done:

A group of activists, Women's Voices for the Earth, organized a "Mine Your Jewelry Box, Not the Blackfoot" movement that inspired hundreds of women to raise resistance money by donating heirloom gold jewelry; a group of river residents, The Blackfoot Legacy, hired renowned economist Ed Whitelaw, of the University of Oregon, to do an independent, nonpartisan study of the McDonald Project that ended up blowing the corporate portrait of the mine's "benefits" out of the water; Don Peters, a state fisheries biologist whose career focus has been the study of the threatened trout of the Blackfoot, has taken a scientifically flawless and courageously vocal role in depicting the biological dangers of the proposed mine; Bill Leachman, a Virginia stockbroker and thirty-year veteran of Blackfoot fishing trips, logged hundreds of hours sleuthing out the weird financial dealings and wheelings of the corporate owners of the mine site; attorneys Cal Souther and Jeff Rentz donated hundreds of hours of legal advice; scores of whitewater and fishing guides wouldn't let clients on the water till they vowed to write letters protesting the mine; the Patagonia clothing company threw a chili-cookoff/microbrew fund-raiser; a half-dozen filmmakers made fine Blackfoot documentaries without hope of even covering their costs; one of them, Gene Bernovsky, donned a T-shirt that read PURE WATER IS MORE PRECIOUS THAN GOLD, parked himself beside the mining industry's opulent booth at the '97 Montana State Fair, and gave away copies of his documentary, *A River Cries,* to anyone who'd chat about the mine—till he was grabbed by police who'd been told that his backpack full of videos was a bomb; scores of artists donated a fortune in artwork; pilots donated flights to give scientists and filmmakers aerial perspective on the site; musicians Greg Brown, Jen Adams, Jimmy Dale Gilmore, Keb' Mo', and Bonnie Raitt put on fabulous benefit concerts that sold out in support of the river; writer Dick Manning gave a year of his life to *One Round River,* a nonfiction tour de force on the Blackfoot's history and fight for life; writer Annick Smith donated her time, even as she was losing her father, to compile *Headwaters,* a literary anthology in which thirty writers celebrate the ways a healthy Blackfoot serves us all; thousands donated cash, auctionable gifts, great food, high spirits, and volunteer hours to keep resistance alive; thousands more carried news of the threat to river access points, fishing lodges, fly-fishing magazines and catalogs, metals market investors, football games, concerts, classrooms, parades, National Public Radio, *Sports Illustrated,* CBS, *The New York Times,* the Turner Network, and all over the nation; and one small river watchdog group, The Clark Fork Coalition, fought off lawsuits, slim funding, gloomy basement offices, and the rancid ass of despair to serve as a clearinghouse, coordinator, instigator, and/or inspirer of almost all of these efforts.

On September 29, 1997, our long resistance met with an unhoped-for result. In a document titled "An Open Letter to Our Montana Neighbors," the Phelps Dodge Corporation, a true mining superpower, announced that it was abandoning the McDonald Project, ceding their 72-percent share to their minority partner, and leaving Montana. The project was now in the hands of Canyon Resources—a deeply indebted company with such terrible credit that no American bank would lend them money. The irrational hope of 1996 had become 1997's reasonable one: the Blackfoot had a hell of a chance at survival. For our ragtag river army to take credit for Phelps Dodge's departure would be foolish. Falling gold prices and the colossal cyanide-gold investment fraud known as Bre-X were contributing factors. But the ferocity of the Blackfoot's defenders remains a surefire third factor. This region is a jostled beehive. In reaching for "easy honey," Phelps Dodge was stung again and again, and the stings weren't just annoyances; they cost *money.* Phelps Dodge claims to have spent $26 million on its futile quest for Blackfoot gold.

The story gets better. For more than a century, Montana state government and Montana mining have been virtually the same entity, all prospective mines were deemed good mines, and all mining damage was left to posterity. The war for Norman's river has changed this forever. Seeing river after river threatened with something close to death while gold profits slipped away to Toronto and New York corporate accounts, Montanans realized en masse (as Wallace Stegner predicted) that Rocky

Mountain waters are a far greater treasure than Rocky Mountain minerals will ever be. What's more, "the Treasure State" is also the Manifesto State: if you came here by the summer of '98 wearing much in the way of gold, Montanans would *lecture* your ass. Thanks to the Blackfoot, thousands of us now knew that 84 percent of gold becomes jewelry, that gold more than sufficient to even vanity needs is produced by recyling or as a by-product of safer kinds of mining, and that a six- or seven-hundred-year supply of gold sufficient to global industrial needs is already out of the ground. To celebrate a romance or a special occasion with gold that arrives over the dead bodies of cyanided aquifers, wildlife, and watersheds, a lot of Montanans would now tell you, is not very god-damned romantic. The most popular bumper sticker in the state for four years running has said, THE BLACKFOOT RIVER IS MORE PRECIOUS THAN GOLD. A close runner-up simply advises, BOYCOTT GOLD.

Then came the knockout punch: when Montana's Republican governor and senators continued to serve international mining corporations instead of their own citizens, the people led their leaders. In November 1998 we collected signatures for, and passed, an unprecedented ballot initiative that *bans all new cyanide heap-leach gold mines from the state forever.*

A greater Montana grassroots victory against our extraction-industry-serving government has perhaps never been won. Though corporate gold-diggers are trying to overturn our anti-cyanide law—though the war for Norman's river may not in fact be over till the sin of greed departs the human heart—Norman says it best: "All good things—trout as well as eternal salvation—come by grace and grace comes by art and art does not come easy." Corporate miners still lurk in our watershed. But tens of thousands of poignantly disorganized river lovers now have their eyes glued to the clean green flow, and vow to mount as many ballot initiatives, concerts, lawsuits, protests, and expressions of love as it takes to keep heap-leachers off Norman's river till kingdom come.

8.   Suddenly the whole world is a fish and the fish is gone. . . .

—*A River Runs Through It*

In the Blackfoot's high mountain headwaters, snow falls for seven months or more each winter, collecting in immense, sun-defying banks. Then the planet tilts toward solstice, the angle of sunlight grows acute, and the banks begin to pay out their wealth. Drop by drop, the clean, pure riches melt, congeal, obey gravity, start seaward, filling everything they touch with life.

Immersed to the waist in this vast liquidation, I watched a tiny fiction ride an apricot strand of water. Then the pale evening dun that was not a dun reached the point where the broad-browed trout had risen. And it rose again. I lifted my rod. The trout slammed it back down. I gulped joy. The trout gulped Blackfoot. Disbelief in our opposite fortunes froze us for a moment. Then the trout, with great tailfuls of river, began trying to douse the sky's single star—and a tiny answering splash promptly sounded behind us: *Doip!*

I laughed out loud.

The big trout took off, running so fast downriver he might have made it to the Pacific in a day or two. But as Huck Finn said, "I been there before." I set out on a river-hampered run of my own, using my magic wand to slowly charm the fish into staying in Montana with me.

Four pounds easy, the threatened West Slope cutthroat I finally held under a fully starred, moonless sky. Yet her cold sides, as I freed her, shone even by starlight a hint of the sun-made pinks, teals, and pumpkins that filled the world all evening.

Back home later than late, I greeted wife, dogs, and daughters with an apology so bogus, so brimful of the joys I'd stood immersed in, that I may as well have been toting an I'M NOT SORRY! placard around the room. I didn't dare ask forgiveness when it was obvious even to the dogs that I'd gladly do it all over again. What I did ask, the very next evening, was whether my six-year-old cared to join me on the Blackfoot, my thought being that her limited endurance would force domestic grace upon me.

What happened instead was that the rafts again left the water, the wind ceased in the pines, the convergences, comedies, and ecstasies that are a Blackfoot River evening rise descended, and my little girl embraced, comprehended, and refused to relinquish it all. Now she too is a joy-junkie, incapable of guilt, the teals and apricots gleaming in her eyes. Now it's me going, "Jeez, we gotta get home for dinner," while she cackles, "*Never!* It's not dark! See the stars in the river!"

May her love live and grow.

10. The 1872 Knee-Mining Act & Your Exciting Financial Future!

Apologia

One of the most anachronistic and devastating pieces of "corporate welfare" legislation in the world is America's 1872 Mining Act. In November 1996, I wrote a farcical fable hoping to draw attention to this farce of a law, for a Nature Conservancy fiction anthology called *Off the Beaten Path*. The composition of this fable was, I confess, no attempt to make great art. (The term "activist art," truth be told, strikes me as close to oxymoronic.) I wrote this tale simply to preserve my health—because I was on the verge of apoplexy at the time, thanks to the recent appearance of Montana's governor, Marc Racicot, at the dedication of a Nature Conservancy–brokered wildlife corridor newly established on the Blackfoot River.

While I admire the Conservancy's nonpartisan approach to conservation, and have written and stumped for them on several projects, free of charge, there's a time and a place to draw the line. For years, Governor Racicot had been shilling for the proposed Blackfoot River cyanide heap-leach gold mine, paraphrasing corporate propaganda claiming that the mine would be "cutting edge," hence "safe," and a "boon" to Montanans. Mines with identical technology have killed entire rivers, most recently (summer of '99) destroying the upper Danube. My beef with the Conservancy, then, is obvious: to allow a cyanide heap-leach proponent like Governor Racicot to preside over the dedication of a beautiful living stretch of mine-threatened Blackfoot corridor was rather like inviting a weasel to serve as pediatrician to a nestful of baby grouse. Or asking a wad of *Tubifex tubifex* worms to baby-sit a school of trout. Or inviting me to organize a Republican or Democrat fund-raiser.

I therefore wrote the following clanging, banging, therapeutic train wreck of a story—and sincerely thank the Conservancy for suspending their usual perfect diplomacy long enough to help me heal myself, by publishing it.

The 1872 Knee-Mining Act and Your Exciting Financial Future!

Ty Coburn was a Montana cattle rancher. He didn't go to church. Didn't smoke, or drink to speak of. Didn't golf, or bowl, or even fish the Big Blackfoot River, though it ran right through his little spread near the prairie-dog-sized town of Ovando. He did shoot a couple of deer each fall, usually one on his own tag and one on his wife Annie's. But that was work, not sport. Hunting by tractor (towing the usual hay bales on the trailer so the deer wouldn't suspect), Ty took five or ten minutes to bag the two best bucks, and the rest of the day to carve, package, and freeze them.

He didn't mind the endless work, though. The fact was, Ty had never wanted "sport" or "relaxation." His two kids, six horses, and varying-sized herds of cattle, his hay fields and water rights and addiction to Skoal were all he'd ever wanted. "This ranch is my country club, church, and whorehouse all balled up in one," he liked to say— when Annie was well out of earshot.

Lucky for the marriage, the ranch kept Annie satisfied, too, as long as she could add one outside ingredient to the mix: though she rose at dawn and worked the same double-shift days as Ty, late every night she watched the CNN News, over and over and over.

"Connects me to the world," was Annie's explanation.

"Disconnects her from rememberin' our total economic dependence on a buncha stupid cows," was Ty's theory.

"It's her mantra," opined their six-year-old daughter, Rhett, who was getting weird ideas at school.

"It's *boring!*" roared three-year-old Russell with cattlemanly authority.

Whatever it was, seven in a row was Annie's CNN record, and three per night was her norm. She didn't doze while she was watching, either. Annie could tell you which news clips were fresh, and which were repeats from the past half hour; she noticed every time Lynn Russell changed hairdos and David Goodnow changed suits; she never stopped wondering why Bob Lozier (whom Ty called "Bob Loser") always wore the same smirky smile no matter how grim the news.

Of course, Rhett and Russell threw fits about their mom's one-show obsession—especially after she tried to defend it by calling it "educational." But Ty had long ago noticed how Annie's monopolization of the tube bored the kids into an early bedtime, which left him and Annie a quiet hour or two together. And to his delight Ty discovered that, once a week or so, after he'd triple-checked the kids, Annie was not averse to having sex to a CNN accompaniment. He loved the crazy buffalo rug she'd take down from the shelf to lie on; loved the way her body looked in the flashing blue light; loved it that he was the one thing on Earth that made her ignore her insufferable show. Hell, he finally even grew fond of CNN itself, if only by association—though he did sometimes wonder, when they were hard at it, whether he and Annie might be the reason for Bob Loser's smirky smile.

One night after Ty dozed off, Annie caught a CNN clip on the dangers of cholesterol. Because she was head chef of a family that daily inhaled serious quantities of home-grown beef, the CNN story scared Annie the way disease-plagued elk farms scared Ty. The following morning she drove to OK Books in Helena, bought *The Next-to-No-Cholesterol Cookbook*, hurried on to Wholly Foods (an establishment Ty would soon be calling "that goddamned hippie feed store"), spent a small fortune, returned home, and proceeded to revamp the family diet.

153

"I blame Ted Turner for this!" Ty roared the instant he set eyes on the tofu-and-vegetable stir-fry Annie had concocted in lieu of his customary catcher's-mitt-sized, drippingly rare steak.

"You should *thank* him for it!" Annie retorted. "I'll bet your blood looks like sausage grease. I want you to get it checked."

A modest request in most families. But the only medical problems for which Ty Coburn ever opened his wallet involved his kids, horses, wife, or events that knocked Ty himself unconscious, hence unable to resist. He agreed to check nothing. He said hard ranch work purged the blood. He did eat the stir-fry—hating every bite, feeling hungry again an hour later. It was a thankless act of courage: the next night Annie served up something called tempeh that had Ty looking back on the tofu as if it had been steak.

Things went from bad to worse. Bulghur-oatmeal burgers. Rice so wild it drove little railroad spikes between Ty's teeth. Four-pound loaves of bread that tasted like stagnant pondweed. Soybeans that tasted okay drowned in ketchup, but later produced enough methane to heat the house.

The weird food began to terrorize Ty's dream life. He dreamt he went shopping for dangly earrings—for himself! He dreamt he joined PETA. He dreamt he changed the name of his favorite horse, Butkus, to "Shakti." He dreamt he rode Shakti out into his fields, took a pair of bolt cutters to his own barbed-wire fences, and set all his cattle "free." He'd wake in a terrified sweat, usually needing to fart. It upset him.

Ty took action by trying to joke Annie's health kick away. The kids' pinheaded collie dog, Boofus, had been chewing up pine cordwood lately, and pugging out splintery loaves afterward. Ty sneaked out in the yard one freezing cold night, picked up half a dozen Boofus loaves, stuck them in a Ziploc bag, hid them in the freezer, made a trip to Helena a few days later, borrowed a few hippie feed-store food labels, returned home, and informed Annie, "Stopped by Wholly Foods. Wanted to set eyes on the Enemy myself. But I found these—skinless soy sausage with toasted almond slivers. Sounded worth a try."

Annie was so pleased by Ty's sudden cooperation that she had the things frying in olive oil and garlic, and was quadruple-checking the kids' shoes for dog do, before she figured things out. Ty, peeking in from the living room, was rolling on the floor and sobbing by then. Annie was not amused.

Things went from worse to awful. A pair of four-wheel-drive ruts appeared on Annie's forehead every time she glanced at Ty. A mask of saddle leather replaced Ty's face whenever he eyeballed Annie. Russ and Rhett ate so little of the Next-to-No cookbook concoctions that they began to look anemic. Annie started fixing them separate meals of their former diet. Ty took to clearing the table, just so he could sneak scraps from the kids' plates. Boofus skulked miserably about, watching Ty snorf up what used to be *his* food. The TV-lit lovemaking went the way of the rare steaks. Bob Loser kept smirking at them anyhow.

"Six hundred tons o' cattle surroundin' us day an night," Ty finally bellowed over his string-squash and Swiss chard one night, "an' I'm *always hungry!*"

"A blood test costs *twenty damn dollars!*" Annie bellowed right back.

Neither wives nor husbands survive long on ranches without being heroically stubborn. The next time he drove to town, Ty showed Annie, Ted Turner, Bob Loser, and all the rest of 'em how a real rancher operates—by *again* refusing to see a doctor, toting home his first bottle of whiskey in years, and matching every CNN his wife watched that night with two double shots of Rebel Yell. But Annie knew a thing or two about ranching herself. Seeing Ty's game, she just sat back and watched CNN so many times in a row that Ty finally got the whirlies, dashed in the bathroom, and did some rebel yelling down the toilet.

The next morning, Ty, looking as if he'd had Boofus sausage for breakfast, loaded up the hay trailer, climbed onto the tractor, drove down by the Blackfoot, watched the opal-green river flow as the cows chewed and crapped and lowed, and felt his stubbornness suddenly melt away. He missed Annie's smile something awful—not to mention her buffalo rug, her long, slow kisses, the blue flashes of *The Hollywood Minute* and *Dollars and Sense* upon her body.

"I surrender," Ty told the Blackfoot, who thought no less of him for that.

So, at age forty-one, feeling as strong as a wild bull elk, Ty Coburn swallowed his cowboy pride, drove into Helena, and splurged on a complete physical for himself and a dozen red roses for Annie.

Turned out he was right about hard ranch work: his cholesterol matched his weight at 195.

"Not bad for a decrepit ol' carnivore," Annie admitted as they lay in front of the TV that night, as naked as the steaks they'd devoured for dinner, with Annie loving her roses and Ty loving Annie and Bob Loser's smirk making perfect sense again.

But when Ty woke to a ringing phone in the middle of the night,

155

something did not make sense. It was his doctor, saying that Ty's blood tests had revealed more than a cholesterol level: they'd confirmed a condition known as "Miner's Knee." What's more, the doctor said, he worked for a corporation known as SurgiCorp International. "And on SurgiCorp's behalf," he informed Ty, "I'm staking claim to both your knees."

Ty chuckled at this nonsense. He thought his sawbones must have taken a shine to him, and was now trying but failing to pull off some complicated joke.

But there was no punch line. "SurgiCorp's corporate prep team will be out to see you in a few days," said the doctor. *Click,* said the phone.

In preparation for the "corporate prep team"—whatever that might be—Ty drove down to Missoula and the University of Montana library and did some homework. "Miner's Knee," he was appalled to learn, was a genuine condition: a mineral buildup that occurs on the kneecaps of one in five hundred people. The condition caused no pain or loss of mobility, and posed no health risks short-term or long, if the minerals were left alone. But way back in 1849, researchers at the newly formed National Institute for Profitable Surgeries (NIPS) began looking for ways to make money on Miner's Knee deposits. And they found one: a common knee mineral known as "glod" could be removed and fired into a malleable yellowish metal, then fashioned into jewelry.

That a knee-born metal had been discovered at all amazed Ty. That a glod wedding band, necklace, tongue-stud, penis-ring, or cuff link would eventually become the desire of millions of men and women seemed preposterous. But within a decade of the mineral's discovery, glod lust became a national epidemic. Citizens suspected of having Miner's Knee deposits were soon being mugged in broad daylight, ripped open in back alleys, crippled for life. Doctors gunned each other down over knee rights to a single patient. Indians, Chinese immigrants, poor whites, and Southern blacks were herded by the thousand through glod-extraction facilities that were little more than slaughterhouses for human legs. Then, in the 1870s, glod fever became government policy when President Ulysses S. Grant, venting years of pent-up battle fury, signed into law The Knee-Mining Act of 1872—a piece of legislative inanity that allowed the holder of any type of medical degree, from any nation on earth, to journey to this country, locate Americans with Miner's Knee, and legally operate upon them.

Coming down, as he read, with a terrible case of psychosomatic knee pain, Ty learned how, for the past 125 years, glod had been gouged, suctioned, blasted, and drilled from tens of thousands of his fellow citizens by quasi-Hippocratic opportunists from all over the globe. Hundreds of Americans had died from glod surgery; thousands had contracted cancer from chemicals used in the extraction process; thousands more ended up in wheelchairs for life. And Grant's antique Human Butchery Law was still on the books! To this day, Ty discovered, any dentist, any ophthalmologist, any proctologist or chiropractor or boob-job specialist on Earth possessed the right to rip open the knees of any American in whom minerals had been discovered! Worse still, the glod industry had made a minuscule number of people so stupendously rich that they'd hired lawyers, public-relations firms, spin doctors, politicians, and hit men: every time a protest, scandal, ballot initiative, or grassroots protest threatened the 1872 Knee-Mining Law, an election was bought, a PR brainwash took place, a key activist vanished, and the maiming of American knees remained legal and rampant. The new transnational knee-mining corporations even had the gall to call their butcheries "cures."

What Ty learned, in a nutshell, was that he and his knees were in surreal but perfectly genuine trouble.

SurgiCorp's corporate prep team came jouncing up the Coburns' drive in a lost-looking white Lincoln Town Car with the words SURGICORP: CUTTING-EDGE SOLUTIONS FOR YOUR GLOBAL GLOD NEEDS stenciled on both front doors. Ty had given some thought to their arrival; early that morning he'd turned forty head of cattle loose in the yard. As he opened the door to greet his guests, he was gratified to see fresh manure splashed to the windows of the Town Car's four doors. But the two briefcase-toting men and the beatifically smiling woman who stepped from the car proved nimble; they made it to the porch in their three immaculate gray suits without greening even the soles of their shoes.

Annie, too, had prepared a special greeting. After leading the reps into the living room, she served a triple-strength herbal tea that Wholly Foods called "Last-Ditch Laxative." With huge thanks and broad smiles, the reps each downed a twelve-ounce, honey-laced mug. Ty and Annie watched, poker-faced. When none of them showed discomfort or asked to use the bathroom, though, the Coburns felt their first true rush of fear: these were three competent-looking, well-dressed, determined people skilled at ignoring, sidestepping, and squeezing in every kind of shit imaginable.

Ty decided to end the team's visit with one fell speech: "I just flat refuse to be operated on," he announced, giving each rep his slowest, most ominous Old West stare. "I won't be part of this. End of discussion. You may now leave."

But the beatific lady rep just beamed more brightly. "Yours is a common first reaction, Ty," she said with a warmth that sounded almost sexual. "But it's not, I'm afraid, a *legal* reaction. If you cooperate, your cure will take place in the private hospital of your choice. If you defy the 1872 law, it will take place in SurgiCorp's state-of-the-art, fifty-five-foot traveling operating room outside your cell at the state penitentiary in Deer Lodge. That choice is yours, certainly, Ty. But rest assured, the cure *will* take place."

Ty was stunned to silence.

Annie took up the fight. "Those forms you sent about a compensation check. Are they *real?* Is the U.S. Government actually saying that the payoff for Ty's maiming is *five dollars per knee?* With no funding for physical rehab? No assistance for wheelchairs, wheelchair ramps, bathroom alterations? No compensation for time off work? Or were those forms a sick joke?"

"The five-dollar-per-knee compensation," the lady rep replied, "is a proud American tradition more than anything else, Annie. That price was set by President U. S. Grant himself—one of the heroes, I'm sure you recall, of the successful war against slavery in this country!"

"But his mining law is a form of the very thing he fought to end!" Annie shouted. "Any halfwit can see that!"

"But Congress can't see it," said the rep with the thickest briefcase, who turned out to be one of SurgiCorp's army of lawyers. "If you don't like the law, Mrs. Coburn," he said, "by all means, fight it! That's your right as a citizen. Of course, it'll be time-consuming. And *expensive*. If you lose, I imagine it could even cost you this lovely ranch. But do feel free. And may the best team of lawyers win!"

While Ty and Annie reeled at this prospect, the lady rep produced a pile of elegant four-color brochures, spread them across the coffee table, and, in the hushed tone of a TV golf announcer, said, "What these illustrate, what we really came to discuss with you two, are some of the exciting new options in glod-extraction methods! Over the past couple of decades, SurgiCorp's world-class research team has developed safe, efficient new ways of extracting glod from American mineral owners. Ask anyone in the business. We're cutting-edge!"

The reps all turned out to love this phrase: "cutting-edge." Ty noticed how much they loved it, because every time they used it his anus seized up in some sort of sphinctoidal arrest. The first illustrated Surgi-Corp's extraction method consisted of removing the patient's knees completely and replacing them with metal joints—made of "cutting-edge aerospace metals." The large color photo showed a voluptuous, bikini-clad postoperative victim in a poolside lounging chair, smiling seductively at her own shiny titanium knees. Gaping at the gorgeously maimed legs in horror, Ty felt his anus *and* his penis seize up.

The second extraction method—the one the lady rep said "we'd be *thrilled* to see Mister Ty Coburn choose!"—was called Cyanide Knee Leach Extraction. Hearing the name alone, Ty grew clammy and faint. Opening the appropriate brochure, the lady rep showed Annie and a fast-fading Ty how two plastic bladders, like colostomy bags, were strapped to the patient's knees, and a hose running from each was attached to a powerful pump. The bladders were filled with cyanide . . .

("Yes, the *famous deadly poison*," the lady rep tittered in response to Annie's furious question. "But what a way to put it, Ms. Coburn! Our safety engineers are on *your* side. How about a little *trust?*")

. . . Next, the patient was fully anesthetized. Then—in a series of illustrations that even the intrepid lady rep dared not describe aloud—the caps of both knees were, as the brochure put it, "traumatized" with repeated blows from a hardwood mallet, until "healing fluids" (more commonly known as water-on-the-knee) formed . . .

(Ty was so faint by now he had to stuff his head down between his potentially doomed knees. But Annie was CNN-tough. She paid attention.)

. . . Once the "healing fluids" formed, a hole was drilled in each knee, a second hose was inserted into each knee hole, the opposite end of the hose was attached to the cyanide bladders, the pump was activated, and lethal quantities, stupendous quantities, unbelievable quantities, of sodium cyanide solution were pumped through the smashed knees of the patient in order to draw out the glod.

"But won't the cyanide just *kill* my husband?" Annie cried.

The SurgiCorp team let out a unison chuckle. "We're a cutting-edge operation!" the technician exclaimed—causing Ty's anus to burrow like a terrified gopher clear up into his small intestines. "There's no sense confusing you good folks with complex terminology," the technician added, "but you'll be glad to know that knee fluids are what we call *discrete,* and that the only way cyanide can enter the bloodstream is through what we call an *indiscretion.*"

"And *what,* in the name of *Satan,*" Ty rasped from down between his knees, "is an *indiscretion?*"

"A burst hose would be an example," the technician said. "But, need I say it, SurgiCorp's bladders and hoses are absolutely—"

"*Cutting-edge,* yes, we know, we know!" Annie snapped. "But Ty read that SurgiCorp, operating earlier this decade under the name Knee Source Incorporated, shot cyanide from burst hoses into the blood of three hundred patients in a year!"

The reps enjoyed another group chuckle. "SurgiCorp International is *not* Knee Source Incorporated, Mrs. Coburn," the lawyer cooed. "SurgiCorp was built, from the ground up, with *public safety* as its *number one priority.*"

"Ty read that you just restructured Knee Source to dodge a barrage of lawsuits," Annie retorted.

The lawyer turned as pink as a ham and began groping through his brain wrinkles for a reply. But the radiant lady rep, smile unscathed, silenced him with a look. "Your husband," she told Annie, "no matter what extremist literature he's been reading, will receive the benefit of *millions* of dollars' worth of cutting-edge research. I know this is hard for laymen to grasp. But you needn't fret much longer. We've scheduled Ty's cure for next week!"

Ty raised a bloodless face in protest, but had to drop down between his knees again. Annie began looking around the room for a weapon.

"One more thing," said the lawyer. "Miner's Knee is, of course, hereditary. We've staked claims to little Rhett's and Russell's knees. Of course, we'll wait till they're physically mature to operate, to maximize yield. Don't mean to bore you, the details are all in the claim forms, filed in Helena. But I *do* need to mention that Russ and Rhett are required by law to sign those forms on the day they turn eighteen. And if, God forbid, they become parents in the interim, our right to any legitimate or illegitimate offspring's knee minerals goes into effect from date of birth."

Determined to throw them out now, Ty tried to let out a roar, but it emerged as a mere gasping groan as he flopped forward off the couch, slammed his face and chest into the coffee table, exploded all four of its legs, and sprawled, unconscious, on the ruined table and floor.

The SurgiCorp crew stood as if choreographed. "Dear me!" said the technician. "Ty's having the darnedest time retooling his thinking."

"Don't worry, Ms. Coburn," said the lawyer. "He'll come around."

"Thanks so much," cooed the beaming lady rep, "for the yummy tea!"

Annie was speechless as they trooped out the door. But they weren't two seconds into their Town Car before she picked Ty's pockets for his keys, unlocked the gun cabinet, and began cleaning both deer rifles, both shotguns, the .22, and Ty's antique Colt .45. She then drove up to Lincoln for fresh ammo.

Lyle Croft, the gunsmith, was an old schoolmate of Ty's—and when he saw the fury in Annie's eyes, he was worried for his friend. "What's with the fireworks, Annabelle?" he asked. "Gonna Unabomb the Tyster?"

"If those SurgiCorp geeks think they're cuttin' *my* family," she fumed, "they got another think comin'."

Lyle usually stared when he spoke with Annie, who was awfully easy on the eyes. But now his gaze veered off. "If Ty an' the kids got Miner's Knee," he said, "them SurgiCorp folks got every right to cure it."

Annie gaped. "Could you repeat that?" she whispered.

"Let 'em operate," Lyle said, avoiding her face. "Ain't the end o' the world."

Up till now the whole glod threat had given Annie a muffled, foggy feeling. Lyle's words cut through this fog like a hard slap. "Then is it the end of the world," she asked, "if they *don't* cut my family? Give me one good reason why we should let this happen, Lyle. So kids at the high school can wear glod rings in their eye sockets? So some already-rich shareholder can get richer? So Ty can sit in a wheelchair growin' fat an' suicidal while the kids take over the ranch at the ages o' six an' three? So our grandkids' lives can be ruined before they're born? Come on, Lyle! One good reason!"

"Eighteen-seventy-two Knee-Minin' Act," Croft replied. "The law's the law."

"Till *you're* ready to drive drunk or poach an elk!" Annie retorted.

Lyle shrugged. "I read in the paper," he said, "how there's enough undiagnosed Miner's Knee in western Montana river valleys to keep a hundred surgeons busy for twenty years. Them surgeons make big bucks, Annie. Then spend it places like mine. I'm lookin' out for number one, I admit it. You an' Ty'd do the same in my shoes."

"In the first place," Annie seethed, "your shoes *reek!* An' in the second, those surgeons aren't *from* here! They don't care about us! They'll cut Ty up an' leave! Whereas you an' he grew up together, remember? You've footballed an' rodeoed an' hunted an' worked the mill—hell, you stole Ty's slut of a high-school sweetheart an' saved him for *me,* remember? An' we go way back as your customers, too, Lyle. That ain't big bucks, I know. Ty's a good shot, is the problem. But is betrayin' us your economic answer? Is a little *glod* trickle-down worth more to you than lifelong friends?"

"Annie," Lyle said, at last meeting her eyes. "You an' Ty are mosquitoes in a blizzard on this one. Me, I choose to be one of the snowflakes. This glod deal's way bigger'n any of us. Now take your ammo an' go, 'fore you make me mad."

When Annie got home with her pathetic bag of bullets, she collapsed on the couch. No sooner had she done so than Ty tore downstairs, grinning.

"Did some research while you were out," he said, a little self-importantly. "Turns out there's a Clean Blood Initiative on next fall's ballot that'd make Cyanide Knee-Leach surgery impossible in this state. So the fight with SurgiCorp isn't international after all. This is a *state* deal, Annie! An' think who I'm friends with!"

Ty left a silence so Annie could answer. But she was stumped. "Butkus?" she asked. "Boofus? Not Lyle Croft, that's for sure."

"Bobby Robocot!" Ty cried. "Governor Robocot's kid brother! Remember my baseball days? Bobby an' me were the all-league keystone combo two years in a row. An' there comes a time to play the old-boy game. Go grab the extension an' listen, Annie. Me an' Governor Robocot're gonna have us a chat!"

Annie went to listen. What a nightmare!

"Great to hear from you, Ty, you bet I remember!" Governor Robocot began. "Like clockwork, you and Bobby, turning those double plays. And I'll remember you next week, too, when you work with SurgiCorp on this exciting glod deal."

"Whoa there, Guv!" Ty said. "That's why I called. I'm doin' no such thing! They've staked claims to our *kids,* for chrissake!"

"Now back up, there, Ty," the governor said. "SurgiCorp doesn't cure anyone under eighteen. And think of the jobs you'll be creating!

An entire *team* of surgeons, nurses, anesthesiologists, caregivers! Think of the income that brings this beautiful state! A lot of fine people are depending on folks like you, Ty. And hey! That's a nice ten-dollar compensation check you'll be gettin' in the bargain."

"I don't want ten dollars!" Ty roared. "I want poison-free blood! I want kids who can walk! An' there *is* a way to fight this, Governor. Come next fall, election time, you've got to—"

"Ty, Ty, Ty," Governor Robocot cut in. "I've been *good* to cattlemen. Good to you and yours, partner. But I'm a public servant. And you're saying, 'Side with the radicals, not the public!' You're saying, 'Turn your back on the unemployed.' You're saying, 'Reward me for playin' ball with Bobby twenty years ago.' Let's get the sentiment out of this, Ty. What good are knees upon which no one operates? How does that create jobs? My mind's open as ever, you know that. But your facts and figures, Ty. That's what we need.

"Great talkin' with you!" the governor concluded.

Click, said the phone.

"This can't be happenin'," Ty groaned as the anesthesiologist lowered the mask over his mouth. He opened his eyes wide, to memorize the son of a bitch's face so he could kill him later—but instead saw Annie drawing away from him, her face blue for some reason, her body blue, too, and naked. Embarrassed, Ty sat up to cover her, but the instant he moved, the anesthesiologist vanished, he and Annie were on the buffalo rug, Bob Lozier was smirking out of the TV, Rhett and Russell were undoomed, his ranch and knees were safe, his life was worth living again—and Annie was *still* blue-bodied and naked. Ty couldn't believe his luck!

"We fell asleep," Annie whispered, "till you started whimperin' like a dog on death row. What on *Earth* were you dreamin'?"

"Worst nightmare o' my life!" Ty gasped.

"Tell me," Annie said.

So they lay back on the buffalo and Ty did tell her—beginning with the 195 cholesterol count, which was real, and the condition in his knees, which, thank Glod, was not. And with his ranch-bred eye for detail and in his joy at being awake, Ty soon had Annie gasping with laughter. The absurd intricacy of the dream: cyanide extraction! cutting-edge anal cramps! 1872 Knee-Mining Acts! While Ty was still spinning out corporate threats to Rhett and Russell's unborn offspring, though, Annie suddenly sat up and cried, "My *God!*"

She sounded so scared that Ty took to his feet. *"What?"* he whispered, listening for coyotes, for troubled calves, for sounds outside the house.

"It's *real*," Annie said, staring straight ahead into the dark.

"What's real?" Ty asked.

"Only your knees aren't knees," Annie said, still staring at nothing. "They're that giant gold mine proposed for the Upper—"

"Oh don't *start!*" Ty groaned.

"—for the Upper Blackfoot," Annie finished. "An' your blood isn't blood. It's water, the life's blood of this valley. So what's at stake isn't one family's ability to walk. It's *worse*, Ty. It's the health of every water-drinkin' human, animal, fish, an' bird in this watershed. It's the—"

"Bullshit!" Ty snapped. And he was pissed. Because they'd *had* this worthless argument. They'd fought for months over the proposed Blackfoot gold mine and, last November, had canceled each other's votes on the one related ballot measure. By Thanksgiving, though, they'd agreed to bury the hatchet forever. And now Annie was using *his* nightmare to throw *her* fears for the river back in his face. "Bullshit," he repeated. "It was *my* dream, Annie. An' I say it's pure random craziness. I say it's one cowboy's phobia 'bout doctors an' agin' knees. An' I'm awake now, Annie. Dream's over. So let it drop."

"Have it your way," she said. "The hammers an' pumps an' cyanide they wanted to take to your knees have nothin' to do with *real* explosives an' two-hundred-ton earth-wreckin' machines an' two-mile holes in the ground an' whole *reservoirs* of cyanide. An' your dream fears for Russ an' Rhett? Silly! What's *real* poison groundwater or mountain-sized toxic dumps or a river of heavy metals flowin' past us got to do with *them?* It's random craziness. Ol' Ty an' his doctor fears . . ."

In a quiet, painstakingly controlled voice, Ty said, "I see you're out to wreck an evenin' I was countin' among the best o' my life. But I just won't fight you on this, Annie. An' for everything else this evenin', up till now, I still thank you."

Annie took this speech in. Mulled it a full quarter-minute. Then said, "An' I thank *you*, Ty. For your toughness, which helps us survive, even if it makes you vote the straight macho ticket. An' for the love beneath the toughness. For me an' the kids, this ranch, that river out there. You got a big heart, Ty, much as you hate to admit it. An' it's as scared of upstream poison-spewers an' jewelry-wearin' fools as *my* heart. It's why I can stand to live with you. How I can love you back. So I thank *you* for that."

Ty's toughness had to stare at Annie a long time before his heart could break through enough to let him mutter, "Welcome."

They kissed then, a perfunctory peck of truce, and went up to bed, where through the wide open window they listened—in a long, not-at-all perfunctory silence—as the Big Blackfoot went on talking.

Now if only it will go on living.

I grow utterly absorbed, as I age, by two things: love, thorough or insufficient, and grace under duress. Only those two.

—Brian Doyle, *Credo*

Damn the kind of mind that's in two places at once!

—Kabir, *The Bijak*

11. Beauty/Violence/Grief/Frenzy/Love: On the Contemplative Versus the Activist Life

I became a fiction writer, after long, painstaking apprenticeship, at the age of twenty-nine. I did so out of a sense of calling, out of gratitude for the sustenance that novels had given me, out of raw heartache for humanity, out of a desire to write antically of humanity's antics, and out of an overtly contemplative yearning for the loss of self that occurs during the daily making of fiction, in the belief that "he that loseth his life shall save it."

I became a nonfiction writer—after no apprenticeship whatever—at the age of forty. I did so not out of a sense of calling, but out of a sense of betrayal, out of rage over natural systems violated, out of grief for a loved world raped, and out of a craving for justice.

In donning a second literary hat, I became chronically self-conflicted: every page of nonfiction I now write, no matter how valid it seems on its own terms, feels like a betrayal of the fiction writer I originally set out to be. Yet every work of fiction I write, no matter how proud I might be of it, forces me to feign obliviousness toward the abuse of the loved and endangered places and creatures that constitute and share my home. I admire fiction boundlessly. Artistically speaking, I would always rather create fiction than try to give voice to a dying river or vanishing species. I just don't feel my world gives me this choice. Once upon a time, only Rome burned while we fiddlers fiddled. Nowadays the entire planet grows scorched, and the wild diversity that is our children's lifeline shrivels. When I feel this happening, I can't always keep the fiddle to my chin. When events are local, corporate-propelled, politically spun, directly devastating, and the people of my watershed are being scammed and lied to, the need to make nonfiction sometimes leapfrogs my fiction, becoming the most direct means I have, in an industrialized world of ideas, of championing the industrially dispossessed.

The fiction writer in me is contemplative to a fault, self-abnegatingly self-absorbed, and happiest when he's so lost in the wilderness of imagination and music of words that the travails of this world exist only in the Valmikian palm of his hand. I see my fiction-writing persona as a benign monomaniac; a self-giving narcissist; a *Glasperlenspieler* so absorbed in his *spielen* that he doesn't care whether anyone but he even knows what *Glasperlenspieler* means.

The nonfiction writer in me is also lost—in *incredulity* at the agonies and extinctions that industrial humanity is inflicting on our planetary home; he is therefore, of necessity, a public figure, aiming his work toward the most timely and largest possible voting audiences. I see my activist persona as a dithering desperado, constantly near tears at the vastly reduced world he'll be bequeathing his kids, as sincere as a larva-toting ant on a crushed anthill in his desire to preserve what remains—and in constant dire need of Lao Tzu's boomeranging reminder that "he who strives to be of use in this world soon burdens the people with his own insufficiency."

My inner fiction writer is a complete and demanding personality. My inner nonfiction writer is a complete and demanding personality. How does it feel to have two demanding literary personae crammed into my one head and body, fighting for possession of my pen? *Gnarly!* But if we reclusive artists and contemplatives, we confrontation-haters, we humans, do not rob our private selves often enough to give voice and succor to the primordial and life-sustaining, I believe we'll soon live in a land so reduced and desperate that such delicate art forms as fiction will not exist. This is not prophecy. It's just a peek into neighboring lands, where a literature-killing desperation is already in place.

One blue-then-crimson-then-starry-skied evening last July, I had a parable of a dinner with the triple-hatted lepidopterist/author/ activist Robert Michael Pyle (henceforth "Bob"). Bob writes from and fights for the damaged landscapes closest to his life and heart: the Willapa Hills of Washington; the High Line Canal of Denver; the habitats of Bigfoot and of butterflies.

Bob had spent our dinner day negotiating two hundred miles of one of the most scenic backroads on earth—Idaho's Lochsa River Highway—yet had managed to perceive hardly a scene. Why? Because Bob, being Bob, had his eyes glued to the air in front of his car, trying with all his might to avoid collisions with the abundance of butterflies. I can only imagine his pain. I guess an equivalent day for me would involve driving a car sixty miles an hour *underwater* up, say, the Big Hole River, splattering trout after innocent trout all over my windshield and grille. Bob Pyle is a man who worships butterflies: a man who goes into instant ecstasies at the sight of inert obtect pupae that normal people mistake for bird turds; a man I once saw reduce eavesdroppers to tears as he told of the violent death of his lifelong female companion— till the listeners realized the deceased lover was Bob's favorite butterfly net. He is a man who had *me* near tears with his descriptions of what the killing pollen of Monsanto's millions of acres of biochemically altered, insecticidal corn is doing to North America's monarch butterflies. At our midsummer night's supper, though, something besides butterflies had fought its way to the front of his lobes.

We had just finished eating when Bob donned a conflicted expression doubly troubling for its presence on the face of such a sublimely jovial man. Confessing how difficult he'd been finding it to wear his author, activist, and lepidopterist hats all at once, he dumbfounded me by expressing admiration for the "graceful" and "seemingly effortless" way I juggled my own two writerly hats. He then asked for my "secret."

The poor unsuspecting man! Bursting out in an incredulous cackle, I blored, *"How do I do it? HAHAHAHAHAHA! How do you think? Unwillingly! Schizophrenically! Antagonistically! Badly!"*

Beauty/Violence/Grief/Frenzy/Love

Looking, for a moment, as though he'd just witnessed the murder of another nubile butterfly net, Bob finally managed the sort of exhausted, responsibility-lashed smile that Santa would smile if he were real. He then sighed, "So much for helpful hints."

More calmly, but no more helpfully, I told him that I feel as though I am inhabited by two good men who detest each other despite their goodness, because there will never be enough of either man to go around.

Hoping to compare pathologies, Bob asked how far this detestation went.

I told the truth: each of my inner writers would like to see my other inner writer assassinated at once, and buried without tears, ceremony, or headstone, preferably in a toxic landfill, so that memorial visits would be impossible.

Bob nodded three times—once for each of his hats. We then attacked the red wine with the thirst of the fivesome we collectively are, and for a few hours grew so satisfyingly subtracted that we were just two half-snockered nature-dweebs enjoying a perfect Montana evening.

But of course we woke the next morning, a bit hung, as a fivesome again.

Who is this amorphous enemy that drives so many nature-lovers into multiple-hat-wearing and career schizophrenia? Aren't we citizen/activists being ridiculous to fear such cooties as "corporate power"? Doesn't Monsanto, on some level that Robert Michael Pyle has missed, have the best interests of consumers, farmers, and butterflies at heart? Isn't it more likely that Bob and I are a couple of paranoid, sixties-style nutbags than that the megacorporations are out to destroy the world? Wouldn't a better therapy than frantic activism be a relaxing round of golf on some beautifully groomed, only modestly herbicided links—say the Jack Nicklaus–designed course built over ARCO's Superfund slag heaps here in Anaconda, Montana?

FUCK NO! The people who work for, invest in, and rely upon multinational corporations (nearly all of us) try to maintain that corporations are "just people." But this is just not so. By dictionary definition and under authority of law, a corporation has "a continuous existence independent of the existences of its [human] members," and possesses "powers distinct from those of its members." This existence is real, this power vast. Yet the legal owner of the power does not eat, drink, or breathe, hence has no particular allegiance to pure food, clean water, clean air. It possesses no beating heart or soul, hence fears no God and suffers no karmic consequence for its actions in any kind of Hereafter. In obedience to bylaws and shareholders, a corporation is a serenely calculating, bloodless, bodiless profit-machine. When such an entity hires humans, it does not suddenly embrace the finest values of those humans; on the contrary, a bloodless job description predetermines the role of every human hired. Corporations *contain* humans the way a cult, a sedative, or a "consumer-conditioning" TV set contains humans. Far from being influenced by the humanity of its employees, the typical corporation *prevents* employees from expressing their full humanity, their long-term vision, their thrift, their compassion, their respect for the natural world—except as required by law, which the corporation of course sculpts relentlessly to serve its own nonhuman needs.

"Judge not, lest ye be judged" was addressed to no such entities as these. I *do* judge. With rare exceptions, the megacorporations *are* out to unify, dominate, monoculturize, dehumanize, and exploit the living world and its increasingly disenfranchised populace. Every environmental dispute judged by the all-powerful World Trade Organization since its formation in 1995 has ruled in favor of business and against increasingly frayed ecosystems. The top two hundred corporations possess twice the assets of 80 percent of the world's populace. The wealthiest 20 percent of the populace hoards 86 percent of the world's goods, while the poorest 20 percent scrape by or die on 1 percent. This disparity between top and bottom quintiles has doubled in the three corporation-serving "free trade" decades. Are Robert Pyle and I sixties dinosaurs? Sure. But listen to a man who has incomparably better credentials than Bob's or mine, articulating his fear back in the other wild and crazy sixties: the *1860s*: "I see in the near future a crisis approaching that unnerves me and causes me to tremble for the safety of my country. As a result of the war, corporations have been enthroned and an era of corruption in high places will follow, and the money power of the country will endeavour to prolong its reign by working upon the prejudices of the people until all wealth is aggregated in a few hands and the Republic is destroyed."

The writer: Abraham Lincoln. And the arguably less honest but even more visionary Thomas Jefferson, half a century before Lincoln, expressed the very same fear in these words: "I hope we shall crush in its birth the aristocracy of our moneyed corporations, which dare already to challenge our government to a trial of strength, and bid defiance to the laws of our country."

Who are Bob Pyle and I to discount the fears of Lincoln and Jefferson?

For the corporations' tendency to concentrate and corrupt power, for the spiritually suicidal way in which they force employees to behave, for the way they misinform, exploit, overwhelm, insult, and control our minds and our governments, for the damage they've done to the beauty, inhabitability, and inheritability of this world, I seek the transformation of these run-amok institutions. And if transformation is impossible, I seek their disempowerment. I believe corporate transformation is the crucial (in)human topic of our time.

But it's not my topic. My topic is the five-people-at-once whom Bob Pyle and I feel we have to be in order to earn a living while also decrying the havoc that corporate power is wreaking upon the butterflies and salmonids to which we've sworn our allegiance. My topic is the hash that fleshless, bloodless "independent existences" are making of the contemplative and artistic lives of the fleshed and blooded. My topic is the grief and frenzy that daily invade every sincere human's attempts to simply pursue a vocation that expresses gratitude and respect for life.

The great Trappist contemplative Thomas Merton had strong words of warning for those suffering the type of inner division I've described in Bob Pyle and me:

> *There is a pervasive form of contemporary violence to which the idealist . . . easily succumbs: activism and overwork. The rush and pressure of modern life are a form, perhaps the most common form, of its innate violence. To allow oneself to be carried away by a multitude of conflicting concerns, to surrender to too many demands, to commit one's self to too many projects, to want to help everyone in everything is to succumb to violence. More than that, it is cooperation in violence. The frenzy of the activist neutralizes his work for peace. It destroys his inner capacity for peace. It destroys the fruitfulness of his own work, because it kills the root of inner wisdom that makes work fruitful.*

My inner fiction writer would embrace Merton, if he were alive today, for having made this statement.

My nonfiction-writing activist, however, would sit down and write the Trappist a stern corrective letter.

"*No!*" my fiction writer would yell at my activist. "You don't know *anything* about the contemplative life! Leave Merton alone! He's right! You're wrong!"

But of course my inner activist would ignore him completely.

His letter to Merton would begin with an autobiographical poem penned by one of Merton's favorite contemplatives—the T'ang Dynasty poet Wang Wei:

In my middle years I became fond of the Way
And made my home in the foothills of South Mountain.
When the spirit moves me I go off by myself
To see things that I alone must see.
I follow the stream to its source,
And sitting there, watch for the moment
When clouds rise up. Or I may meet a woodsman;
We talk and laugh and forget about going home.

In this poem—written in an unimaginably different time yet in our same basic world—Wang Wei portrays a life that smote Thomas Merton, and millions of my own generation, with yearning. In his twenties, Merton grew so fond of "the Way" that he left an urbane circle of friends and a teaching position at a New York college to become a novice at Kentucky's unheard-of Gethsemane Abbey. In my own twenties I grew so fond of the Great Way that I created a fictitious Wang Wei, made him a fly fisherman, moved him to the Oregon Coast, let him spend his days "seeing things that he alone must see." And when my protagonist's yearning resonated with other denatured Americans and my novel made money, I too was freed—from a career of urban lawn mowing and cardboard recycling—to follow in Wang Wei's footsteps.

But I arrived at my coastal "South Mountain" in 1980—the very year President Reagan enthroned corporate timber executives in the U.S. Forest Service, converting it into the largest, least sustainable timber company in the history of the planet: arrived, in other words, just in time to see my "home in the foothills" quickly stripped, raped, and beaten into an industrial coma from which it will take centuries to recover. What did I do as the rape proceeded? Practiced my art. There was only one writer living in me then. Fighting to remain in touch with "the root of inner wisdom that makes work fruitful," I worked hard and, arguably, well. If nothing else, my second novel represents seven years of contemplative concentration: seven years spent ignoring chain saws and falling trees.

Once that novel was birthed, though, and I opened my eyes wide in the wake of my South Mountain's rape, my sense of literary accomplishment collapsed. And, to this day, I need only explore the Coast Range's billion stumps, its Doug fir monoculture, its salmonless, silted rivers to feel the very "frenzy" that Merton decries rev up in me like a chain saw. What I want to ask Merton is, aren't there situations in which the rapacity of industrial plunderers demands an answering frenzy? When the monastery is ablaze, doesn't the contemplative life itself become "cooperation in violence"?

Talk to us, Thomas.

Once we've been scorched by our own capacity for frenzy, we seem to develop an eye for spotting it in others. I remember once climbing on a bus in Berkeley, California, to find the folksinger Pete Seeger in a state so frenzied that he could not stop raving, to everyone on the bus, about a lethal madman he called "Hitler Kissinger." There were listeners on that bus who considered Henry Kissinger a sage. Frenzy made Seeger both insensitive and fearless. I have fished, birded, and taught alongside the naturalist/activist/Zen priest/novelist Peter Matthiessen, and have twice seen him reduced to something like frenzy, both times in front of large audiences. The first time, in Key West, was in response to a scurrilous, FBI-friendly *Outside* magazine article that damaged the decades-long effort to free Leonard Peltier; the second time, at the Orion Society's millennial conference, was in response to a retired ARCO executive saying that America's corporations were doing a good job of protecting the environment. In both cases, frenzy made Matthiessen arguably tactless, and devastatingly eloquent. I've watched Terry Tempest Williams, in a frenzy of nature grief and love, embrace every member of an audience of two-hundred-plus listeners in hopes of accomplishing God knows what: two hundred embraces speak for themselves. I've bumped a few times into Doug Peacock—the inspiration for Edward Abbey's dam-hating insurrectionist, Hayduke—and found that Peacock's more-or-less nonstop battle frenzy, in my Lincoln- and Jefferson-respecting eyes, gave his wild trajectory a cogency I couldn't find in Hayduke himself. I've swapped thoughts with Earth First!ers and Greenpeace co-founders, AIM and anti-AIM Indians, wildlife-loving madpersons, conservation kings, and eco-feminists galore. I've witnessed the belly-aching and PC pieties and anti-PC impieties, seen the puritanism and promiscuity, hard living and hyperactivity, witnessed the lawbreaking, the self-righteousness, the endless burning rage, and it has all driven me to an invincible conclusion:

I pray God sends this sweet Earth a billion more of them!

Is this contemplative heresy? Is it distrust of Merton's and my own prayer life and love for God? Is it a failure of faith to want to fight back physically for the sake of the physical world? Or is the physical world the one God loves enough to send a physical Son?

Perhaps the most frenzied activist I've ever met—in terms of the "multitude of conflicting concerns, too many demands, too many projects" that Merton warns against—is my Montana fiction-writing *compadre*, Rick Bass. I don't know how to describe Rick other than as a man crazed, every day and all at once, by beauty, violence, grief, and love.

How it happened, no one knows. A little-known short-story writer, seemingly named after a pot-gutted fish, moved from Texas to the northern Rockies' Yaak River valley for the same reason we innocents all move to our South Mountains: to "follow the spirits' movements"; "laugh and forget"; "watch clouds rise." He wrote of his Yaak love-at-first-sight with such rapture that even the excesses were magic; his umpteen-page description of cutting forty cords of firewood, for instance, has induced stigmatalike blisters on the palms of inert urban readers ensconced in La-Z-Boy recliners. But when this man's entire beloved quadrant of Montana became a timber-industry sacrifice zone, his literary aims, work pace, voice, public readings, and private correspondence all changed—and Thomas Merton's quote seems to nail the change.

Rick Bass appeared to become "frenzied." Even his most casual notes—to friends, enemies, editors, me, you, anybody—began to include his now infamous, home-brewed "Don't Hack the Yaak!" propaganda. Even the most literary of his public appearances now ended with a list of northwestern Montana's diverse but vanishing wildlife, followed by a plea to write or call state representatives, senators, governors, followed in tedious turn by addresses and phone numbers. As he stumped against the stumps, Rick continued to publish prodigiously—nonfiction and fiction both. Some of his readers feel that the fiction, too, changed once the forests started to fall—that the dwindling animals, fouled streams, lost habitat, wounded Rick to the root. I've heard admirers of Early Bass fiction refer to Later Bass advocacy as "annoying!" I don't so much want to argue as to aim the critical tone at a more proper target: the timber companies and politicians that are together destroying northwestern Montana.

A better word for the change in Rick himself is "inevitable." Consider the frenzied thrashing of a mother wood duck when we step too close to her hidden chicks; consider the rage of the sow bear whose cubs are threatened; consider the redwing's insane strafing of even eighteen-wheeled log trucks when they pass too close to her nest. Writers are human. Humans are animals. Rick is of the Yaak, and the Yaak is being destroyed. When a loved one or a loved home is threatened, frenzy is the animal's way. In language that is now both powerful and afflicted, Rick fights (and fights and fights) the affliction that has engulfed his home. Even his motionless posture seems afflicted to my eye: the man stands still at a dead run. My Yaak-adoring friend has, in short, become a poster boy for "the frenzy of the activist," the ravaged "inner capacity for peace," the reckless endangerment of "the root of inner wisdom that makes work fruitful."

But the plot thickens. The name of the good man who sent me the Merton quote on the activist's self-defeating frenzy? Rick Bass.

I'm not sure Rick sent the quote on purpose. His missives, during the half-dozen years we've corresponded, have all been semi-legible, flash-of-the-Bass updates hand-scrawled on the backs of his own reject manuscript pages. Sometimes *embarrassing* reject pages. When you live amid fresh clearcuts and realize paper is forest, you start recycling *all* your used tree bits, content be damned.

In the handwritten letter in question, Rick touched on essays we'd recently exchanged, described his latest good hunt and good hike, and ended, as always, with which five politicos I should write, fax, or phone with my "Don't Hack the Yaak!" pleas. I sighed at this ending. I then turned, with a pleasantly prurient sensation, to see what sort of reject prose skulked on the back of Rick's letter—

And there lay Merton's warning against frenzy. What really got me, though, was a small addition. In the margins of Merton's words, in a scrawl even more frenzied than his letter to me, Rick had written to no one, to himself, or to the late Thomas Merton,

Yes. but NO
Can't do it! Not yet.
Not now

These ten hangdog-looking, self-divided words looked so helter-skelter in the margin of Merton's focused warning, so overpowered by Merton's warning, yet so helpless to heed the wisdom of the warning, that a lump the size of South Mountain rose in my throat. My heart went out to Rick. My heart went out to Merton. My heart wanted Tom and Rick to take two long hikes together: first, through the forested foothills of Gethsemane; then through the deforested foothills of the Yaak. Why? Because the instant I envision two such hikes, serious disagreement between the two men becomes inconceivable.

On both the Kentucky and the Montana hikes, I picture Tom and Rick walking fast. They're both known for it. I picture them comparing the number of times the legendarily incompetent motorist, Merton, put cars in Gethsemane ditches to the number of times the legendarily incompetent gearhead, Bass, has shot himself in the face with pepper spray in the Yaak. I picture them in stitches, at some point, comparing the tin-eared ecstasies that Gethsemane induced in the young postulant, Merton, to some of the over-the-top enthusiasms young Rick spurted out on behalf of the Yaak. *"What in the world would be wasted is here all God's, all for love!"* the monk rhapsodized upon arrival in his monastic home. *"O Earth! O Earth!"* he cried. *"When will we hear you sing? . . . / When will you wake in the green wheat / And all our oaks and Trappist cedars sing?"* That Merton! Stoned as a Deadhead on the prophet Jeremiah. Taking woods walks, loaded on Bible, hallucinating Old Testament energy balls . . .

On their Yaak hike, though, I picture the laughter vaporizing and the good monk freezing in his tracks as the landscape itself suddenly raises the question: *What Trappist cedars?* Because in the scenario Rick faces—the scenario every ancient forest defender in much of the world has faced since 1980—the ancient cedars are on the ground or falling fast, the air round the stumps is so thick with the fragrance of violated heartwood that even the sawyers sometimes work in tears, and while corporate shareholders spend profits on security systems and country-club dues, and while noncorporate citizens fund Forest Service debt, we present and future lovers of source streams and the Great Way are left to sing: *O pucker brush! O skidder scars! Oh 2-4D-sprayed slash and mudslides! When will you wake and sing for love?*

There is little doubt in my mind that this kind of alteration, inflicted upon the forests of Gethsemane, would induce in the nature-adoring Trappist the very state his contemplative self abhores: *the frenzy of the activist.* When your heart's home is being annihilated, your peace and serenity are in deep shit and that's all there is to it. When the money-men took over the holy temple, even Christ succumbed to actions far from peaceful or serene.

That said, I still love Merton's careful defense of the contemplative terrain. Even my inner activist agrees with Merton's warning against the shallowness and shoddiness of too much work done too fast. His warning might mean beware of too many causes, too many easy op-ed generalizations, too many abstract attacks on amorphous enemies; he may be warning against the dissipation of our focus and energy via response to too many declared states of junk-mail emergency, too many heartfelt letters to dead-hearted political nimnams, too many scattered impulses, unnurtured loves, untethered thoughts; he may be telling us to go slow and be silent for a while each day, even if we've got to go faster the rest of the day to make room for the slow silence; he may be telling us to keep our small spiritual practices, our family and community life, our prayer and dream life, alive no matter what. But I can't make the monk's words on frenzy mean that we should stop bleeding inside, and fighting back, when our very world is going down. To grieve and rage when our world is dying slope by slope; to sally forth wounded, even in "frenzy"; to keep fighting even when others think us "annoying" or fools; to refuse to disobey Christ's "Love thy neighbor as thyself"; to include in this Self every wolverine, lynx, woodland caribou, ancient cedar, living tributary, and future generation of our watershed, *is* to remain in touch with "our root of inner wisdom."

Like Bob of the Butterflies and Rick of the Yaak, I don't know how to balance contemplative need with gut response to this beautiful world's ruin. But I believe that America's most famous contemplative lived the same painful paradox, occasionally referring to it by the catchall term "the Cross." Consider the following assembled "conversation," Merton's portion coming from a day of 1947 monastic life as recorded in his journal, *Entering the Silence,* Rick's part coming from his 1999 credo, *Brown Dog of the Yaak:*

Tom: "Snowed under with even more work . . . I wish I had the sense to avoid so many plans. . . . If God wants me to stay here (at Gethsemane), as He apparently does—in fact it is morally certain—it means the renunciation of any hope of the pure contemplative life. . . ."

Rick: "I argue myself left, I argue myself right. Art, or activism, and if art, what kind? Is the strain of trying to keep the two separate ultimately as debilitating as any imagined detriments brought by mixing the two? . . . Each letter to Congress, each activist essay about the Yaak, feels most days like nothing more than another damn piece of wild moraine, ten pounds, chunk, into the sled and down onto a purposeless stone wall. . . ."

Tom: "The same old distractions, and worse still!! my mind full of business and vanity . . . I am destined for the frustration and denial of every natural and even supernatural desire I may have in this life. That is to be my purgatory. . . . And I suppose the biggest and strongest desire I have is this one of being a contemplative with a capital 'C'. . . . The work I do does not mix with contemplation—not pure contemplation. . . . OK. *Fiat.* I am leading the active life. Forget about the question. Try to pray and get the amount of contemplation that people in the active life get. . . ."

Rick: "Art, or activism? Why not both? Why worry about burning out in activism, or failing in art? What else are our lives but diminishing tapers of wax, sputtering already in long flame? . . . Art [and] activism shadow one another; they destroy one another: but they share the same inescapable, irreducible bedrock fuel—passion. Love, or fury. Love, and fury . . . I would rather fail at both than be disloyal to one. . . . I would rather be ragged-thin and weary than brittle."

Tom: "I feel in my bones that I will never have any peace until I kiss everything goodbye, even my highest ideals and aspirations. . . . This thing will die hard. If I can make a little less fuss about it in the future, I will be satisfied. . . . Holy Spirit, fill me with Your simplicity and teach me to avoid getting myself into useless works by my own blind and impetuous will. . . . Love will be my beatitude—in darkness, on the Cross. . . . My heart burns within me with joy."

For my part, I thank heaven for all such splendidly conflicted companions, with their self-enditched cars and self-peppered faces, their huge injured hearts and sow bear/redwing frenzies, their agapé leapings from beauty to violence to grief to frenzy to confusion and ever, back to love. If such imbalanced passion leads to "the Cross" and "darkness," well, the cross at least is balanced. The destroyers of human cultures, of biological systems, of irreplaceable homes, however they define themselves legally, are our enemies. And the enemies of our enemies are our friends. In honor of Lincoln and Jefferson, in honor of Earth, in honor of present and future generations, divine love, human and animal fury, let us suffer, fret, fear, research, rise up, urge, testify, march, moan, hoot, howl, and roar.

Even in darkness.

And may our hearts burn within us with joy.

*Rivers and streams in which the salmon are found or to
which they resort shall not be obstructed by dams or
otherwise, unless such dams or obstructions are so
constructed as to allow salmon to pass freely up and down
such rivers and streams.*

—Oregon Territorial Constitution, 1848

*The public must retain the control of the great waterways.
It is essential that any permit to obstruct them for reasons
and on conditions that seem good at the moment should be
subject to revision when changed conditions demand.*

—President Theodore Roosevelt, 1908

*He whose braveness lies in daring, slays.
He whose braveness lies in not daring, gives life.
Of these two, either may be profitable or unprofitable.
But 'Nature hates what it hates. . . .
He who grudges expenses pays dearest in the end;
He who has hoarded most will suffer the heaviest loss.
He that works through violence may get his way,
but only the mountains, rivers and heavens endure.*

—Lao Tzu, *Tao Te Ching*, circa 400 B.C.

12. A Prayer for the Salmon's Second Coming

Introduction to "A Prayer"

One day in the summer of 1969, an X-Acto blade pierced my left hand
and turned me into the fisherman I'd set out to be as a boy. One day in the
fall of 1987, a statistic pierced my conscience and changed me back into a

civilian again. In between those two changes, for twenty wonderful years, I fished the salmon and steelhead rivers of Oregon only slightly less fanatically and no less joyously than the fish-crazed hero of my first novel. Focusing on five small streams near my eventual Tillamook County home, fishing the back end of rainstorms as the waters dropped and greened, I landed an average of thirty winter and summer steelhead, five chinook salmon, thirty jack salmon and sea-run cutthroat, and fifteen adult coho salmon each year.

I often fished, accidentally, for a multitude of species. Among the thrills of coast-stream fishing are the many times a one-rod, one-reel search for a particular kind and size of fish puts you over much larger quarry for which you're laughably ill-prepared. A mint-bright, cartwheeling, seven-pound coho hen on a cutthroat fly and a little 4-weight fly rod, for example. Or the bright twenty-eight-pound, thirty-five-pound, and forty-pound chinook I hooked on the 6-weight fly rod and damp fly with which I chased summer steelhead. The forty-pounder—my largest salmon ever—was, frankly, a lolling bore: I'd as soon play a dairy cow on a fly rod. The twenty-eight-pounder, though, took a grease-lined Freight Car at the end of a long cast at dusk, did one quick subsurface thrash, then lit out on a half-mile downstream run that had me gulping my heart down my throat as I chased it for half an hour, believing I'd hooked the steelhead of a lifetime.

During my coastal decades I was a man of estuaries and mountains: I never fished the ocean, never fished the crowded bays, never fished in a crowd, period. Excellent maps, serious backroad exploration, and rough hiking were required to make this solitude possible. Even today, though, I know a few coastal canyons where salmon and steelhead outnumber fishermen by hundreds to one. And I'll share their locations gladly—if you hold a knife to my throat.

It's not for the fishing that I'm secretive. As wild salmon runs, throughout those decades, grew ever more fragile, my killer instinct, then even my catch-and-release instinct, faded, then vanished. I love to eat fish, and for a long time killed ten or so clip-finned hatchery steelhead and jack salmon per season. I also, each November, killed a single, mint-bright wild coho. A late autumn dinner of barbecued coho with, say, huckleberry muffins, local greens, and a chanterelle soufflé, shared with friends, was the true coastal Thanksgiving feast. The indigenous food did not just feed us, it accomplished the impossible: it made beautiful, edible sense out of all that rain.

A hundred twenty inches per annum in the valley where I lived. Half of those inches, it seemed, in November. Rains to put moss on your teeth; rains that set orange witches' butter growing from the seat of my Rambler

American even as I drove it; rains that drove some residents to divorce, some to Southern California, some to hallucinogenic mushrooms, some to Prozac. Thanks to the coho, though, the rains were nothing but beautiful to me. I grew to sense their approach and size by smell and barometric mood. The big fronts would blow in, the birds would be rammed south, the folks with seasonal stress disorder would jet to Arizona—and I'd be out in the downpours, thrashing happily down the middle of some stream too small to be blown out, my grandfather's spiked golf galoshes on over my waders for traction, blissfully chasing my small allowance of ocean-fattened, heaven-summoned coho.

So many beautiful things would happen. I sat waist-deep in a November creek, in Neoprene waders one afternoon, and watched two otters not fifteen feet away share an entire coho's spawned-out body, discussing its complex flavors in urbane otter chitter the entire time. I fished one canyon so misty and wild that a blacktail doe walked up to me out of the gray, scrutinized my face, sniffed the very tip of my fly rod, then strolled leisurely upstream and did the same to my fishing partner. I watched water ouzels stroll the half-rotten backs of still-living, still-spawning chinooks—the ouzels, too, chittering blithely as they danced upon the salmons' very death. I watched coho spawn for days and nights, stand guard over the redd for more days and nights, then weaken, drift, and die; watched their carcasses hang from branches or flutter from the bodies of sunken cars; watched them lie dead in the quietest water, turning black for days, white for a few more, finally sending out pale clouds of ghostly green growth that let me see decomposition as a kind of blossoming. I watched the coho's own alevins nibble these blossoms the way the faithful nibble the body of Christ. I glimpsed, as we all have in rivers, the death, the resurrection, and the life.

The last wild coho I killed was in November 1987. A bright eight-pound hen. And its flesh again worked the magic: my friends and I turned our eyes skyward and sincerely thanked our Maker for the rains. Not long after that last coho rite, though, I was stunned to learn from the local fisheries biologist that there'd been an estimated seven spawning pairs of coho, total, in the river from which I'd taken that hen. Turned out the Department of Fish and Wildlife had been botching their statistics for years. The coho were vanishing from Oregon.

Who doesn't know the story? My favorite form of worship had become species extermination. Our sacramental November feast had become sin. Those blithe, golf-galoshing jogs down wild green currents had become unconscionable. I try to avoid vows amid a life as uncertain as this one, but without even vowing, I realized I'd never kill a wild Oregon salmon again. And the instant I came to this realization, the magic coho rains became plain, cold November rains.

I share this bit of history not in lament, but to introduce the admittedly demanding piece of writing that follows:

The Pacific salmon's biological and migratory needs force them into intimate contact with landscapes dominated by humanity. Because of this, salmonids can continue to exist only if humans enable and encourage them to do so. Most Northwesterners desperately want this. Year in and year out, polled majorities of citizens swear their willingness to make financial sacrifices and lifestyle adjustments for salmon, and fresh waves of schoolchildren love and coax salmon back into a few preposterously unlikely industrial streams.

But a powerful minority disagrees with such love and willingness. This minority sees rivers not as arteries of interwoven life, but as hydraulic engines meant to crank out industrial profits. In defense of their profits, the same minority has diligently emitted a rhetorical smog around the topic of wild salmon. The chief themes of the rhetoric:

1. It is not we who threaten salmon; it is salmon who threaten us.
2. By passing through *our* lands in migration, so-called endangered salmon in fact endanger *our* jobs, *our* crops, *our* electricity, *our* prosperity.
3. *No* sacrifices should be made for these romanticized creatures of the past. If they can't survive while we do as we please, let them die of industrial causes. As a prominent southern-Idaho cattle rancher put it, "We're gonna miss them salmon about as much as we miss them buffalo."

Such rhetoric has not just created a media smog: it has stalemated the decision-making process needed for salmon recovery. Lawmakers seeking honest recovery strategies have also been buried in specious scientific studies of farcical faux-complexity, the most ridiculous of which have been penned by the very agency responsible for salmon recovery under the Endangered Species Act. The news media in turn, assuming such an agency has the salmon's best interest at heart, plays directly into these false stewards' hands by "objectively" reporting their "scientific" balderdash. As a result, honest people who care deeply about salmon have nevertheless come to feel that anadromous fish and contemporary humanity can't coexist.

This is a disastrous misunderstanding, inculcated by ingenious industrial cynics. Pacific salmon are not just "canaries in a coal shaft." They're the signature wild creature of the Northwest—a creature upon which millions of humans, fauna, and megafauna depend for their very existence. A "modern Northwest" that cannot support salmon is unlikely to support "modern Northwesterners" for long. I have therefore tried my utmost to construct a narrative—readable, I hope, in one espresso-fueled sitting—that pierces the cynical rhetoric and depicts the genesis, the true value, the crisis, and the potential salvation of the most crucial population of wild salmon left in the lower forty-eight: those of the Columbia/Snake river system.

"*In the beginning*" say the very first lines of the Bible, "*God created the heavens and the earth. And the earth was without form, and void; and darkness was upon the face of the deep. And the Spirit of God moved upon the face of the water.*" The best way I know to begin to grasp the seriousness and scope of the Northwest's salmon crisis is to sit down in a quiet place and try to imagine the mysterious movement, across the black waters of pre-creation, of the spirit of God. Imagine a quickening that pierces the Pacific—the entire ocean suddenly invested with *being,* suddenly restless, inhaling and exhaling the moon-coaxed breaths called tides. Limn this vast being with glaciers in the north, volcanic fissures in its depths. Imbue it with the same blue, gray, and green surfaces and glass-smooth-to-mountainous textures as the Pacific; same molten-to-frozen temperature ranges; same unknowable, 36,000-foot depths; same power to produce wonder, terror, beauty, death, and life.

Imagine this being is your biological mother—because, in a very real sense, she is. Imagine the Sun is your biological father—because, in equally real, life-giving ways, he is. Imagine that after the spirit of God touched them, your distant but brilliant father and 70-million-square-mile mother not only fell in love, but began making love: imagine Ocean and Sun in coitus for eternity—because they are. Imagine your ocean mother's wombs are countless, that her fecundity is infinitely varied, and that her endless slow lovemaking with Sun brings about countless gestations and births and an infinity of beings: great blue whales and great white sharks; endless living castles of coral; vast phalanxes of fishes; incalculable flocks of birds; gigantic typhoons; weather patterns the size of continents—because it does.

Now turn your imagination inland toward North America. Follow the cloud banks into the mountains and up against them. See how every raindrop and snowflake, every skyborne molecule of H_2O that falls upon the Rockies, Sierras, Sawtooths, Cascades, Bitterroots,

Salmon Rivers, Clearwaters, Blues, is also a child of Ocean and Sun: a literal offspring of their endless coition. See how, when Sun and Ocean's liquid offspring congeal, obey gravity, and start back down the slopes toward their mother, the result is every life-giving trickle, creek, and river in the land. See how those streams and rivers, as Aldo Leopold pointed out, are "round," running past our feet and out to sea, then rising up in great tapestries of gravity-defying vapor to blow and flow back over us in oceans of cloud, fall once more upon the slopes as rain and snow, then congeal and start seaward, forming the perpetual prayer wheels we call watersheds.

Picture the Columbia/Snake Prayer Wheel: two joined wings of a single **Y**-shaped flow, really; each wing a thousand miles in length; the swiftest river of its size on earth. Picture the Prayer Wheel entire: cloud formations as big as Alaska easing one after another in off the Pacific, shedding rains and snows on range upon range of mountains, forming the countless snowbanks, marshes, seeps, and rills that start downward in obedience to gravity, forming a filigree of tributaries more intricate than our own veins and arteries, converging, gaining power, converging again, more power, becoming the hundreds of rivers that form the Columbia/Snake and carry the collective flow, industrial effluent, and riverine reproductive power of two Canadian provinces and six American states—260,000 square miles of continent, all told—back to the sea.

It's hard to imagine anything as mighty as the Columbia/Snake Prayer Wheel in trouble because of the antics of anything as ephemeral as human beings—yet it is. It's even harder to see how anything as fecund as the reproductive power of Ocean and Sun could possess limitations—yet it does. For all the diversity of life they've given us, Sun and Ocean have managed to bequeath us just one—count them: *one*—family of creature capable of journeying back and forth between the high-altitude valleys of our continent's interior and the green ocean swells a thousand miles away. That family is the anadromous fish, the most celebrated of which, for a hundred poetic and pragmatic reasons, is the wild salmon. And in just twenty-five years, four Snake River dams have destroyed 90 percent of these beings, extirpating scores of distinct runs for all time.

The corporate and federal beneficiaries of the inland Northwest's hydroelectric system—with their huge taxpayer subsidies and gargantuan appetite for the rivers' life-giving currents—claim that salmon are "just a fish of diminishing value." The Columbia/Snake system has changed, they say. Salmon haven't, and that's too bad for salmon. But in "today's world," river industrialists argue, in terms of "practicality" and "profitability," there is nothing so necessary about salmon that we should sacrifice anything at all to preserve them. *"Remnant species,"* Senator Slade Gorton (R-Wash.) calls the survivors.

I never cease to marvel at such pathologically self-involved minds: completely oblivious of the natural forces that daily sustain their own 78-percent-H_2O, solar-engined, wind-breathing, protein-needing bodies; completely forgetful of the fact that we can't *eat* electricity; completely embarrassed by the fact that for the majority of Northwest citizens, for our native tribes, for our Catholic leaders, for an emerging socially responsible, Earth-awake corporate culture led by Yvon Chouinnard and hundreds like him, and for a few long-memoried Celts like me, salmon are not just a vanishing species: they are a holiness, a divine gift.

Perhaps the separation of church and state means the state *must* define salmon as "just a fish." Let's assume it does. Let's temporarily refuse—like a congressperson with a lobbyist's brass ring in his nose— to see our wild salmon as anything but protein units. We run into problems even so. Because even insofar as salmon *are* "just a fish," so is Earth just a warm, wet, finite ship sailing a sea of cold and uninhabitable space. And in irrevocably annihilating one of Earth's invaluable food species, we rip irreplaceable planks from the hull of our ship for all time.

This in itself is reason enough to save them. But I would begin at the very beginning—*Bible,* page one—and remind our lawmakers that four federal dams are unmaking a holiness, that four dams are performing a hysterectomy upon the Columbia/Snake Prayer Wheel, that four Snake River dams are uncreating the primordial waters' response to the touch of the spirit of God.

Migration + 16 Dams

The inland West's wild salmon awaken, at birth, to the pebbles and clear flow of a high mountain stream. The tiny fish thus bond not to a parent fish, but to the parenting stones and flow of their birth-stream. For a full year, in some cases two, fingerlings cling to this unlikely madonna, imbibing her unique chemistry, memorizing all they can about her. Then, at the nautically unpromising length of five inches, they obey their blood and the parent stream's incessant downward urging and set out on a journey that rivals, in terms of wonders, horrors, steadfastness, and distances, that of Odysseus himself.

Juvenile coho, sockeye, steelhead, and the three surviving strains of chinook all make the marathon swim from the inland West's mountains to the Pacific, but it's the way spring and summer chinook do it that really gets me: fasting like holy pilgrims, five-inch bodies quivering like flames, these two-year-old naifs travel the entire distance—eight hundred miles or more—*backwards*. As the current sweeps them seaward tail-first, they gaze steadfastly back upriver toward the mountains, like kindergarteners backing ruefully away from home toward a first day at school. They've got plenty to be rueful about: 99.7 percent of them won't live to see their birth-stream again.

Because they fast all the way, the smolts' migration must be swift or they starve. There is also a limited window during which they can make the metabolic transformation from fresh to salt water. In the pre-dam era, the Columbia/Snake's mighty spring runoff carried smolts up to nine hundred miles in two weeks or less. Now, with eight dams and slackwaters in place, the same journey takes six weeks or more.

Gale Ater—of Gouge Eye, Idaho—is one of four intrepid souls who swam the upper half of the astounding sockeye smolt migration route from Redfish Lake, 7,000 feet up in the Sawtooth Mountains, down to the first of the four notorious dams. In the unfettered Salmon River, Gale said, the swimmers were carried an effortless thirty miles a day by "just stayin' afloat and watchin' for rocks." Then they hit the forty-mile slackwater behind Lower Granite Dam. "You hear the word 'impoundment' different forever," Gale told me, "once you've approached one by swimmin' four hundred miles of free-flowin' river. Soon as we hit slackwater, a ten-day emotional high became the Bataan Death Swim. Headwinds, three-foot whitecaps, the same boring chunk of basalt in the distance though you've swum for hours. Our interpersonal dynamics went to shit. Five miles a day was torture. We almost gave up."

Still far from the dam, the swimmers saw a fleet of boats approaching. It was the Nez Perce—the same tribe that kept the Lewis and Clark Expedition from unraveling two hundred years before—come to honor the group's gesture on behalf of salmon. The swimmers found fresh strength, made it to the dam, were made honorary members of the tribe and given a feast. "How cool is that!" says Gale.

Very. But at the point the humans faltered, the fasting smolts still have seven slackwaters, eight dams, and four hundred miles left to traverse. And in each slackwater the salmon encounter an array of predacious fish (bass; walleye; the smolt-devouring artists formerly known as squawfish) whose populations have exploded thanks to elevated water temperatures. Lack of current brings migration to a near standstill. The fasting juveniles waste energy seeking elusive river flow. The John Day slackwater alone is eighty miles long. The desert country in summer is a furnace. The same temperatures that give voracity to warm-water predators are, by July, deadly to smolts. Schools of salmonids sometimes circle slackwaters for weeks, unable to sense the way to the sea. When their metabolic-transition clocks run out of time, they become baitfish. Sport fishermen aren't fools. The bass lure of choice in all eight impoundments is a four-inch Rapalla the green-backed color of a bewildered chinook smolt. And of the smolts that somehow survive and return as adults, 40 percent will be killed, before they can spawn, by the same dams.

When they reach the dams, the young salmon that travel deep are torn apart by sheer pressures and crushing currents, 5 to 15 percent at each dam; eight dams in all; end of story. The smolts that travel shallow, though, are blasted over spillways, which kill just 2 percent per dam—but only if river current is sent over spillways rather than through turbines. To the region's hydroelectric profiteers, this means that "their" generators are being "robbed" of kilowatt dollars by juvenile salmon. Hence the long, bitter fight for the very flow of this river—and the shocking hatred, among industrial river users, of five-inch travelers, fasting as they drift, gazing back toward long-lost, mothering mountains. Only because of the Endangered Species Act have these embattled innocents begun to encounter spillways and fish bypass systems instead of turbines.

The lucky, starving smolts that reach saltwater encounter fresh trials, such as a sterile shipping channel where a food-rich estuary should be, and a man-made island of dredge spoils now harboring the world's largest colony of smolt-eating Caspian terns. But the fish that reach the Pacific, even today, put on silvery muscle fast, and, for the next two to three years, travel distances that put every inlander but circumpolar birds and long-haul truckers to shame. Some Idaho chinook swim ten thousand miles at sea. They've been caught off the coast of Japan, the Kamchatka Peninsula, the Aleutian Islands. Diving so deep at times as to be untraceable, swimming too far, too fast to be followed, oceangoing salmon maintain the ability—so troubling to those who would control them completely—to elude the radar of human knowing.

Yet no matter how far they rove or how big and strong they grow, there comes a day when they hear in their blood the song that leads them to abandon the sea and seek again their high-mountain place of birth. The journey is always fatal. Every salmon undertakes it even so. And if and when they again conquer the eight-dam gauntlet, parse the currents, rediscover the mothering stretch of pebbles and snowmelt, they begin—despite all they've endured—to make love.

But not to a mate. On the eastern edge of Idaho last fall, seven hundred miles from the sea, I watched a single female chinook, with great, crimson-gilled gasps of effort, turn her ocean-built body into a shovel and dig, in the unforgiving bone of the continent, a home for offspring she would not live long enough to see. I watched her lay eggs so tender the touch of a child's fingertip would crush them, eggs exactly the color of setting suns. I watched the darker, fierce-kyped male ease in front of those suns without once touching the female, and send milt melting down into her nest of stones. I watched the paired chinook circle their pebbled redd, tending it, guarding it—I want to say "loving it," if the State will allow. Yet only incidentally, as if by accident, did they touch each other. Because they weren't making love to each other. They were making love to the very land and water, to broken bits of mountain and melting snows.

I left them to die, as salmon do, their clutch of eggs orphaned in a frigid gravel womb. As I write these words, winter has snapped down hard in the Rockies. Snow is mounting high. But in that ice-covered streambed nest, which the female covered with protective pebbles with her last few strokes of life, tiny eyes are even now appearing in her sun-colored eggs.

There is a fire in water. There is an invisible flame, hidden in water, that creates not heat but life. And in this bewildering age, no matter how dark or glib some humans work to make it, wild salmon still climb rivers and mountain ranges in absolute earnest, solely to make contact with that flame. Words can't reach deep or high enough to embody this wonder. Only wild salmon can embody it. Each migration, each annual return from the sea, these incomparable creatures climb our inland mountains and sacrifice their lives, that tiny silver offspring may be born of an impossible watery flame.

These are the beings, the "remnant species," that we are eradicating from the American West and the Pacific for all time.

Irreplaceable Genetic Treasure

The three most crucial refugia of Pacific salmon on Earth—three giant evolutionary nexus in which salmon species are created and served to the world, thriving and whole—are the Sacramento, Yukon, and Columbia/Snake river systems.

The Columbia/Snake's hundreds of streams required millennia to evolve their hardy indigenous salmon stocks. The entire population of the upper Columbia portion of that system—the salmon of eastern British Columbia, a third of Washington State, and northern Idaho—were destroyed in a day, by the Grand Coulee Dam, half a century ago. This is too easy to say: it is crucial to imagine it. Hundreds of crucial salmon strains, ancient as gods, doomed to annihilation in a day. Tens of thousands of people thrown out of sustainable outdoor work and forced to rote factory jobs. Scores of indigenous tribes impoverished if they were lucky, destroyed and dispersed if they weren't.

The surviving anadromous fish of the Columbia/Snake now depend utterly upon the Snake River migratory corridor to reach Idaho, eastern Oregon, and the southeast corner of Washington. And though not many realize it, these last wild strains are the genetic engine that continues to give us all Pacific salmon—even those raised in net-pens and hatcheries. Dolly the Sheep notwithstanding, human beings do not know how to create and maintain a viable race of salmon. All "man-made" stocks are ephemeral because all are, essentially, big batches of identical first cousins rapidly inbreeding themselves into genetic inferiority and nonexistence. "Homeless seagoing Spam," salmon bard Tom Jay calls hatchery fish. It is our resilient, diverse wild stocks alone that give artificial stocks a fleeting viability before they are destroyed by technological incest.

The wild fish of Idaho—the ones the Snake River dams are extirpating as I write—are adaptive geniuses, utter standouts among salmon. Every winter, for example, anchor ice forms in their high-elevation birth-streams, freezing the streams almost solid in places. Idaho salmon smaller than my little finger know to move out from under this ice and winter over in deep pools. Coastal salmon stocks, introduced to the same inland waters, stay put in the seemingly benign runs as the ice forms, then freeze to death en masse. Idaho's wild genius fingerlings also know, as they migrate during July heat, to gather in "summering holes" cooled by depth, shade, and in-stream springs. Introduced coastal smolts grow stressed and oxygen-deprived in the heated shallows, and become easy prey.

This kind of indigenous genius is a primary reason why the countless attempts to "repair" or "replace" the inland West's dam-annihilated salmon with hatchery fish have a forty-year history of failure. Musically speaking, we are trying to replace Bach, Mozart, and Beethoven with Yanni, Yanni, and Yanni. Sorry to pick on Yanni. He *looks* like a composer—just as hatchery fish look something like wild salmon. But cloning someone who merely looks like a composer, then stuffing concert halls full of him, does not resurrect Bach, Beethoven, or Mozart. Borrowing fertilized eggs from a techno-alien species, dumping them in a high-mountain Idaho tributary, and expecting these newcomers to magically acquire survival instincts and migrational genius acquired over thousands of years is like putting a gun to the head of poor Yanni and ordering him to perform Bach's Goldberg Variations or die.

For Pacific salmon, the hatchery programs are a failed industrial dream. The insurmountable problem: God and Nature are infinitely smarter and more nuanced than Industrial Man. The longer the migration, the more dismal the hatchery failures. The vanishing sockeye of Idaho's Redfish Lake, to cite one of countless such failures, were replaced with 3 million Canadian sockeye eggs three years in a row. Millions of healthy smolts were duly released for the Pacific. The number of sockeye that adapted to the river, the slackwaters, the dams, the sea, and returned to Idaho as spawning adults: zero.

Wild Snake River salmon are the irreplaceable genetic treasure that safeguards *all* Pacific salmon, "farmed" or wild, inbred or free.

Cold War Relics

A dam is not a biological treasure, and it is not a holiness. A dam is an inanimate, river-altering tool, created by humans to serve humans. Most of our 75,000 dams were built before negative biological, economic, or cultural impacts were a consideration, hence many have done more harm than good. Learning from our mistakes, we've created laws that weigh some of the long-term damages of dams against their benefits. When a river-altering tool is shown to be more injurious than helpful to a majority of humans and to the health and wholeness of the land, we now occasionally recognize our obligation to retire that tool before it injures further.

Americans have, historically, not been fast to retire dangerous tools, because tool retirements come with a price tag. We're getting faster, though. Only by paying the price to retire tools fiercely defended by profitmakers has America ceased to be the land of thalidomide infants, asbestos-ceilinged schoolrooms, DDT trucks dousing residential streets, Dalkon Shield IUDs, and explosion-prone cars. The Snake

River dams have earned an early retirement alongside those other once-loved products in the American Museum of Fabulously Treacherous Tools.

The eight federal dams that bar the inland West salmon's journey are not created equal. The four on the Columbia have brought both benefits and disasters. Among the disasters: mass salmon extinctions; the impoverishment of hundreds of fishing communities and salmon-dependent Indian tribes; and the 1956 inundation (behind the Dalles Dam) of the lower Columbia's Celilo Falls—for ten millennia the greatest tribal gathering place west of the Mississippi, drawing salmon celebrants and Neolithic traders from as far away as Central America. Celilo's inundation was an act of cultural annihilation that did to American Indians what it would do to New Yorkers if the Army Corps simultaneously flooded Yankee Stadium, Madison Square Garden, Fifth Avenue, and the New York Stock Exchange. To those not victimized by this act, however, the four lower Columbia dams have brought hydropower, navigation, flood control, and, thanks to abundant electricity, the aluminum that became the aircraft that helped win World War II. The four Columbia dams have also been retrofitted to accommodate safer salmon passage and now assist, albeit awkwardly, in flushing migratory smolts to sea. With changes in operations policy (particularly at John Day) and an unbiased look at the no-longer-strategic aluminum industry's deadly waste of hydropower, these four dams could keep salmon mortality at a viably low rate until sustainable energy alternatives come on line, making giant, river-killing hydroelectric projects a rarity.

The four dams on the Snake are an agonizingly different story. Conceived at the height of the Cold War, they are deadly relics of that brutal era. It's a mistake to forget or to underestimate this. The four Snake River dams are a conception of the same vintage of federal pathology that gave us the House Un-American Activities Committee's Hollywood blacklist, J. Edgar Hoover's hatred of Martin Luther King, the Nevada nuclear test sites, Rocky Flats, the Hanford nuclear leak site, anthrax, 3.5 trillion lethal doses of nerve agent released by the Pentagon into Mormon- and Navajo-populated deserts, thousands of army troops ordered to lie in fresh atomic fallout, millions of civilians unwittingly exposed to the same fallout, encephalitis-carrying mosquitoes released by Defense Department scientists upon destitute civilian volunteers, 45,000 American radioactive sites, 1,140 carcinogenic uranium mining sites in Utah alone, and a present-day epidemic of cancers that we will never be able to tie to its Defense Department sources.

The four dams on the Snake are the Cold War's killing progeny. And even in the political climate of the 1950s the dams were bitterly opposed for the damage they were sure to inflict on the salmon-dependent Northwest. Among their opponents were President Dwight D. Eisenhower; the Corps of Engineers, which later built them; the Oregon and Washington departments of fish and game; the region's thirteen native tribes; the West Coast's multibillion-dollar fishing industry; and the majority of the region's salmon-loving populace. But the 1955 Congress, craving a four-dam hydropower "saber" to rattle at the Soviets at any cost, liked the proposed dams' meaningless proximity to that other monument of Big Stick diplomacy—the Hanford Nuclear Reservation—and so approved them. The four dams came on line. The river route to and from wild Idaho was quadruply blockaded. And wild salmon runs and related economies crashed as predicted.

Something few people know: the four Snake River dams are of a type known as "run of the river"—which offer no flood-control storage. The Northwest's far right foretells catastrophic floods with the dams gone. It's a lie. The reservoirs of these dams must be kept within three feet of the top to run navigational locks for barges. Two more absurdities: for months at a time these desert dams turn just one or two turbines (the Columbia dams, on average, turn ten or more); nor do the Snake River dams provide storage for irrigation: thirteen agribusinesses use just one reservoir, Ice Harbor, for irrigation, and with the dam and reservoir gone they can simply run intake pipes to the river—a fraction of a week's work for an irrigation crew. The truth is, the four dams, beyond their limited hydroelectric function, were a pork-barrel present to the inland town of Lewiston, Idaho, whose D.C. insiders had a nature-whuppin' hankerin' to be a "seaport"—450 miles inland from the sea.

This so-called "port," the salmon's bane, is living proof that subsidies can be as dangerous as drugs in causing harm to neighbors. The Lewiston "port" is primarily a trucking depot. Its "marine" portion receives no oceangoing vessels and would be insolvent without federal and county subsidies. Most ludicrous of all: its barges plow alongside railways and highways that until 1975 carried the region's cargo at no cost to salmon, or to U.S. citizens—who have so far pumped billions into dam and port construction and operation, and $3 billion more into failed efforts to redress the deadly effects of the dams.

The usual media term for the species being eradicated—"Snake River salmon"—is a tragic understatement: Lewiston's "port" places a hangman's noose round an entire crucial Pacific salmon refugium, including Oregon's Imnaha, Grande Ronde, Wenaha, Lostine, Minam, Wallowa, and Powder rivers; Idaho's South and Main Clearwater, North, South, and Middle Salmon, Selway, Rapid, and Lochsa rivers; and many more, strangling the economies of towns throughout the region, along the Columbia, up and down the Pacific Coast. In 1993 the sport fishery for just one Snake River species—the summer steelhead—generated $90 million and created 2,700 jobs, even with the run in semi-ruins. That same year, the Lewiston "port" directly employed twenty-two people. The four dams' removal, even according to the Corps of Engineers, will create between 13,400 and 27,700 jobs immediately. Independent economic studies say that dam removal plus an even modest recovery of Snake River–dependent salmon stocks would generate as much as $2.6 billion of new regional income, annually. But the dams of the Snake have not just impounded life-giving current: they've created a quasi-culture of slackwater politicians whose hysterical rhetoric has instilled vague yet paralyzing fear in the hearts of federal lawmakers.

What is the substance of these fears? Who are the regional "leaders" trying to convince us to ignore biological reality and spiritual integrity in favor of a "self-interest" that permanently destroys the web of life? Helen Chenoweth-Hage (R-Idaho) asks how Idaho's salmon could possibly be in trouble when she sees canned salmon stacked in her local supermarket—ignoring the fact that it's *Alaska* salmon. Slade Gorton sees in the removal of Snake River dams a new "domino theory" that will bring down all dams, everywhere, and leave us in a "Mad Max"–style postindustrial wasteland ravaged by biblical floods (caused, no less, by the removal of four dams that offer no flood control). Gordon Smith (R-Ore.) responds to rigorous Corps of Engineers analyses linking salmon with jobs and prosperity by accusing the Corps of being stoned. The ruling Republicans of Idaho, meanwhile, have quietly gained control of all state fish-management decisions and fisheries science. As a result, Idaho is now exploring the possibility of building a 400-mile-long water-filled pipe down which to flush endangered juvenile salmon from the state's pristine interior to the lower Columbia, like turds. On the day a slackwater politician comes up with a single cogent, altruistic reason to sacrifice the inland West's salmon to their agendas, I'll eat my trout flies. All five boxes.

A Prayer for the Salmon's Second Coming

Ian Gill is chair of Ecotrust, an organization regionally famous for developing intelligent, sustainable economic opportunities for small communities like Lewiston. I asked Mr. Gill (a Canadian) for a nonpartisan take on the Lewiston port. Fresh back from a trip to that very town, Gill declared the port "fatuous beyond any rational understanding! Lewiston's barges are so misplaced they remind me of the Werner Herzog film—*Fitzcarraldo,* wasn't it?—whose crazed hero stopped at nothing to drag a sternwheeled riverboat over a mountain in Brazil. We need to be cognizant of the era in which things are conceived. There was a Conquistador mentality afoot during the Cold War. Here in Canada they talked of building a canal from Winnipeg to Hudson Bay, of reversing the flow of a major river, of building thirty-mile bridges from the mainland to Vancouver Island when the ferries already served. The fifties mentality explains the Lewiston 'port,' but doesn't excuse it. Do we live with fifties acts of idiocy, or do we set to work to undo them?"

So far, we live—and salmon die—with the idiocies. The Ice Harbor, Lower Monumental, Little Goose, and Lower Granite dams came on line in 1962, 1969, 1970, and 1975, respectively. Their legacy so far:

- *1986: all Idaho, Oregon, and Washington coho dependent on the Snake River migratory corridor, extinct*
- *1990 through 1999: 20 sockeye, total, returned to the same vast system*
- *1997: all surviving Snake system salmon and steelhead threatened or endangered*
- *1998: 306 fall chinook returned to the system (down from 100,000 or more per run)*
- *1999: Idaho spring/summer chinook, once the largest run of its kind in the world, down to 2,400 returning adults, leaving many key streams with no spawning for the first time in history*
- *2017: system-wide extinction predicted*

The Snake River dams' proximity to the defunct Hanford nuclear weapons works is painfully revealing as Cold War metaphor: once a tool in our lethal duel with the Soviets, and *the decisive factor in the '55 Congress's approval of the dams,* Hanford is now so full of irreparable subterranean radioactive leaks that it has become, according to the U.S. Department of Energy, "the single largest environmental and health risk in the nation," hence an incomparably greater threat to American well-being than modern Russia or China. "This world in arms," President Eisenhower said of the Cold War, "is not spending money alone. It is spending the sweat of its laborers, the genius of its scientists, the hopes of its children. This is not a way of life at all in any true sense. Under the cloud of threatening war, it is humanity hanging from an iron cross."

The Soviet Union is dissolved; the Cold War over. Yet salmon and their people remain on an iron cross. The two hundred dams of the Columbia/Snake make it the most overindustrialized river system on Earth, mirroring the grandiose, and famously fatal, engineering schemes of the USSR under Stalin. To give up 3.5 percent of the region's hydropower frightens some, because no one's done anything like this before. *But no nation on Earth has erected 75,000 dams before.* Looked at in human and biological terms, it is the *unwillingness* to give up a mere four deadly dams that terrifies me—because no person, no family, no country, and no civilization in history has remained viable for long without engaging in corrective acts of self-criticism, self-sacrifice, and restoration.

Three-point-five percent of a region's hydropower is not strategic. Its biological and spiritual web of life is. Lewiston, Idaho, can ignore its railways and highways and enjoy a piddling barging operation—or the interior West can have wild Pacific salmon and the vast web of wildlife that salmon support. We can't have both.

I a g o

A century ago our government defined salmon as a "commercial species," thus bequeathing the problems of salmon not to fish people, but to money people, namely the U.S. Department of Commerce's National Marine Fisheries Service, aka "NMFS" (pronounced "nymphs"). Shakespeare wrote a play concerning a general, Othello, whose life is destroyed by a brilliantly false adviser, Iago. NMFS is the salmon's Iago.

NMFS is, so to speak, "the mind" and the Army Corps "the muscle" of salmon recovery under the Endangered Species Act. In three decades of NMFS/Corps "stewardship"—the primary feature of which has been a disastrous juvenile-salmon barging program that I'll examine in a moment—salmon runs have done nothing but collapse, while even the most murderous, cost-ineffective dams under their jurisdiction have remained standing. But NMFS's performance is *far* more treacherous than this. In 1993, deep into the dam-inflicted extinctions in Oregon, Idaho, and Washington, NMFS scientists brazenly announced that they had studied the Columbia/Snake hydro system thoroughly, and concluded that the system "poses no jeopardy" to the recovery of Snake River salmon! This from the salmon's scientific "champion" under the ESA!

"I am not what I am," whispers Iago.

Outraged salmon lovers were forced to take the agency to court, where Judge Malcolm Marsh, in a landmark decision, found NMFS's science "arbitrary and capricious" and ordered it to rewrite its biological opinion, this time incorporating the expertise of state and tribal fisheries biologists. Seeming chastened, the NMFS/Corps team instigated the most comprehensive analysis of a fish species and watershed ever conducted on this planet. The renowned effort, known as the PATH study, included a carefully defined procedure, a review process, a 1999 deadline to honor the fact that salmon would be going extinct as research proceeded, and a federal vow that PATH science, being the best that humanity has, would determine the course of wild-salmon recovery action.

After five years of arduous effort, the comprehensive study concluded that existing strategies of river use will lead to certain extirpation of inland salmon; that barging smolts around dams cannot restore viable runs; but that if the Snake River dams are removed, our endangered salmon have an 80 to 100 percent likelihood not just of surviving but of flourishing.

Salmon lovers were ecstatic. After thirty years of federal indecision, it was time to act. What happened instead? The PATH conclusions began to be squelched, falsified, and politically spun not just by the far right (whose hysteria was expected) but by the salmon's Endangered Species Act champion. Suddenly, NMFS began to raise "other threats" known to salmon lovers all along—ocean conditions, overfishing, habitat degradation—as *arguments against dam removal.* This is like refusing to remove a terminal tumor from a man with a broken arm because his arm is broken. It's also a sickeningly familiar tactic. Here is a 1965 medical expert hired by the tobacco industry: "Research . . . indicates many possible causes of lung cancer. . . . There is no agreement among the authorities regarding what the cause is. . . . More study is needed." And here are NMFS "salmon experts," cited and paraphrased in the October '99 *New York Times:* "The salmon involves our whole way of doing things. There is no simple, easily defined enemy." "[Salmon] could be rescued by some means short of breaching dams." "One option would be to wait."

"This may help to thicken other proofs that do demonstrate thinly," whispers Iago.

Dangerous and superfluous dams are being removed all over

America—465 of them as of January 2000, with many more scheduled to go. And when dams go, anadromous fish return. On Butte Creek, a Sacramento River tributary, dam removal has helped turn a 1987 chinook run of fourteen fish into a 1998 run of 20,000. The pre-dam Snake system produced great salmon and steelhead runs in the 1960s despite the Columbia dams. The wild salmon of the Hanford Reach of the Columbia are thriving today, though they traverse the same four Columbia dams as the vanishing salmon of Idaho: the sole, quantifiable difference between prolific life and annihilation: the four Snake River dams. Yet NMFS is using R.J. Reynolds–style public-relations gimmicks to subvert their own best science and defend the dams. It's as if the Marsh Decision and the PATH study never took place. Wild salmon have no Endangered Species Act champion; they have an Iago.

"My lord," wheedles Iago. *"I would I might entreat your honour to scan this thing no further. Leave it to time."*

Iago is a subtle betrayer. Consider the famous "juvenile salmon transport" barging and trucking programs. At mind-boggling taxpayer expense—$3.5 billion as of fall, 2000—the NMFS/Corps team ostentatiously "saves" migrating smolts from turbines and slackwater—by removing the fish from their river completely, ceding the river to its industrial abusers, trapping fragile smolts at every Snake River dam in multimillion-dollar Inspector Gadget gizmos, handling and tagging them (often fatally) in the name of research, shooting them through whirligig "bypass systems" that disorient like Disney rides, sluicing them into overcrowded trucks and barges, shipping them like coal or plywood for three hundred miles, and dumping them—with no notion of what planet they're now on—below Bonneville Dam, where a crowd of slackwater industry officials and media stand cheering on the bank while, down in the river, an unphotographable horde of predators awaits a disoriented-smolt feast. NMFS then solemnly counts the dead 2 percent left floating in its state-of-the-art, taxpayer-duping barges, defies the science of every salmon-loving state, Indian, and nongovernment biologist by refusing to factor in the 40 to 60 percent of barged smolts that later "mysteriously disappear," calls their barged and dumped fish "saved fish," and proclaims their transport program "a 98 percent success." (*"There's millions now alive that nightly lie in those improper beds which they dare swear peculiar,"* says Iago. *"Patience!, or I shall say you're all in a spleen. . . ."*)

NMFS's "scientific" defense of its barging program is salmon-betraying drivel. NMFS's spokespersons continue to claim that because of their $3.5 billion transport program they have "fixed the dam problem," yet it has been proven repeatedly, by every "non-NMFS" Columbia/Snake fish-passage study we have, that barging *does not come close to matching the success of migrating smolts that are simply left in the river to deal with the eight killing dams and slackwaters unassisted.* Even Commerce Department biologists know that the only meaningful measure of recovery is the number of adult salmon that return from the ocean to spawn in home streams. By this measure, juvenile transport is an unmitigated disaster. The smolt-to-adult return range needed for salmon recovery is 2 to 6 percent. *The average adult return under NMFS is a dismal 0.25 percent.* In the real world, employees with this kind of "success" rate are fired. In the federal world, the ESA's Iago just spins the statistics of failure, says "let's study it further"—and Congress and the White House continue to fund this anti-scientific, money-wasting balderdash.

In spring 1999, the NMFS/Corps team released yet another "new" environmental-impact analysis of the Snake River dams. This report was literally *three feet thick*: thousands of pages of charts, graphs, and brain-scrambling pseudoscientific and engineering jargon as thick as the wall of a dam. We the people spent $22 million on it. Yet by deliberate NMFS/Corps decision, this study did not examine the fact that the four dams *destroy 40 percent of returning adult salmon.* It only examined juvenile salmon. Twenty-two million dollars for a "scientific" study that assumes salmon migration is one way, not a round-trip! The study also makes no mention of the estimated annual $2.6-billion net economic benefit of breaching the dams; it mentions only an estimated $300-million-per-annum net loss—and even this loss has been proven specious. (See "Dam Breaching Myths" by economist Ed Whitelaw, *Oregon Quarterly,* Autumn 2000.) The Corps' study calculates long-range economic loss by predicting that every person who becomes unemployed due to breaching *will never find a new job,* and *will remain unemployed for the next one hundred years!* The Corps also neglects to mention that the number of people so affected amount to just one of every five hundred workers in the few counties in which dam-influenced jobs exist. Yet, under NMFS's "endangered salmon stewardship," this three-foot-thick, calculatedly incomplete, dam-worshiping, specious techno-propaganda is now the chief body of "scientific" and "economic" literature upon which the recent federal decision to delay breaching is based.

At a March 2000 Corps "salmon hearing" in Seattle, Rob Masonis of American Rivers rolled in a hand truck stacked five feet high with previous NMFS/Corps Columbia/Snake salmon studies and demanded that federal officials stop "studying" and *act*. I couldn't agree more. *"Nature hates what it hates."* To create more salmon, we must return some of the stolen rivers in which they evolve, return the clearcut forest slopes that purify those streams, return the worse-than-clearcut seas that once sheltered and fed them—solutions so obvious that American industrialists and their political and scientific minions loathe it. So they rustle up "salmon task forces," kick it around a few more decades, kick its brains out, and bury it deep with the advance-degreed, politically spawned and spun, Phillip Morris–style NMFS/Corps propaganda that now passes as federal *science*.

The babble of "salmon management" rhetoric has taken a river of prayerful human yearning, diverted it into a thousand word-filled ditches, and run it out over alkali. When migratory creatures are prevented from migrating, they are no longer migratory creatures: they're kidnap victims. The name of the living vessel in which wild salmon evolved and still thrive is not "fish bypass system," "smolt-deflecting diversionary strobe light," or "barge." It is River. And this is the last thing the NMFS/Corps team is willing to give to the endangered salmon whose fate they now control.

Salmon Theology 1: Biblical Mandate

In 1999 the salmon's defenders were powerfully joined by the Northwest bishops of the Catholic Church, who, in an unprecedented document, *The Columbia River Watershed: Realities and Possibilities*, defined the Columbia and Snake Rivers as "a sacred commons," "created by God," to be shared and lovingly cared for by all. In this document the bishops argue against "arbitrary policies and practices based primarily on the greed and politics of power." They call for holistic, watershed-wide solutions that take into account "the needs of native peoples of the watershed, the economic benefits of jobs and property taxes for communities provided by all commercial fishers, [and] respect for salmon and trout who are God's creatures and share the commons with us."

A crucial value the bishops bring to the table, in corroboration of the tribes: it is impossible for individuals or governments to comprehend, effectively analyze, or defend a living holiness from a purely quantitative point of view. Federal government has lost all sight of this.

Politicians with two- and four-year dispensations of plenary powers are making decisions that annihilate God-given gifts and biological processes that required millions of years to establish themselves upon Earth. Any analysis that places a 260,000-square-mile watershed's permanent loss of a fundamental biological component—or the tribes' loss of a ten-millennium spiritual tradition—on a par with the annoyance salmon are causing wheat bargers and beer-can manufacturers, is no analysis at all. It's a reasoning so reductive it vivisects. Yet it is federal reasoning.

Wild salmon are not economic units. They are transrational beings whose living bodies bring far-reaching blessings to a watershed. Their self-sacrifice in migration is a literal and symbolic magnificence. Their flesh is one of Earth's perfect foods. Their existence puts us in touch with ultimate questions. Their hounding from existence puts us in touch with ultimate consequences. They are, first and foremost, a spiritual gift, so their loss is first and foremost a spiritual loss. In the face of such a loss, the federal failure to consider religious and moral roots is more than remiss. Indians aren't the only people with ancient stories that establish the sacredness of this species. It's time non-Indians recalled their own. On the very first page of the Bible, for instance, the sublime Creativity that has given us wild salmon is celebrated in these words:

And God said, Let the waters bring forth abundantly the moving creature that hath life, and fowl that may fly above the earth in the open firmament of heaven. And God created great whales, and every living creature that moveth, which the waters brought forth abundantly, after their kind, and every winged fowl after his kind: and God saw that it was good. And God blessed them, saying, Be fruitful, and multiply, and fill the waters in the seas.

Who can read this and not see that, for believers at least, the preservation of salmon is not just American law; *it is biblical mandate.* The annihilation of creatures whom God created, blessed, and ordered to fill the sea is the repudiation of a divine gift and spiritual impoverishment of a people. The bounty of Creation is daily evidence of a living, giving Creator. In the Northwest there is no more moving evidence of such giving than a huge, healthy run of salmon. Speaking from lifelong experience, I can say that the sight of these massive ocean travelers in a clear flow before me, hundreds of miles inland, thousands of feet above the sea, is a literal answer to unspoken prayer. Words aren't needed in the presence of such an answer. There it swims in the water before me: Genesis blessing, *the moving creature that hath life.*

What we are stealing from our children and their children, via the glib operation of four unneeded Cold War dams, is this literal answer to prayer. What we are removing from every future generation's intuitive reach is the awe, faith, and gratitude that such gifts inspire. What politicians are treating as a two-party rhetorical bauble is a holiness promised to all people by Moses' beloved God.

Salmon Theology II: Cattle, Fishes, and Dominion

On the same page of the Bible I keep quoting sits every dam-defender's, anti-salmon industrialist's, and bigot's favorite verse: *"And God said, Let us make man in our image . . . to have dominion over the fish of the sea, and over the fowl of the air, and over the cattle, and over all the earth. . . ."* What clear-eyed reader of American history hasn't seen the way generations of self-styled Christian lords of the land have used this passage, with its totalitarian-sounding D-word, as an excuse for everything from the morally exultant enslavement of Africans to the murder and robbery of Indians to the mass eradication of buffalo to today's status-quo slaughter of salmon? This passage, many honestly believe, is biblical justification for the annihilation of salmon, and of Indian culture along with them. Yet no interpretation of the ominous D-word could be further from biblical truth:

The Hebrew word translated as "dominion" is *rạdah*, which simply means "rule"—and the nature of this rule is fine-tuned by hundreds of Bible passages. In Genesis, men and women are made in the image of the God who just created and *blessed* all creatures and their *ability to multiply,* and Adam is placed in Eden merely "to dress it and keep it." In Exodus, the Sabbath rest is given to animals as well as humans. In Leviticus, humans are told by God to tend the land carefully and not treat it as a possession, because "the land is mine, and you are but aliens who have become my tenants." In Deuteronomy, when the harvest of wild stocks such as salmon is discussed, we're told we may take eggs from a nest we find in the wild, but must leave both birds and nest intact, that they might replenish their kind. In Ezekiel, God gives to his people, as a permanent component of the Promised Land, a desert river flowing out to the sea, healing all it touches, *"and there shall be a very great multitude of fish, because these waters shall come hither . . . and every thing shall live whither the river cometh. And it shall come to pass, that the fishers shall stand upon it . . . to spread forth nets; their fish shall be according to their kinds, as the fish of the great sea, exceeding many. . . . And ye shall inherit it, one as well as another. . . . This land shall fall unto you."* Then in the Gospels we meet, in Jesus, a lifelong friend to fisherfolk and a leader who defines "dominion" as *"Thy will be done, on earth as it is in heaven"*: a leader who lives a life of "kingship" culminating in a salmonlike act of self-sacrifice, and characterized throughout by supreme sensitivity toward the meek, the weak, birds, field lilies, the voiceless, the disinherited, the prostituted, the poor, and all other forms of life. There is, in short, no such biblical thing as a "dominion" that allows the status-quo obliteration of an invaluable species. It seems ridiculous to have to say it, but *there is no way to rule a subject that you have driven into nonexistence.*

Something far more interesting to me, in that same abused "dominion" passage, is the mention of "fishes" and "cattle" as equally "blessed" by God. I would ask ranchers to consider this. I'm a lifelong fisherman—same as any rancher is a cattleman. When the God of Genesis blesses "fishes" in the same breath as "cattle," I take that blessing as deeply to heart as cattlemen do. Consider the two species. Transpose them. How many ranchers aspire to a "dominion" that would drive *all* of their livestock into irrevocable extinction? How many would tolerate a federal "dominion" that allowed outsiders to come in and exterminate their prize bulls, brood cows, entire herds, for any reason under the sun? What cattleman would say yes to an offer of "unneeded hydropower at the cost of all your cattle for all time," or "a subsidized barging scam for Lewiston at the cost of all your cattle for all time"?

These questions are insane. The sustainable health of diverse livestock is the life's blood of the entire ranching enterprise. *So why is the same inalienable right to exist* not *being extended to the diverse wild salmon stocks that are the life's blood of our fishing enterprises and tribal cultures?*

I trust any rational soul on Earth to see that the permanent destruction of the lower forty-eight's last great genetic cache of wild inland salmon is just as unconscionable as would be the permanent destruction of all of the same vast region's cows—and if that rationality excludes our federal government, it is a dark day indeed. If there is any point upon which even theologians agree (I phoned two Baptists, two Catholics, and a Methodist to quintuple-check this), it is that the Genesis account of Creation was set down to guide humanity for all time, that it contains, so to speak, both our ultimate set of fishing regulations and our ultimate manual of viable dam operation, and that its eternal instruction to humankind is to help salmon *be fruitful, multiply, and fill the waters in the seas.* And yes, our *rạdah* mandates and celebrates grateful harvest, and other uses of the waters including dams. But *not at the cost of a species' ability to multiply. Not at the cost of extinction.* I can think of few acts more anti-biblical, more Luciferian in grandeur, than the permanent, man-made negation of God's Genesis blessings to Earth and man.

Another Forgotten Treasure

In the summer of 1965, a Washington State geologist named Roald Fryxell visited the banks of the free-flowing Snake, shortly before its inundation by Lower Monumental Dam. Knowing slackwater was on the way, Fryxell was committing the archaeologically indelicate but expedient investigation method of walking along the riparian behind a bulldozer driven by one Roland Marmes, the property's owner. Beneath a basaltic overhang, Fryxell looked down in the bulldozed rubble and discovered, several feet below the ash line created by Mount Mazama's eruption 6,700 years ago, a group of ancient bones.

The bones were human—and turned out to be between 9,000 and 11,000 years old. The discovery stunned the archaeological world. Not only were these the oldest human remains ever found in North America, they overlay remains of evidence, resting layer upon layer, of consecutive human use of the basalt overhang for ten millennia. In one small area—condensed and well preserved—Roald Fryxell and Roland Marmes had unearthed one of the great archaeological finds on any continent, ever: extensive remnants of *a hundred consecutive centuries* of human history.

The "Marmes Rockshelter," as it was dubbed, was world-renowned within months. A Fryxell-led crew soon discovered hundreds of fabulous artifacts: animal bones from as far away as the Arctic; tools, including handmade blades sharper than modern surgeon's scalpels; a treasury of ancient weapons; a perfectly preserved sewing needle, perhaps the oldest ever found; more human remains. Scientists began piecing together unprecedented information about how these river people hunted and lived, what they ate, how ten millennia of climate changes affected regional flora, fauna, and human culture. For two years the team dug and sifted, removing 5,000 cubic yards of dirt, much of it with hand trowels, tiny brushes, dental picks. A wealth of priceless artifacts continued to be unearthed. The archaeologists needed time. And like the salmon, they didn't have it. The Corps of Engineers' inundation of the riparian behind Lower Monumental Dam remained on schedule—ironically, to "protect" migrating salmon.

Because the Marmes Rockshelter was by then famous, President Lyndon Johnson approved federal funding enabling the Corps to build a levy around the site. In February 1968, they began to fill the reservoir. The levy sprang leaks. Water burst into the Rockshelter at 45,000 gallons a minute. Giant pumps were put in place, but failed to expel the flood. The reservoir was temporarily lowered. Fryxell's crew was allowed to cover the Marmes site with sheets of plastic, and to anchor the plastic with dump-truck loads of dirt. The Corps then ordered the area evacuated, and archaeologists watched forty feet of water bury what remains one of the great prehistoric sites in North America. And Marmes was not the only such Snake River site—only the most studied. Strawberry Island, Alpowa, Davis Bar, Windust Caves, Thorn Thicket, Wawawai, Squirt Cave, Granite Point, Three Springs Bar, and other sites await the tribes when the dams go.

A distressing study in contrast: In 1995 the Corps of Engineers discovered the skeleton of a man on the banks of the Columbia near Kennewick, Washington—a man who apparently lived in the Northwest some 9,000 years before Europeans were supposed to have arrived, yet who seemed to possess Caucasian facial structure. "Kennewick Man," he was dubbed. And the sensation he caused brings to mind the thirty-year-old Sinatra. An indigenous North American white guy! What a mind-bending contradiction! Scientists and journalists descended on the bones like fleas and flies. Magazines as varied as *The New Yorker,* *National Geographic,* and *Hustler* weighed in. A confederacy of bigots, thrilled by K-Man's honkizoidal cranium, began chanting "We were here first!" at Indian tribes. Specious books, harebrained doctoral theses, and prehistoric fantasy films starring the likes of Brendan Frazier began to brew. And when the tribes begged to differ, invoking federal antiquities laws guaranteeing their right to rebury all such bones, they were ordered to leave the disturbed remains to (white) scientists.

Is there a discernible direction here? Unneeded dams standing, salmon species extirpated, railroads abandoned, smolts kidnapped in barges, the fishing sites, homes, burial grounds, art, and evidence of an elegant Indian culture drowned from Celilo Falls to the Rockshelter, while we break our own laws to exaggerate the bones of the lone possible prehistoric White Boy? The bias here is so concerted, it reminds me of the Taliban's recent destruction of the pre-Islamic art of Afghanistan. And, valuable as the Snake River archaeological troves are, they're a mere aside to this grim story. Placing ancient artifacts aside and racial, biological, economic, and religious issues front and center: the ongoing operation of the Snake River dams is one of the most overtly racist projects funded by our own, or any, modern government.

Kamiakan's Lip and the Coming Lawsuit

Four dams created by Cold War paranoia and sustained by a subsidy-addicted few are wiping out the sacramental fish, sustainable economy, and ancient religion and culture of the Northwest's sovereign tribes for the sake of no industrial good, service, or commodity that can't be replaced by profitable and sustainable equivalents. To add insult to injury, the tribes are now so hated in right-wing circles for standing faithfully by salmon that they are being publicly accused—by the PR flacks of slackwater industry—of bringing about salmon demise by simply exercising their treaty-guaranteed right to fish.

Northwest Indians catch and eat salmon for two reasons. The first is the reason that cattleman eat cattle: it's who they are, what they do, and what they have. The second is the reason that Catholic celebrants eat bread and wine at Mass: Northwest Indians are the humans for whom the grateful catching and eating of salmon was a sacrament centuries before the birth of Christ. The Columbia and Snake rivers are the Indians' place of worship, their "church." Salmon-killing government and industry are simultaneously destroying the tribes' place of worship and vilifing the tribes for still worshiping.

Under the Marsh decision, the Umatilla, Warm Springs, Yakama, and Nez Perce people, represented by the Columbia River Intertribal Fish Commission (CRITFC), became fully empowered participants in the scientific and managerial struggle to save endangered salmon. But NMFS has given CRITFC's calm, clear voices no more weight than the calm, clear voices of blacks were given in the courts of Alabama in the 1950s—and for the same reason: the four dams on the Snake are like four whites-only drinking fountains. Their life-giving, job-generating flow is being illegally stolen from Indians and salmon and converted into dollars reserved for Anglo industrialists. If this is not federally defended racism, I don't know what is. Columbia/Snake River economic and cultural apartheid is carefully enriching one race of people while deliberately impoverishing another.

What should it mean to be "co-managing" the river and its salmon with the Yakama, Umatilla, Warm Springs, and Nez Perce people? Shouldn't it mean that we listen with respect when tribal leaders speak, and give their worldview legal weight even when that view feels a little foreign? The tribes' openly expressed appreciation of salmon as fellow beings, for instance, feels a little odd to those who prefer to consume less-than-fellow creatures—until we remember the wine and blood of the Mass. Isn't it racist, in management venues, to write off the tribes' regard for salmon as sister and brother beings as "Neolithic" and "irrelevant"? We lament a crisis in American leadership and express near-ubiquitous lack of faith in our politics. The tribes, meanwhile, are often decisively led by men and women whose common sense and open spirituality move us. Yet we consider it credulous to incorporate such spirituality into our politics. So back we go to special-interest-serving, negative-campaigning, mealy-mouthed "leaders." Where can we turn for a rejuvenation of ideals if not to genuine idealists?

Last summer a scholarly Warm Springs Indian friend, the poet Elizabeth Woody, learned that I was writing of the inland West salmon's plight and surrounding thicket of politics. Her response was a wonderful non sequitur. She mailed me a John Corsiglia/Gloria Snively monograph on universal values drawn from the traditional sciences of the world's long-resident indigenous peoples. Here are four of those ancient values:

1. Humans and nature are inseparably linked in a universe pervaded by consciousness; spiritual essence suffuses all forms; all life forms are thus intrinsically valuable and interdependent; we are all relations.

2. Animal souls survive and are reborn; animals are social beings, with thoughts and feelings, and must be treated with respect; respecting an animal means honoring its spirit, using every part of its body, and allowing it to reproduce in sustainable numbers; all creatures can be our teachers; though we may readily affect other life-forms, we needn't see ourselves as superior.

3. All natural and supernatural objects have power to harm or help humans; it is not only wrong but spiritually dangerous to wantonly destroy or take more than one's share of other life forms; justice is

208

unavoidable; wrongs are not so much 'punished' as brought before the inescapable light of justice.

4. Spiritual essence persists while forms change; all humans return to face their mistakes, in this life or the next; the truth of situations always becomes known; there are no secrets; death is less to be feared than shameful actions.

After years of listening, I haven't heard a public word from a Columbia River Intertribal Fish Commision salmon spokesperson that was not in keeping with these values. I'd wager that thousands of Americans still remember the words of CRITFC's Ted Strong, to President Clinton, at the 1992 Timber Summit: "American Indians, natives to this land, hope and pray that the pen you wield will be guided by the sacred beings who created and authored the perfect laws of nature by which all mankind has existed since the beginning of time."

When I compare such guiding principles to the Iagoan ploys of NMFS, or to an Idaho far right that mandates extinction because of the "threat" salmon pose to subsidy arrangements, or to the BPA's need to slaughter smolts in order to service a $7-billion debt caused by the Reagan-era failed-nuclear-plant debacle we Northwesterners call "WHOOPS," or to the barging scam of a railroad-refusing Idaho town that is bringing extinction to a hundred rivers and economic harm to hundreds of towns, my heart feels like a smolt barged and dumped into God knows what caustic flux and moral vacuum.

It's time Americans listened to the tribes, for two reasons. The first: we have, in the Columbia/Snake region, a clear and dire choice to make between what is sacred (the health and wholeness of life) and what is profane (the worship of wealth at all cost), not just according to Indians, but according to *all* the world's major religious traditions. (See the Appendix to this book.)

The second reason to listen: dire financial repurcussions, besides all those to which I've already refered. A powerful legal document known as the *treaty* grants sovereign rights to native peoples for all time. Among those rights are hunting and fishing privileges in "usual and accustomed places" throughout the Northwest. Those privileges are not something "given" to Indians, like welfare. They are a table-scrap tossed to the tribes by an inadequately shamed U.S. government as Indian lands, languages, and lifeways were being ripped away. This is why, when I hear highly paid, posturing corporate flacks inciting the meat-and-potatoes public by saying the cause of salmon decline is Indian fishing, I open Dante to enjoy his descriptions of the particularly heinous circle of hell reserved for malicious slanderers. The tribes were given hunting and fishing "privileges" over the dead bodies of men, women, and children and against their will. When Kamiakan, chief of the Yakama, signed the 1855 treaty that ceded his tribe's lands in perpetuity in exchange for fishing and hunting "privileges," his lip dripped blood from biting it in the effort to contain his helpless rage. And as CRITFC's Chuck Hudson told me in October 1999, with an admirable restraint I couldn't share, "From 1855 till now, there has not been one good day to be an 1855 treaty Indian."

For a century and a half, 1855 treaty rights have been dishonored and negated. Many "usual and accustomed places" are on private land, with legal access illegally denied. When access isn't denied, there's often nothing to fish for. When there *are* fish, Indians have to fight for their "guaranteed" right to catch them (witness the fisherman David SoHappy's courageous legal battle and its famous result: the Boldt Decision). Many "usual and accustomed" fishing sites are now buried under slackwater. Thousands more have been sterilized of their salmon by dams. A court in Idaho recently ruled that though the Nez Perce have a right to fish in usual and accustomed rivers, they have no right to ask white irrigators to leave water in those rivers. And now the federal government threatens to outlaw even the last Columbia/Snake tribal ceremonial fishery "to protect the salmon"—while the same government murders smolts by the millions in its dams and barges in violation of its own Clean Water Act, its own Endangered Species Act, its own taxpayer-funded science, and its own binding treaties.

In the fight to preserve the salmon, the tribes have been heroically patient. They seek the return of their sacred fish, not court battles. But when sovereign rights and viable recovery strategies are ignored again and again, Indians are left no choice but to litigate. And in treaty-inspired legal wars, they haven't lost a major battle yet. Treaty rights are potent and damn well should be. Indian treaties, as even the conservative senator John McCain puts it, "were written in exchange for a significant portion of America." The right to fish for ghosts of salmon is hardly just recompense for "a significant portion of America." The extinction of salmon is not nature's doing; it is being *inflicted* on Indians by state and federal "river management" racism. If NMFS continues to make a mockery of the ESA by allowing a coterie of industrialists to drive salmon into extinction, we the people will be sued for treaty violation, and the settlement will be huge: $10 to $20 billion, even according to NMFS estimates—and I've heard methods of analysis that double that figure.

We're well on our way to paying it. The dwindling fish counts at Snake River dams should be posted daily—in the nation's financial pages.

A Prayer for the Salmon's Second Coming

Every dam on Earth has a life span, and sustainable forms of energy are rapidly on the way. The removal of the four Snake River dams is inevitable—later if we heed slackwater rhetoricians, subsidy beneficiaries, and NMFS; sooner if we heed the tribes, the Northwest bishops, salmon-loving scientists, and the spiritual foundations of our own culture. So let's envision, for a moment, the restoration process that so horrifies the far right:

Once federal approval is given, removing the earthen portion of the four dams—according to the men who built them—will be an engineering piece of cake. The revegetation of the drained reservoirs, removal of silt, and rebuilding of riparian communities and recreation sites will be hard work, but will create thousands of jobs. As for the feared changes: breaching the four dams will not touch 96.5 percent of the region's hydropower, will not cause a single home or business to go without electricity for even a minute, and will soon strengthen the financially troubled Bonneville Power Administration by relieving them of their multibillion-dollar Endangered Species Act burden. Breaching will cost us *no irrigation, no flood control, no needed energy,* no "national security," and no industry save an immediately replaceable, scandalously monomanical barging operation. Breaching will not harm a single cattle rancher, southern Idaho potato grower, or farmer. Indeed, it will help the thousands of farmers, ranchers, and reservoir recreationists and merchants throughout the region, who, under the Endangered Species Act, must now squander massive amounts of stored irrigation and recreational waters, right before the hot season, in order to flush endangered smolts through the four Snake River slackwaters.

The regional grain growers now dependent on Snake River barging almost all farm to the north and west of Lewiston—nowhere near the Snake River. Those growers, sans dams, will simply begin moving their grain south to barges at Pasco, Washington, by truck and train, instead of to barges southeast at Lewiston. A glance at a map reveals both the shockingly small distance that has wiped out the region's salmon, and the lightly traveled new four-lane freeway (U.S. 395) that will support increased grain-truck traffic. It's also worth noting that the towns that once served the grain growers were economically harmed by the Snake River dams when barging forced the abandonment of their rail lines, grain elevators, and the commerce stimulated by both. Breaching would restore to those towns the vitality they possessed before the dams.

There *will* be some employment changes: over the agonized bellows of Lewiston, Idaho's worst minds, breaching will protect the rest of America from this multibillion-dollar boondoggle of a "seaport" and transform a failed Portland-wannabe into the revamped, world-class outdoor recreation and sportfishing destination it should have been all along. Over more agonized bellows, Snake River breaching will put hundreds of bureacrats, "salmon managers," political propagandists, and Iagoan scientists out of work, creating tens of thousands of *real* jobs instead.

Best and most crucial of all, Snake River breaching will protect the long-term genetic health of *all* Pacific salmon by protecting Idaho's paragon wild genius salmon; it will honor treaties and racial diversity and preserve our continent's oldest sacred culture; it will create a half-billion-dollar-a-year commercial fishing industry, will put tens of thousands of sportfishing men, women, and children back on the free-flowing waters of Idaho, Oregon, and Washington, and will enliven every riverside town and coastal fishing port in the process; it will attract tourists, fly-rodders, kayakers, birders, botanists, Lewis and Clark buffs, and rubberneckers from all over the globe to ogle the mothballed dam remnants, study the returning plants, birds, and wildlife, marvel at some of the world's most ancient tribal treasures, ride the seventy new whitewater rapids, hunt the newly revealed side canyons, fish the newly revealed steelhead riffles, and watch the spawning of fall chinook; it will bring, in the form of an abundance of salmon, a flood of health, income, marine nitrogen, and energy to hundreds of Northwest biological and human communities, and a source of hope, happiness, and gratitude to every riverine creature from insects to kids to angels, preserving not just our way but our very web of life.

The poet Jane Hirshfield writes: "As water, given sugar, sweetens / given salt, grows salty / we become our choices." The Columbia/Snake, given current, creates salmon, biological richness, and reverent cultures; given Snake River dams, creates electricity, polarized rhetoric, extinction, and heartbreak. We become our choices. I pray there are leaders in Washington who will weigh this choice before we become it: 96.5 percent of our electricity intact and the interior West's salmon thriving; 96.5 percent of our electricity intact, *102 major Columbia/ Snake hydroelectric dams still intact, 217 major (100 feet or taller) Columbia/ Snake dams intact,* but four Cold War dams gone, that our tribal and fishing cultures may thrive and our rivers again burgeon with their living symbol of generational sacrifice.

Who are we, with our seventy-year life spans and 225-year-old nation, to pretend we know better than humanity's most ancient and sacred laws? If the lives that God and His instruments, Sun and Ocean, have placed in our rivers and oceans are not holy, what is? If the first page of the Bible doesn't convey truth, what does? If the heroic migration and dying sacrifice of salmon are not exemplary, what is? If Genesis is meant to be believed, God blessed the chinook, coho, steelhead, and sockeye the waters brought forth, pronounced them good, and as they took their part in the panoply of creation, He upgraded that to "very good." To honor the Creator's gift to all generations, to embody a true *radah,* to restore to our fellow blessed creatures their indispensable path to and from mountain birth-houses, we have four dams to unbuild in a hurry.

To that end, a prayer: from my friend Sherman Alexie—registered member of one of the Columbia/Snake's many salmon tribes now stripped, by Cold War anachronisms and economic apartheid, of every last one of the creatures that so recently and beautifully defined them:

I release these salmon
I release

I release my father and mother
I release

I release my sister and brother
I release

I release these salmon
into their personal rivers

the river of bitter root
the river of broken bone

213

the river of stone
the river of sweet smoke

the river of blood and salt
the river of semen and sap

the river diverted
the river dammed

I release these salmon
I release

I release these salmon
I release

o, salmon, I release you
o, salmon, I pray

o, father and mother
o, sister and brother

return to me
return to me

My Story as Told by Water

13. River Soldiers

In the beginning, on the volcanic cone back in Southeast Portland, there was nothing much going on. Dehydrated industrial Martians seemed to dominate the terrain completely. So I fastened the family hose to an azalea bush at the summit of a flower bed, turned on the faucet, created a little liturgical river (*arka*). And as a three-inch-tall blue plastic U.S. Cavalry dropout stood in that river, the stock of his upraised rifle converted into a fly rod, I lay on my belly, cheek to the ground, listening to the tiny current curling round his thighs, watching his line work, eyeing the bend in the tip of the rifle-rod, till on the best days the rod dipped and we actually hooked, in sunlit riffles, tiny sun-glint fish.

Four decades later I live amid a web of sunlit, life-giving streams in Montana. And I relish my time on those streams. Yet I couldn't help but notice, while reflecting on existence one recent summer's day, that I was in fact glued to my writing desk in a Venetian-blinded study, ignoring streams and sunlight in order to fight for the who-knows-how-manyth time for the life of some river, creek, or salmonid in urban Washington, desert Oregon, mining-crazed Montana, french-fry-crazed Idaho. "How have I come to this?" I asked myself. "What makes me take on these feisty, endless jobs?"

Then a recognition swept through me and I started to laugh Those tiny scientific nativity rivers . . . The three-inch-tall soldier with the rifle fly rod . . . There was the culprit! There should have been a warning label on the damned garden hose: CHILDHOODS SPENT MESMERIZED BY TOY RIVERS LEAD TO PERMANENT TRANSFORMATIONAL DAMAGE. Because somehow that little dude has *become* me. I'm a life-sized, lifelong River Soldier.

Since the moment of recognition I've been trying, as pop psychologists recommend, to "own" my permanent damage. But it's a strange thing to describe at, say, cocktail parties. "What were you up to today?" someone asks.

"Me? Oh, a little soldiering. Tedious work at times, but I've gotta do it. I enlisted as a kid, actually. I'm a River Soldier."

"River Soldier. Hmm," people say. "Is that a branch of the armed forces?"

"Armed forces, legged forces, winged and finned forces," I answer. "If water's part of it, we River Soldiers are a branch of it."

"Well, uh, what's the political orientation?" some ask. "Is river soldiering more of a Republican or a Democrat type deal?"

"Different spectrum," I answer. "Most voters seem to adhere to a left-to-right political spectrum. River Soldiers adhere to a high-to-low-elevation, mountain-to-ocean spectrum. We humans are 78-percent water, you know. Being true to this 78-percent majority, regardless of anyone's left to right political concerns—that's the work of the River Soldier."

"So what do you do from day to day?" some want to know.

"Seek justice," I answer, plundering my favorite William Stafford quote, "via millions of intricate moves."

"Such as?" people ask.

Such as my dentist here in Montana loves rivers, same as I do. And my dentist also proudly calls himself "as right wing as you can get." This is not a good description of how I conceive of myself. But it's my dentist's skilled and gentle hands, not his right wing, that so painlessly fix my teeth. A River Soldier, in such a dentist's chair, endeavors to be like a river. You meander away from the hot buttons, oxbow around the shared passions, hone in on the water molecules. You marvel at the umpteen trout the dentist caught on the Bighorn, then he marvels at the moose you saw chase an otter, as if playing with it, in a marsh by the river last week. Why judge, why argue, why alienate the best dentist you ever had, because of an alleged right wing you can't even see, when you can calm down and talk water instead?

Another example: Say that, at the same cocktail party, somebody tries to spike the social punch by bloring: "I just *love* Rush Limbaugh!" Causing a second person to turn crimson and bark, "Well, *I* love Dave Foreman." Or probably they both already *were* crimson, if they love Rush and Dave.

A River Soldier response: "Well, Limbaugh and Foreman, like you and me, are 78-percent clean water, and 100-percent dead without that water. So let's focus on the inarguable. Rush and Dave, like it or not, are 78-percent molecularly identical."

What can they say in objection? The worst-case scenario is: *"I 22-percent disagree with every damned word you just said!"*

I can 78-percent live with that. Why define the most life-giving, apolitical substance on Earth politically? Why define even people who dirty, steal, or kill water politically? The River Soldier's allegiance is to the water itself: to the life and health of the unjudgable, apolitical, forever-flowing substance that no man, woman, child, plant, or animal will ever survive long without.

Norman Maclean's father was one of us. When he fished the Big Blackfoot, the Reverend Maclean carried a Greek New Testament in his wicker creel. His River Soldiering habit was to catch a few trout, clean them, sit down under a pine, pull the Gospels from the creel, put the trout where the Gospels had been, and read Blackfoot and Greek both at once. Turning from sunlit riffles to hovers of insects to water running over stones to the primordial Word, λόγος, he saw it all as a single beautiful text.

Norman was one of us. Of the same Blackfoot he wrote: "Heat mirages danced with each other, and then they danced through each other, till eventually the watcher joined the river and there was only one of us. I believe it was the river."

Tom McGuane is one of us; he calls "every refractive glide of water a glimpse of eternity." Izaak Walton was one of us; he wrote that while fishing, he was sometimes "lifted above earth, and posses'd [of] joys not promised in my birth." Sir Philip Sidney was one of us; he concluded, five centuries ago, that rivers are "one self same continual and inseparable essence, which hath neither foreness nor afterness, save only

in order and not in tyme," hence, "rivers are like God." Lorian Heming-
way is one of us. Returning in her forties to the rank home creek of her
Mississippi childhood, she "looked down the clogged channel . . . at
the sedge broom, wild holly, sawgrass, brambles knotted up like barb-
wire, and watched the clean red feather of a cardinal drift from the
open limbs of a sweet gum tree, spin like a maple seed caught on a draft
of wind, and land on water just short of my outstretched palm, an invitation home." Jim Harrison is one of us. Walking "the same circular
path today in the creek bottom three times," he suddenly saw that his
life depended "on the three-million two hundred seventy-seven / thousand three hundred and thirty-three / pebbles locked into the ground
so I / don't fall through the thin skin of earth / on which there is a large
coyote-turd full / of Manzanita berries I stepped over twice / without
noticing it, a piece of ancient chert, / a fragment of snakeskin, an owl
eye / staring from a hole in an Emory oak, / the filaments of eternity

hanging in the earthly / air like the frailest of beacons seen / from a ship
mortally far out in the sea."

River Soldiers. Dangerous people in their way, mucking peacefully
around in water, stirring up idle love for minnows, mud, and eternity's
filaments when there's hard cash to be made. Obeying 78 percent
of Christ's love-thy-neighbor order by loving the fluid 78 percent of
everyone, whether they believe in Christ or not. Creekophiles. Stone
skippers. Aquatic bug lovers. Idlers. Weirdos. There ought to be a law.
There are some, actually. But it's hard to outlaw River Soldiering completely without outlawing love and life itself.

We're not out to make trouble for the money-driven—though we
do like to remind them that water is essential even to the manufacture
of the paper their money's printed on. We're not anti-progress, anti-
profit, anti-politics. We just happen to have discovered that once you
start spending time in the wet, glimpsing eternity in glides, or being
lifted above earth by joys caused by nothing but water's flow, you tend
to stop fretting the gross national product. Less gross but equally
national products such as *Ephemeroptera* swarms, ouzel squats, the eyes
in frog eggs, the chitter of baby kingfishers, start to tilt your needle
instead.

We're not on the make for converts. If you're a Mountain Soldier;
Desert Soldier; Ocean, School, Neighborhood, or Parish Soldier, we
already work for the same Boss. If you insist on joining us, we're not in
the phone book, but you'll sooner or later spot us on creek or river.
Don't call us even then, though. Let the rivers and λόγος call you.

The life and health of the waters flowing into our lives; the life and health of the same waters as they flow out of our lives: this is the news that absorbs us. Our kind of news doesn't make many headlines, but there's a newsworthy reason for this: eventually there may be only one of us.

Norman believes it's the river.

We call ourselves the River Soldiers.

14. Strategic Withdrawal

any movement inward

—as into a chair by a window the light of which you use only to stare into a cup of tea

—or as into a habit of tea-drinking, as opposed to coffee, because the former behaves so much more quietly within the body, so softly helps open the eyes and the mind

—or as in letting the eyes come to a standstill, in some space on the page of a book you've been reading, in order to stare at nothing, or at something inside, or at something neither inside nor out—an association-sprung scene, an entire small world, maybe; a place so pungent you leave your body to stand in it for a time

—or as in turning over a handwritten letter, before or after you've read it, to run your hand across the blank side, the written words invisible now, yet palpable in the impressions the pen left in the paper, the strange backward slant you never think of as being there, the earnest weight of the writer's departed hand, physical track of her thought still traceable, the "handicraft" evident in the paucity of words; the whole page, though we think of paper as "smooth," as idiosyncratically and subtly bumpy as the skin of your love's body, in which also dwells a reverse side, unseen side, of breath, blood, inchoate words, nonverbal language

strategic withdrawal: any movement backward, away from the battle lines of one's incarnation (as in the phrase "spiritual retreat" but without the once-in-a-blue-moon connotations of those two words, because the backward movement needed, the spiritual retreat required, is moment to moment and day to day)

strategic withdrawal: any refusal to man our habitual political or psychological trenches or to defend our turf, for though the turf may be holy, our defenses, when they grow automatonic, are not

any refusal to engage with that testy or irritating or ideologically loud or theologically bloated person in your life—you know the one: the agitatedly racist or religionist, politically powerful or compulsively processing pedant, co-worker, parent, friend, or (God help you) spouse whose opinions are too poorly formed, too loudly held, or just too incessantly divulged to allow you to achieve peace in the presence of so much clanging banging editorializing mental machinery

any retreat (however ignominious it may seem to the will or the mind or the ego) not just from all such exchanges but from the underlying tensions and history that launch the exchanges (*your* side of the tensions and history, anyway: the side you've an inalienable right to retreat from)

any movement away from one's "urgencies," one's "this-is-who-I-am" nesses, one's responsibilities, agitations, racial guilt, sworn causes, shames, strengths, weaknesses, memories, workaday identity, public or secret battlefields

any movement toward formlessness

silence

emptiness

primordiality

any movement toward a beginning, as in Genesis 1, John 1, Quran Tao Te Ching Diamond Sutra Mahabharata Kalevala Mumonkan Ramayana Torah Gita 1

and toward one's own "in the beginning"

toward one's *origin* (root of *originality*); toward one's ignorance (that underrated state the embracing of which precedes every influx of fresh knowledge); toward one's amorphousness (state of all clay before the potter conceives a form, wedges the clay, centers it, and begins throwing the cup or bowl); toward one's interior blankness (the state of the paper preceding every new idea, drawing, poem); toward one's wilderness (*wild*: the condition of all worlds, inner and outer, before the creation of the man-made bewilderments from which we are endeavoring to withdraw)

strategic withdrawal:

any attempt to step from a why, however worthy, into whylessness

as in an extemporaneous walk to a destination unknown; a walk during which everything but your movement through God-knows-where becomes the God-knows-what you're doing

or as in going fishing without desire for fish so that desirelessness becomes the prey you're catching

or as in a stroll to a neighborhood café or tavern one or more neighborhoods removed from any in which you're known, which establishment you then enter not to socialize, read the paper, or eat the (probably bad) food, but just to nurse the single slow drink as you soak, without judgment, in the presence and riverine babble of your city and native tongue

strategic withdrawal: any act you can devise, any psycho-spiritual act at all, that embodies a willingness to wait for the world to disclose itself to you, rather than to disclose yourself, your altruism, your creativity, skills, energy, ideas and (let's face it) agenda, myopia, preconceptions, delusions, addictions, and inappropriate trajectories to this world

willingness to drop all trajectories; willingness to boot up with all extensions OFF; willingness *not* to save the world but simply to wait for it to disclose itself, whether anything seems, even after long long waiting, to be disclosing itself or not

an act of faith then, really: faith that the world is *always* disclosing itself; faith that lack of disclosure is impossible; faith that what blocks Creation's ceaseless flow of disclosures is, invariably, *our* calluses and callousness, our old injuries and injuriousness, our plans, cross-purposes, neuroses, absurd speed of passage, divided minds, ruling manias, lack of trust, lack of faith—and overabundance of faith, cf. Thomas Merton: "Prayer is possible only when prayer is impossible"

strategic withdrawal: to step back, now and then, from the possible to take rest in the impossible: to stand without trajectory in the God-given weather till the soul's identity begins to come with the weathering: to get off my own laboriously cleared and maintained trails and back onto the pristine hence unmarked path by moving, any old how, toward interior nakedness; toward silence; toward what Buddhists call "emptiness," Christians "poverty of spirit," Snyder "wild," and Eckhart "desirelessness: the virgin that eternally gives birth to the Son"

strategic withdrawal: this prayer: When I'm lost, God help me get more lost. Help me lose me so completely that nothing remains but the primordial peace and originality that keep creating and sustaining this blood-, tear- and love-worthy world that's never lost for an instant save by an insufficiently lost me

"We're all in the gutter," said Oscar Wilde in the throes of just such a withdrawal, "but some of us are looking at the stars"

strategic withdrawal:

look at the stars

—Shepherdstown, West Virginia; cross country
Delta jet; and Lolo, Montana: summer 1999

Fishing the Inside Passage

Water is earth's eye,
looking into which the beholder
measures the depth of his own nature.
                    —Henry David Thoreau

15. Idiot Joy

Caught a twenty-inch brown trout in my sleep last night, inspired by a real brown lost in the Bitterroot yesterday, and another caught and released on a dry—first dry-fly fish of the year; first fish at all on my home water; its quick take and leaps a miracle after months of cold and silence; running water itself a miracle after a winter spent knowing the river as a hikable white solid. Yet how is it, friends often ask me—how is it, I sometimes wonder myself—that losing or catching mere *fish* can give me this huge sense of well-being? How is it that a cold-blooded creature (endowed, let's face it, with a persona as lacking in nuance as its unblinking stare) can grab a scrap of deceptive flotsam in hope of food, instead find itself pierced, leaping, swimming every direction but the one it intends, and a few minutes later, having clutched this betrayed beauty just long enough to reverse the betrayal, I stand alone in frigid water enjoying the endorphin-flow and pulse rate of a post-tryst lover as I thank creek and Cosmos for the whole weird transaction?

My favorite writer of obese novels, Heimito von Doderer, may have stated the fly-fishing unstatable when he said, "All joy is idiot joy." I step into the Bitterroot alone, winter still filling its waters, still aching my bones. But once the idiot joy of sunlight on river becomes the idiot joy of stream-born insects becomes the idiot joy of foraging fish becomes the idiot joy of the water-parsing fisher—once a trout's *prana,* fear, and willpower comes crashing up the line into my hands—where has my aloneness gone? Fly fishing as we nonhunting nongathering catch-and-release nerds practice it isn't even fishing, really. It links us not to the Food Chain but to the Idiot Joy Chain, which differs from a Food Chain in that it has no top or bottom. Rod in hand on the Idiot Joy Chain, I find myself no more worthy or wise or deserving or in touch with IQ points than the stone-, water-, insect-, fish-, and sunlight-links of the same Chain. And that's exactly what I love about it! I don't fish in order to sit atop some predatory or evolutionary hierarchy. I fish to hook into an *entirety.* I fish to trade self-consciousness for creek-consciousness and self-awareness for rise-awareness. I fish to don dumb-looking but functional waterproof togs and even dumber-looking but functional facial expressions. I fish to share the predatory focus of mink and heron, and to adopt contorted postures as fish-obsessed, and to chitter and honk self-admonitions as blood-simple, as mink's and heron's. I fish in order to feel the great verb Gravity and its sidekick, Sun, filch snow from every sloping square inch of continent and send it oceanward around my legs. I fish in fall to feel the slow tilt of planet and weakening solar rays abandon every waterbug, wild-flower, mating dance, and tree-leaf summer gave us. I fish in spring to feel the same planetary tilt resurrect every creature and joy that autumn killed. I fish to grow as water-witted, sun-dazzled, and implacable as the river itself. I fish to let she or he who is without sin among us cast the first fly, knowing that, in the throes of idiot joy, every one of us is sinless, and worthy of that cast.

I'm back at my desk today, "working," as we say—as if what fly fishers do for fun were not the whole planet working perfectly. It's cold again this forenoon, after yesterday's hint of insect-generating heat. But thanks to a tapered tube of graphite, a steel-hooked, man-made lie, and two bronze-sided, water-breathing shadows, my whole chair-bound body yearns—no more intelligently and no less completely than every unbudded leaf, unarrived bird, and unborn mayfly and stonefly—for the whole sodden planet to keep tilting and solar rays to keep intensifying, that I may wake again to the life-making waters, and the next moment's idiot joy.

16. In Praise of No Guide

My reservations about the average fly-fishing guide are a lot like my reservations about the average spiritual guru. Both can be highly entertaining. Both can also be any of several types of idiot. Both usually charge for their services in either case. Why risk rewarding idiocy in hope of a little guidance?

The majority of Western fly-fishing guides tend to be the sort of folks you meet in the cheap seats at professional sporting events—the sort of decent, working-class personages who call a beer a "brewski," a nymph a "nimp," a lost fish a "long-range release," and a minor flesh wound a "Hertz Donut." That I abhor the riverside company of these perfectly amiable souls might seem snobbish. But a river, when one is fly-fishing, is like a symphony: you need your full concentration to make sense of the thing. Is it snobbery when attending the symphony not to want to sit beside some bloke, however likable, who natters on throughout the performance about their favorite brewski brands, deadliest nimps, and most hilarious Hertz Donuts?

Fly fishing at its best is an unmediated, one-on-one music played by a body of flesh and blood upon a body of water: it is a satisfying duet, till a fish makes it an even more satisfying trio. The average guide renders duet and trio inaudible. The average guide is a Top Forty disc jockey who dictates the day's music. The average guide mediates so relentlessly between you and your fishing that it feels as if you and the river are divorcing and trying to split up the property. The average guide plants an invisible ego-flag on every fish you catch, as if he were a mountaineer, the fish were the summit, and your stupidity were Mount Everest.

Annoying? You bet. But, hey, guides don't just annoy you: they *charge* you for it! All that Guidely Knowledge and gear lead in lawyerly fashion to a substantial transfer of funds in your disfavor.

Of course, your guide, like your lawyer, can give you hundreds of scary reasons to make this transfer: you don't know the river and he does; you'll get skunked and he won't; you'll drown if he doesn't float you, starve if he doesn't feed you, get poison-oaked, snakebit, bum-fupped, predated, and vulched if he doesn't protect you. These are remote possibilities. Far, far less remote is the possibility that at day's end you'll be handing your guide three hundred bucks, shaking his hand, and biting your tongue as you fight the urge to say, "Thanks that the insects you said wouldn't bite did, while the fish you said would, didn't. And thanks, twenty-eight times in a row, for identifying the upcoming stretch of river as 'a sexy hole.' Thanks, too, when I asked about food for the day, for saying, 'Don't worry. The grub and brewskies are on me.' I've never lived for sixteen hours on Busy Bucko Crackers, ARCO Brand Chip Dip, and Moose Drizzle Stout before. The great thing is, when I get home and take off my waders, I'll still have aromas to remember you by."

I qualify all of the above with the modifier "average." There are better-than-average guides. There are *way* better-than-average guides. There are gourmet scholar/artists of the river whose lives I respect, whose intelligences I envy, whose senses of humor create a market for Kleenex, and whose company I cherish. But I still reject the basic service. The unavoidable problem is this:

Fly-fishing guides accept payment in order to help clients circumvent their ignorance. *But ignorance is one of the most crucial pieces of equipment any fly fisher will ever own.* Ignorance is a fertile but unplanted interior field. Solitary fly fishing isolates us in this field, and leaves us no choice but to try to cultivate and plant and grow things in it. A guide, on the other hand, is like a hired farmer who, for a price, drives his tractor into your interior and plants your field for you. When the two of you are finished, *he* may know what's growing inside you. But *you* sure as hell won't. Fly-fishing guides turn clients into the absentee landlords of their own interiors.

I do not say *never hire a guide*. Some rivers are rough, and require pros at the oars for whitewater survival. Some locations are remote, and require pros to pack you in and out. Some clients are so perniciously loaded they have nothing less destructive to do with their fortune than throw chunks of it at nimp and Hertz Donut specialists. And a rare few guides are bon vivants, fly-rod geniuses, or euphonious bawds whose company is treasure.

What I do say is this: Every summer and fall, on hundreds of quiet, user-friendly Western rivers, millions of fly-strafed trout spend the day cowering beneath flotillas of identically hot, claustrophobic craft rowed by battalions of identically unneeded guides for the simple reason that Americans have been taught not by common sense, but by advertising, that guides are indispensible. Ads once said the same of beaver hats.

Before hiring your next indispensible guide, ask yourself this: How many *guides* shell out for an "indispensible guide" when they go fishing? The zero that answers this question is the truly indispensible fly-fishing advice. Any self-respecting guide is exactly as likely to hire another guide to take him fishing as a self-respecting groom is likely to hire a horny pal to help him jump his beautiful bride's bones on his wedding night. To fly fishers everywhere, I say: *Steal this knowledge!* The guide's lack of guide while fishing is the greatest lesson most guides have to teach!

Consider the osprey, the heron, the kingfisher. How much verbiage and instruction do these fish-catching geniuses bestow upon their unschooled young? *None.* These prodigies pass on the primordial art by feeding their young vomited-up trout, which naturally makes the young yearn for nonvomited trout, which in turn makes the young sit up in the nest and observe their folks more and more closely, till it hits them: *Eureka! I don't have to squat in this shithole eating puked-up fish all day! Look at Mom and Dad out there catching fish! Look at my wings, my beak, my talons! I've got everything they've got! What the hell have I been thinking? I CAN GO FISHING MYSELF!*

Anglers! Look at your guides on their days off, unguidedly catching fish after fish! Look at your legs, your arms, your rod! Feel the heft and synaptic whir of your big cerebrum! You've got everything they've got! *What the hell have you been thinking? GO FISHING YOURSELF!* We are a nation plagued with self-annointed experts, pundits, middle-persons. Away with them! Dare to be the bumbling hero of your very own fish story! Chop your psyche in half, make a guru/disciple relationship out of it, seat your humble self at the feet of your sagacious self. Read like a fiend; practice like a fool; find the best possible river on the best possible map; read about it; explore it; stick your body in it; cast into it. If you fall in, get out. If you hook yourself, unhook yourself. Make mistakes! It doesn't matter! Make a half-drowned, half-thrashed rat of yourself. Forgive yourself. Regroup. Do it all over again. And at the end of the day, *pay yourself.* Charge an arm and a leg. Leave yourself huge tips. Remarkably painless, isn't it?

Anyone who teaches that solo experience is not the best teacher is not the best teacher. Solo experience now and then teaches the hard way, but the hard way is the unforgettable way. The moment you're capable of finding water without drowning and of making twenty-foot casts, trust your primordial instincts, your fertile interior, the wisdom of ospreys, herons, and kingfishers, and good company of rivers—and go catch a beautiful fish *all by yourself!*

17. Estuary from an Afterlife

Fishing Log Entry/Montana/ Oct. 15

Casey stops by after work, takes an evening look at what October's doing to the world, says, *How can we go to work tomorrow in this?*

I say, *Who said anything about work?*

So we set alarms for four, drive the two-hour distance and the eight thousand feet up, hike the eight miles in, and find snow falling through sunlight, elk bugling in lodgepole, and cranes, sandhills, singing even more strangely than the elk; find thirty-mile-an-hour cloud-shadows screaming across mile-wide meadows, Indian summer grasses billowing like squash-colored ocean swells, huge fronts swallowing then disgorging the Rockies, sunlight exploding through granite teeth and cumulonimbi, silver rays, gold rays, rainbow rays, every time we glance up a whole new Second Coming till we're overdosing on glory, might drown in the stuff, if our brainless, last-second-kitchen-raid breakfast (day-old shishkabobs/green bananas/gorp) didn't anchor us by the stomachache to what we came for.

Like an estuary, this little river. Eight hundred miles inland, a mile and a half high, yet so like a North Coast coho stream winding through salt marsh that all day I hear distant surf. It even has the shorebirds: sandpipers, and a big lone yellowlegs. And who needs the salmon when we both instantly hook rainbows so brilliant-sided, so crazed in battle, that it's sad to admit they smacked a bottom-crawling, man-made something called a "Woolly Bugger"? Too cold for flying insects and dry flies, though, and too much fun to get more "aesthetical" about things, so we keep dredging up rainbows till we're ashamed of ourselves, then find a hot spring, tiny but piping, and coax blood back into feet and fingers the wintry wind and greed have numbed.

Warm again, we split up, Casey to keep dredging, but I switch to dries despite the cold, "just to watch something float," I tell myself, "just to rest a bit," I lie. "Need a break, all those big 'bows." Right. But I sure enough catch nothing. Stay stubborn. Catch more nothing. Then, way downstream, see a rise so substantial I mark the spot, sit down, and rethink what fly. When you've not seen an insect all day and impending winter wind gusts keep turning the river to chain mail, though, thinking doesn't help. Stumped, I find myself mesmerized by the wind-whipped, fire-colored grasses, then remember the grasshoppers that froze out two weeks ago, and think: *Trout have memories, same as me. And maybe the same nostalgia for summer afternoons. Maybe even the same Ant-and-the-Grasshopper Aesop Fable-hate . . .*

So I tie on my favorite late-season, Aesop-defying hopper (yellow-legged, in honor of the bird I keep seeing) and slough it down toward the rise (careful), down (getting close), give the legs a jiggle*ERUPTION-uptionuption!*salmon-sizedtrout!chest-high leaps!hundred-yard run!smoking reel!*NOOOOOO!*

Yep. It's all over in ten seconds: a cartwheel so centrifugal I'd better spell it 'riftugcenal' throws the fly, dooms me to replay the leap all winter . . .

So let's take a rest, dang it. Enough *fishin'*, ding darn it. Over-priced stick with an idiot on the end. "Just breathe and walk a while," I tell myself. "Look around, leave the river. Here. This trickle: baby spring creek, too small for fish. Check it out . . ."

I follow the rivulet up through crimson-stalked willows, not a thought in my head except, *To hell with trout, let's take a walk.* Damn, though! Even without leaves, what a jungle. Starts giving me 'Nam flashbacks even though I dodged the draft. Then there's light up ahead, an opening—huh? Big spring-fed pond! Midges hatching! Audibly slurping trout everywhere!

How soon we remember what we vow to forget! I tie on a Griffith's gnat, ease into the shallows, make a rollcast, *bam!* instant fish. Nice leaps, scrappy battle. Fourteen-inch 'bow. I land it, release it, cast again, *bam!* This one fourteen, too. *What else you got, pond?*

I forget to rollcast, snap off the gnat in the willows, tie on a ridiculously Christmassy #14 Royal Wulf, rollcast, *bam!* Déjà vu: fourteen inches. Nice. Scrappy. Three for three. But almost too good to be true. Suspicious now, I try a #4 Stimulator that crashes into the pond like a kamikaze sparrow. *Bam!* Fourteen-incher. I start laughing, get selectively ridiculous, try a #2 Mickey Finn—with lots of sixties-vintage chrome—barracuda-stripped right across the surface . . . *Bam!* And fourteen again. I find myself recalling the famous Fishing Myth of the guy who dies, finds himself on a pond like this one, casts a fly, catches trout like these, decides he's in Heaven, high-fives himself, catches more, every one of them *nice, scrappy, fourteen inches.* Tries other flies. They all work. Tries a pine cone with a hook in it. Works. Tries a boot. No problem. Realizes oops! he's in Hell.

But hey. How often do I find myself standing in a real, live Famous Fishing Myth? Possibly even in Hell? I slop out the Mickey Finn, barracuda-strip it: *bam!* What a hellish nonsurprise: fourteen-incher. Scrappy. "Am I dead?" I ask myself. I don't sound like it. I tell myself the Myth is bullroar, tell myself this pond has bigger fare, tie on the biggest fly I own: a four-inch-long weighted sculpin. I wade into shore to move to an all-new pond quadrant—but suddenly find myself staring at moose tracks so huge I suddenly realize how tightly the willows hem me, how I can't see what might be coming from even ten feet away, how "bigger fare" could be smelling me, resenting me, loathing me this red-eyed, huge-racked, tiny-brained instant, its fury-snorts blown the opposite way on the wind.

Damn it, though. A trout on every cast, no sign of slowing, no moose trampling me yet, and you don't get up into places as Afterlife-like as this without being as stubborn as some kind of Immortal Being yourself. I cast the giant sculpin, strip it twice, three times, *bam!* But shit. Look at the poor fourteen-incher. Looks like a little naked me with no arms, trying to swim with a baseball bat in my mouth. Sliding it ashore, I stoop to release it, vow to vacate Hell, then notice my Neoprened knees straddling moose-sized but far fresher *grizzly tracks.* My ears turn into satellite dishes. Dread grabs my nervous system by the scruff of its *nice, scrappy* neck. I feel the light snack I prefer to call "my legs" break into the most involuntary rodent-scurry I've ever scurried back through willows, down the tiny trickle, through the 'Nam flashbacks, out into the great wide open,

where I'm so relieved to spot Casey half a mile downstream that I hike the whole way just to watch the sick man Woolly Bugger another 'bow.

We share the last kabob to freshen up the stomachaches, tell some necessarily tall tales, split up for a final hopefully huge fish, and agree to holler and convene when one of us hooks it—for Casey's one-a-day photo op (one past my personal limit).

But the gods of photography, like Jesus, love their enemies: I haven't walked fifty yards before I find a hotspring-warmed tributary I dub Conveyor Creek for the way it's shunting fat, out-of-season mayflies into a slow, foam-topped river eddy, on top of which a pod of corpulent trout audibly grunt, slurp, and wallow.

I flip open my prayer box, match the hatch, drop to my knees, and approach the foam nebula with the caution of, I don't know, Mary Tyler Moore crawling across a floor covered with thousands of baby gerbils. I check the backbrush, manage a cast, watch my fly alight among the wallowing, where it floats. And floats. Ten seconds. Thirty. Eighty. Then half-sinks and slides, still neglected, into a floating island of foam where I can no longer see it. Shit. And to retrieve it could spook the entire school . . .

As I lift my rod to try to ease the fly out of the foam, though, a snout as big as my own rises up through Foam Island, and I set the hook without even knowing the fish was there. The snout vanishes beneath the surface with surprising calm; sinks leadenly toward the bottom: I think, *What the hell?* Then a single small tremor starts up my rod. A split second later, Foam Island blows like St. Helens and a rainbow is pinwheeling in midair. The eddy's instantly thrashed: I doubt another trout will rise here this year. My trout tries balletic leaps, ballistic leaps, epileptic leaps, then heads downriver on a tear, me gasping after, another pinwheel! another! then off it goes into the backing, Casey acrossbank now, running, aiming, shooting, stealing my soul, but the trout's too, I pray, so we end up together in an Everafter that's not all scrappy fourteen-inchers.

Four pounds, it turns out. Not huge, but huge enough. Greenbacked; silver-sided; female; valentine pink in her 'bow. Best part of the whole deal the revival kneel: half my body and all of hers in the one cold current; her strength returning so soon; my hands so reluctantly opening; the galaxy of silvers/greens/black holes/pink melting so fast back into everything that made them.

More elk and crane songs on the long hike out, but we're out of even bad food, out of safe water, out of legs, words, daylight. And eight miles out after eight miles in aren't the same eight miles.

Yet the same pain that makes the hike purgatorial turns our ugly van into a grand hotel of comfort and a small-town shake, fries, and burger into the same hotel's *haut cuisine.* Then the bull moose the size of Butte on the road driving out; mama moose and calf right on the highway in the pass; the northern lights (due South, of course) and stars, some shooting, horizon to horizon; and the one small back-home bourbon, tasting completely superfluous, since all day we've been so drunk.

"Call me," I rasp at Casey, too tired to lift a ceramic cup the size of an eggshell, "the minute you remember the nothing we could possibly have done to deserve such a day."

"Hnnh?" Casey breathes, his closed eyes, his insides, still standing on a salt-marsh estuary eight miles of trail and eight thousand feet above the sea.

18. Fearless Leader

I recently—and, I believed, thoughtfully—mailed my long-time, incandescent, redheaded, red-tempered, six-foot-six-inch terror of a fishing partner, Jeremiah Ransom, five spools of Umpqua Feather Merchant's new fluorocarbon tippet material, in five thicknesses, in honor of Jeremiah's own assorted thicknesses and his fiftieth birthday. "A spool for each decade," I wrote on the card, honestly thinking that, half a century into his raging incarnation, Ransom might have grown well-done or tired or serene enough to simply accept the leader makings, use them, and possibly even thank me for them.

Even in my forties, how naïve I can be! A few days later I received my five spools back in the mail, along with this fascinating missive:

```
Fine Sir,

    Hell of a nice gift, insofar as the thought is what
counts. But as a huge fan of Homer, I can't help but recall
a certain horse once thoughtfully gifted to Trojans, which
beast convinced me that it is far less dangerous to give
```

than to receive. I therefore look all such horses in the mouth, hooves, legs, belly, front end, hind end, & Etc, returning any I don't fully come to trust.

Here's your Trojan Horse tippet material back at you. And here's why:

What I naturally recalled, upon receiving your "thoughtful" remembrance of my approaching dotage, was our four-day float down the Deschutes late last June, during which you remarked with surprise that my tippet brand was "still Maxima," not the supposedly stronger Umpqua Feather Merchant that you prefer. I'm sure you also recall our first evening, when you and your small nymphs and UFM took a dozen nice trout while my Maxima and dry flies and I caught two doinkers. But the following evening, as you perhaps less vividly recall, 'twas my Maximaed dries and I took the dozen comely fish while your UFMed nymphs caught the dreaded nada.

Since our respective tippet types finished in a dead heat, your attempt to change my brand is clearly not based upon result. What, then, *is* your motivation? I would describe it thus:

While fly fishers' vests are full of gadgets, and gadgets make innocent (if silly) gifts, everything the fisher holds in his casting hand—namely, reel, rod, fly line, tippet, and fly—is not gadgetry at all: it is an extension of the fly fisher himself. Hence when one fly fisher (you) mails his statistical equal (me) a new type of reel, rod, fly line, tippet, or fly, he is not engaged in innocent gifting: he is reaching deep and didactically into the other angler's <u>Weltanschauung</u> and trying, consciously or not, to alter it. And as you know, old friend, I resist alteration. Else why, after all these decades, would I still fish and fraternize with the numb-nutted likes of you?

Listen: I know it drives you men of pseudo-science crazy that after all these years of UFM's and Cortland's and Dairiki's and Rio's and Climax's and Superblica's and Orgasmica's and everybody else's higher-test, thinner-diameter, limper, prettier, UV-proofed, fluorocarbonated, vitaminized leader advances I'm still heaving the same old West German cable at them. But I've been hooked on Maxima since the day it came out. And the very attribute you scientists have lately decided to hate about it is the attribute I love: <u>its stiffness</u>. That's right, buddy: at bottom this is a dick thing. The shortest distance between two points—between Point Me and Point Trout, specifically—is, in a manner of speaking, the _stiffest_ distance. And with the exception of saltwater brands, Maxima is the great hard-on of trout tippet materials. Consider this, my fine Umpqua feathered friend. In matters of the member or tippet, do we really want _pretty_? Do we really want _thinner diameter_? Above all, do we really want _limp_!?

(You do, apparently. That's one reason I've returned your gift.)

I am not, by the by, one of these testes-brained squirt-and-salmo-enthusiasts who believes fly fishing is in any way comparable to recreational or procreational sex. In sex—to cite one irresolvable difference—I need sheath only one bizarre body part in the name of public and personal safety, whereas in cold trout streams, all but my arms and head must be prophylactically enclosed. Sex is also terrifying, repurcussion-wise, for those of us terrified of technology, hence of vasectomization, whereas I can fly-fish myself senseless for life, sheathed or unsheathed, and the only pregnancy that will result, the only gravid swelling, will be that of my fishing vest. I do not, in short, find the joys brought to us via tippet analogous to the joys brought via the Little Idiot of the Levi's. But tossing joy aside to cast an analytical eye on performance alone, there is a characteristic the two pieces of equipment unarguably share, namely: _the greater the stiffness_, _the greater the control_. And the average trout river, even you nymph-soakers must admit, is not so tidily tailored to a trouter as is a yoni to a pube.

A trout river is, face it, a multispeeded agglomeration of fly-dragging, fish-spooking swirls, crosscurrents, curlicues, vortices, upwellings, and downsuckings hellbent on deluding the eye, mesmerizing the mind, harpooning the ego, skunking the butt, and ravaging the fishermanly _joie de vivre_. It is _chaos_ out there, buddy. Is a "Spring Creek supple," limp-wristed, permissive fly leader the best way to impose order on this? As Lefty Kreh is my Ahab, I think not! The best way to countermand hydraulic vagaries, traverse the fluidic everywhichway, and pierce our shining quarry, is to send a stiff, one-pointed, utterly direct line harpooning through the devious wet!

Another brag used to peddle limp tippet materials is this

necromantic notion that one's leader should serve as a "shock absorber" when setting the steel to big fish. Quee-queg and me say bullroar. Shock absorbency is the _rod's_ job. The tippet's job, like the hook's, is to be _decisive_.

Yet another stiff tippet advantage: Say it's dusk on some great Montana or Idaho or Colorado river, July or August, five or six simultaneous cross-grained hatches going on, Caddis, May, Stone, emerging, spent, Horse, House, and every other kind of fly on the water, trout rising all around you reject-ing everything you try, you're switching patterns like crazy, the light is fading, and your eyes, if they're like mine, have imbibed decades of TV and UV, fine print and print-outs, campfire, tavern, diesel, and hookah smoke, sun and wind-burnished road and river glare, and are waning like the light. Yet every time you switch offerings, you face anew the optic ordeal of stabbing semi-invisible tippet at the semi-invisible eye of a semi-invisible goddang dry fly. What, in this situation, is your worst enemy? _Limpness_, of course. Same goes for tying blood or nail knots or jerry-rigging a slim fifteen-foot leader from your skunked nine-foot clunker. Stiff makings are the dusk-victim's and extend-it-your-selfer's and thick-fingered-fifty-year-old's best friend. And of the alternatives, only Maxima is a politically correct **GREEN**.

Please know, in closing, that I'm not saying my brand is best. One reason I return your gift is that I know you'll disagree, shoot holes in, and ignore my arguments, then deploy and enjoy this Umpqua stuff yourself. I'll even admit that limpness of leader may allow you limp-wristed _artiste_ types to go with some sort of numinous flow, result-ing in fish we thick-wristed, technologically retarded workin' stiffs merely prick, so to speak. I'm not foisting my logic on you. I'm just displaying it, since you've insulted it with a gift that implies it doesn't exist.

The Poet in me wishes Maxima did not sport the same name as an overpriced obsolete neo-Datsun, and the American Patriot in me wishes it was manufactured by neo-fascist pinheads in North Idaho instead of urbane entrepreneurs in West Deutschland. But as you know, THERE IS NO POET OR AMERICAN PATRIOT IN ME! I've taken six-pound steelhead and seven-pound trout on the 3-lb. green stuff, eight-pound bonefish, twenty-two-pound steelhead, and a thirty-eight-pound chinook on the 8-lb. stuff, twenty-inch 'bows and brownies on the 2-lb. stuff, and as every barroom halfwit in the West including me loves to declaim, "If it ain't broke, don't fix it."

Give me the stiff stuff or give me dearth!

But I do thank you kindly for remembering my born-date.

Yrs. as ever,

(signed)

Jeremiah

Worship God as though you see Him.

—Muhammad the Prophet

19. Khwaja Khadir

In the late 1990s, the editor of a renowned fishing magazine sent a letter asking me to pen a portrait of my favorite fly-fishing guide. This portrait was to take its place among "a celebrity compendium of great Western fly-fishing guides." A color photo of my guide was also requested.

I'm no celebrity and plan to keep it that way. But I do have a favorite guide—an exceedingly quiet fellow of mixed Middle Eastern extraction, named Khwaja Khadir. I wrote a glowing profile, then found a color photograph of a stretch of empty Montana trout water where Khadir has several times given me superb advice. Empty water was the best I could do, portrait-wise, since Khadir happens to be an Islamic immortal being precisely as photogenic as the Holy Ghost.

I mailed this package off to the magazine.

A week or so later the editor phoned. His first words—delivered in the for-some-reason ubiquitous drawl of fishing magazine editors—were, "Ah lahked your gahd po'truht veruh much."

(Pronunciation key: "Ah" = "I"; "gahd" = "guide.")

I replied, "That's okay. I didn't expect you to print it."

Since the editor had given no hint of rejection, yet rejection was indeed impending, he was flabbergasted by my "clairvoyance." But it was really just conditioned response. Years of interaction with magazine editors have taught me that the phrase "liked it very much" is as close as they'll come to saying, *I wouldn't print this cockamamie bullshit if it was the last skein of sentences on earth.* In fact, even the phrases "I *loved* it!" or "I've GOT to publish this!" don't mean your story will be published. And even signed contracts and publication don't mean you'll be paid. But I digress.

What the editor said next was, "Ah *loved* your strange po'trayal of fly fishin'. But Ah was troubled by your gahd concept, raht from the openin' lahn."

I said, "You mean the line 'For the past two and a half decades I have rarely gone fishing without my favorite guide, Khwaja Khadir, whose chief virtues are that, being silent and invisible, he is the closest thing on the river to no guide at all . . .'?"

"Preciseluh," the editor sighed. "How can Ah include, in mah pro-fawls of great fishin' gahds, a profawl that in effect tells us not to hahr gahds at all?"

"I didn't recommend hiring *no* guide," I argued. "I recommended hiring an *invisible* guide. Big difference."

"Not in your photograph of Mr. Khadir," the editor countered. "But now listen. Ah *do* love the fishin' part o' this. That's whaw Ah cawled. Ah'd like you to cut the refer'nces to invisible Arab fellas, bandage up the cuts, run the result by its lonesome. Ah'd pay twice what Ah could for your gahd po'trait."

"But I *wasn't* fishing alone," I said. "That's why the fishing was so good. What kind of thanks am I showing the best guide I ever met if I brag up my catch but don't mention he was guiding?"

The editor sighed again. Even *it* had a drawl. "Ah'm runnin' a *fishin'* magazine here, son. Evinrudes 'n' Eagle Claws. Hawgs 'n' crankbaits. Meet me halfway, is all Ah'm sayin'. Turn the woo-woo down a notch, you got yourself a payday."

"And a betrayed invisible fishing guide," I said. "Just toss my story, please. Don't feel bad."

"Big mistake, son," said the editor.

"Not my first," I replied.

"Ah won't forgive you," he warned, "till you send me a fishin' yarn as fahn as this one, woo-woo-free."

I said, "Compared to hawgs 'n' crankbaits, my whole life is woo-woo. 'Cept for maybe my mornin' dump."

The editor laughed. He signed off. He returned my "Great Western Guide Portrait," invisible guide intact.

Here it is:

For the past two and a half decades I have rarely gone fishing without my favorite guide, Khwaja Khadir, whose chief virtues are that, being silent and invisible, he is the closest thing on the river to no guide at all. I first learned of my guide not in a fly shop, or a fishing magazine, or by word of mouth, but in a collection of essays on ecstatic utterances of Sufi saints. Midway through this book, way back in the early seventies, I stumbled onto the Arabic word *al-Khizr.* I don't speak a speck of Arabic. I'd never seen this word before. When, at the sight of it, an unfounded thrill of recognition shot up my spine, I paid attention.

Investigating further, I learned from a scholarly friend that al-Khizr is a bodiless divine servant so close to Allah that to be accompanied by the former is to stand in the hidden presence of the Latter. I discovered that Khizr is both the guardian and purveyor of "the Waters of Eternity"—the caretaker/bartender, so to speak, of the elixir of secret knowledge and everlasting life. I learned that al-Khizr is also known as *Khidr,* the Green Prophet, Khwaja Khadir, and other aliases, and that he is as famed in the Islamic world as is the Holy Spirit in the Christian world for his omnipresence, perfect wisdom, and perfect invisibility.

In this age of global tyranny by short-term economic thought, Americans have developed a tendency to equate what is desirable with what is profitable, and what is invisible with what doesn't exist. My life-long fly-rod-in-the-office, wisdom-literature-in-the-fishing-vest habits have made me pretty un-American with regard to this tendency. I figure love is invisible. Intuition as well. Before I was born, I too was invisible, at least to the fellow I am now. When I die, I expect to become the same. To be repelled by invisibility is, then, to be repelled by love, intuition, and my former and future selves. I have, on the contrary, spent my life endeavoring to befriend that foursome. This effort has naturally included my fishing life. Upon learning a bit about the invisible al-Khizr, I did not therefore think, *Weird!* and go turn on *The Dave Show.* Instead, my thoughts ran more along these lines:

"*Invisibility . . . Omnipresence . . . Perfect Wisdom . . . Guardian of Eternity's waters . . . Holy shitwaw!* What incredible qualifications for a fishing guide!"

I then began trying to figure how to get this being on a river with me.

I didn't expect results. I didn't expect anything. I'm ignorant as mud in these matters. But I didn't rule out the possibility of contact, either. Fly fishing, successfully undertaken, builds enormous faith in the human ability to make contact with unseen beings. When you have repeatedly accomplished tasks as unlikely as slinging a size-22 dry fly on a 6X tippet toward a hidden aquatic being rising eighty feet away, only to hook, battle, and drag that being into your hands, you grow reluctant to say what is or isn't possible in terms of contacting things invisible—including even invisible fly-fishing guides.

I won't fib. The first time I hit a high desert river after learning of al-Khizr, I fished my predatory ass off for a day and a half, forgetting all about him. After deceiving, catching, and releasing a fair number of trout, though, my "predatory ass" was pretty near gone. I love this gradual transition from raging fish-lust to inner quiet. Brings to mind the t'ai chi sequence, "Embrace Tiger and Return to Mountain." Nothing strained or "spiritual" about it, really. Deploying ordinary perceptions and movement, normal whoops, curses, and obsession, you stalk and embrace tigerish fish and battle current, glare, brush, wind, and mystery, till your predatory energy begins to gutter out. Of course, we fanatics resist this guttering. But sooner or later even the fiercest fly fishers find their eyes staring without focusing, their mouths literally hanging open, and their brains gone silent, having printed out so much fishing data that their cartridges have temporarily run out of ink. I suddenly had no interest in making another cast. The fishing had gone dead anyway. Far better to bask my tired back in July sunlight, let the current lap against my legs, listen to the call of the canyon wren.

A magpie wandered idly across the river. A blissful, no-reason chill wandered idly up my spine. I thought of the Rumi line, *Love has taken away my practices . . .* I thought of the John Coltrane line, *God breathes through us so gently, so completely, we hardly feel it . . .* And suddenly I was gasping with gratitude for every last thing I could feel, smell, intuit, touch, or see. High desert all around. Fragrance of sage, fragrance of juniper, fragrance of water. Still nothing out of the ordinary here. During the "Return to Mountain" phase, no-reason detonations of this sort greet the devotees of every nonmotorized outdoor sport there is. Typically, though, we greet such visitations with our Throwaway Consumer reflexes: *Wow! What a feeling! But now it's fading. Oh well. Good-bye . . .*

When this particular chill struck, however, I did not say good-bye. Instead, unaccountably, I whispered: *"Khizr?"*

And just that fast: a bolt of yearning pierced me.

"Is this really you?" I asked the air.

And something about the light over the rimrock, heat waves over the road, emptiness of canyon, smell of the desert river, left me feeling the answer was, most emphatically, *Yes.*

I don't know what got into me then, but I began speaking to the empty canyon, the yearning, the air, as if to a friend. What's more, I imagined this friend to be the mysterious Arabic being of whom I'd read, and referred to it as such, by name.

I don't recall my exact words, but I remember their basic trajectory. I told Khwaja that since he is all-wise, he already knew I loved rivers and fly fishing: loved them like a sickness; loved them the way some scruffy Druid might once have loved his god. I then surmised—aloud, to keep it physical and official—that as the eternal guardian of waters, Khadir might be as fascinated by fly fishing as I am, yet might also be unable to try it, despite his great powers, for simple lack of a physical body, a fly rod, physical flies. I then informed the immortal Green Prophet that, if he liked, he was welcome to borrow *my* crummy body, rod, and flies, and go fishing with that.

Boy, did my mind kick up a fuss at this proposal! *You imbecile! Al-Khizr is an Islamic divine mystery! An intimate of Prophets and ecstatic sages. Whereas you are a dopey American fly flinger. Why would the Green One ever want to borrow you!?*

I understood my mind's position. Even in those days, though, I'd read too much wisdom literature to take that kind of shit from the hired help. "If I'm just a dopey American fly flinger," I fired back, "then *you're* just that dopey fly flinger's *mind!* So shut up. I'm talking to al-Khizr here . . .

"Khwaja, ignore that jerk. I know I'm in many ways unworthy. But I also know that Prophets and ecstatic sages—the ones I've read about anyway—don't fly-fish a lick. Whereas I do. So if you're curious to try it, my offer stands . . ."

I stood quietly for a while then, out in midriver, waiting to be "borrowed" or some such thing. But nothing happened. And my mind of course assured me that Whoever or Whatever I'd spoken to hadn't been there in the first place.

A few minutes after issuing my invitation, though, I felt a purposeless urge to leave the glide I'd been fishing and hike, despite the heat, to a fierce, boulder-strewn rapid a mile or so downstream. And upon reaching that rapid, I felt a second urge—as strong, clear, and utterly absurd as any in my previous fishing existence—to grease up an extremely large Dave's Hopper with floatant, cast it into the whitewater, hold my rod straight up over my head as high as I could reach, and skitter the 'hopper back upriver against the ripping current, as if in imitation of a depraved, six-legged water-skier. This strategy duplicated no insect behavior or fishing trick I'd ever heard of or seen. And I immediately hooked, and much much later landed, one of the most beautiful twenty-inch rainbow trout I've ever met. What's more, I felt a joy in the take, the blazing runs, the enveloping sunlight and spray around the leaps, fragrance of sage, roar of water—greater than any I'd felt over the day and a half previous. Which led to a second spontaneous outburst:

"Jeez, Khwaja!" I exclaimed as the green-backed trout left my hands and shot back into green depths. *"Nice!"*

That was the first encounter. And scoffers and doubters, please, *do* scoff and doubt: I'm not selling anything. I just feel compelled, in response to this whole difficult topic of fishing guides, to say that the being I've just so bumblingly described is mine.

I issued that first invitation to al-Khizr some twenty-five years ago. I've continued to issue invitations ever since. I have yet to receive an audible reply. If things do get audible, I'll make an immediate appointment with the best available shrink. What I *have* received in "reply," though—beginning that first day—is an occasional post-invitation urge as palpable yet indescribable as river speech, usually involving some very specific, hitherto-unthought-of fly-fishing strategy. These strategems are often so bizarre that my mind gets highly exercised about their inanity, and even my body feels idiotic if I obey them within sight of other fly fishers. But I *do* obey them. By paying careful heed to all such impulses year in and year out, I have ended up fishing in some exceedingly odd places, using some exceedingly odd techniques—and in so doing have caught way more than my share of exceedingly unlikely and magnificent fish. So go figure.

A number of people who've glimpsed these bizarre impulses and their often ludicrously good results have declared me a "fly-fishing genius." But to accept that compliment feels dishonest to me. The genius, in my experience, is Khwaja.

So here's all the info I have on how to hire him:

Khadir's address, ecstatic poets and Sufi scholars agree, is "the cusp between the Unseen and the Seen." Since there is no way to phone, write, or E-mail this cusp, the sole method of contacting my guide is via direct belief. While Muslim mystics, for centuries, have had little trouble with this, American anglers often find it a stumbling block. If you're the type who needs references, you might like to know Khadir was an intimate of the Prophet Muhummad, that he also served (according to Sufi tradition) as guide to Moses, and that he has been written of glowingly by some of the greatest poets on earth—Rumi, Hafiz, Ibn al-Arabi, Ruzbihan Baqli, and al-Bistami, to name a few.

If and when you meet the Green One, you'll notice he is way more invisible than green, that he speaks a language comprehensible to you almost solely in solitude, and that this language is inaudible even then. His skills, though, make up for his marked resemblance to thin air. Confining myself to just four:

1. Khizr has been on the job for all eternity—which is longer, if you think about it, than all mortal fly-fishing guides put together. That's *experience!*

2. Because he's invisible, he has never spooked a fish—*ever!*

3. Through his omnipresence, intimacy with Allah, and knowledge of waters, Khadir knows where *every single fish on Earth* dwells, knows in advance whether you're going to catch it, knows (karmically speaking) whether you *should* catch it, knows who you and the fish were before you were born, who you'll become after you die, who creates and sustains you, the meaning and purpose of life, how it all comes out in the wash. And so on. Despite the subtlety of Khwaja's presence and guiding style, this kind of know-how makes for reassuring company. And,

4. if, like Muhammad the Prophet, "poverty is your pride," you just can't beat Khadir's invisible rates.

I took a trip with the Green One, just the other day, which nicely illustrated some of his guiding techniques.

Our joint adventure began with me in my Montana study, feeling too restless and word-jaded, at the end of a three-week work binge, to cloister myself on another beautiful July morn. Knocking on the door between the Unseen and the Seen, I remarked to Khadir that I'd heard a seven-syllable rumor concerning a creek not terribly far from my study, and wondered whether this rumor was worth pursuing. I then dangled the syllables before him:

"Big Cutthroats in Small Water . . ."

My guide responded with the usual silence—and he is not just poker-faced, he is no-faced: his position proved, as always, very tough to gauge.

I mentioned that if we left at once I had the time, and would be willing to pay the physical price, to check the seven-syllable rumor out. Khadir showed no interest in this "physical price." Lacking a body, what is physical effort or suffering to him? I feel, though, that if we mortals are to relate to Khizr's undying bodilessness, he in return should relate to our doomed physicality. So I described my impending ordeal: "Ninety-degree heat. Seven miles in, seven miles out. Two thousand feet up, two thousand down. Only today to do the hike *and* the fishing. By sundown you can watch me really hurt, if that turns you on at all. And—thanks to your silence—no guarantee that the rumor is even true. Sound like fun?"

He remained inaudible and imperceptible. Beyond imagination and conception, too. But in all the years I've known him, Khwaja has not, to my knowledge, refused an invitation to go fishing yet.

We were in my old Toyota in minutes, my companion withholding comment on the Richard Thompson tapes I blared all the way to the trailhead. We then hiked the seven miles in and two thousand feet up, me sweating, panting, and working like a pig, dog, and mule, respectively; Khwaja as invisible, sweatless, and tireless as ever.

Deep in wilderness, we reached the creek of rumor. Completely new water to me, running cold and as clear as air. Completely familiar water to Khwaja, he being who he is. I began trying to read the situation. It was a small stream, eight to ten feet wide and only a foot deep, most places. A lot of velocity, but no depth. Far from my idea of good trout water. "Khwaja?" I whispered, beginning to doubt the seven-syllable rumor. "A little help here?"

But straightforward Q-and-A is just not the way he works. Khwaja guides when he wants to, not when I ask him to. That's one of the things I've grudgingly grown to respect about him. William Blake called the intuition "Christ," and worshiped it as such. Khadir's guiding style leaves one little choice, while fishing, but to grow increasingly well acquainted with Blake's Christ.

By a tiny, sunlit pool on a side-channel of the creek, I rested from the hike, rigged my rod, traded hiking boots for wading sandals, and meanwhile studied the insect life over the pool. By the time I'd geared up, I'd seen golden stoneflies, three hues of mayfly, two kinds of caddis, and a random smattering of midges and duns. But no species dominated. And Khwaja kept his own council. I decided not to choose a fly till I found fishable water.

We began hiking upstream, Khadir flying or emanating or whatever the heck he does, me splashing right up the creek to avoid impenetrable thickets on both banks. The stream veered up a majestic, granite-sided valley choked with wildflowers, streamside willows, and stands of stately tamarack. The initial shallow run turned out to be characteristic, and I definitely felt disappointment over that. When al-Khizr's with me, though, I get almost as stubborn as the forces that create creeks and depth, and keep seeking the kind of water I long for, scarcely caring whether I ever find it.

Tiny sandbars formed in the creek each time it changed direction. I noticed elk tracks, beaver tracks, black bear and deer tracks on each of these bars. "No griz or moose tracks," I remarked loudly, to reassure myself—though either could have lurked around any bend. Khadir, being fleshless, could have cared less.

A solitary sandpiper began flitting from sandbar to sandbar just upstream of me, singing a song that sounded as if he hated to complain, but, well, these mountain-creek sandbars sure were tiny, and it was embarrassing to admit this but, dang it, it was true, he *had* managed to lose track of the entire Pacific Ocean and was beginning to really pine for its far more satisfactory sandbars. So would I mind directing him?

Over the rush of the water I hollered, "West!" pointing with my flyrod.

Beeping twice in thanks, the sandpiper shot away.

At last we reached promising water: a long run, four feet or more deep, with overhanging willows and broken boulders for cover. The creek's clarity was amazing. The stones submerged by four feet of water were swirlier-looking, but no less perfectly visible, than the stones lying on dry land. The run appeared fishless, but no trout are better camouflaged than West Slope cutthroats, so I treated the water with respect.

Kneeling in the downstream tail-out, I again tried to get analytical about choice of fly, but now the only visible insects in air or water

Khwaja Khadir

seemed to be a jillion of those tiny, sunlit, mote-sized buglets, which, if you focus your eyes one way, are all flying from left to right over the stream's surface, and if you focus another way are flying right to left.

To my surprise, Khadir suddenly gave me to know—via a wave of goosebumps and a sudden urge to laugh—that he cherished these little guys. His first communiqué of the day, as unpredictable in content as ever.

"Bug-love?" I teased. "From the Primordial Keeper of Eternity's Fountain? How long do these wee buggers live? Half an hour?"

Look at them, I felt Khwaja urge. So I did—and at second glance began to get the picture: if the ethereal al-Khizr were ever to sire any-thing so earthly and tangible as children, these deft, silent, near-invisible zippers might be just what they'd look like. For all I knew, they *were* his kids, and all lived as long as he.

The only other animate life-form was a magnificent six-point whitetail, maybe eighty yards upstream, drinking from the center of the creek. Big bucks are usually the wariest of deer, but this fellow, after one brief glance, decided my fly rod and I were no threat and bent back to the water. "You can tell it's Montana," I remarked to Khadir. "Even the deer are serious drinkers."

No response. My guide does not, I fear, have a sense of humor about drink. Could be the bartending job at the Fountain. Could be an Islamic thing.

Having failed to spot a dominant insect, I tied on a prospecting favorite: a dry fly called a Stimulator. I then crouched down and tip-toed to the base of the run, made a long cast, dropped the fly in the belly of the best water, and waited.

Nothing. And still no advice from my all-knowing guide. I made four more casts. More nothing. Sitting on a rock to reassess, I noticed the buck, after all this time, was *still* drinking, realized he must not be drinking at all, noticed the tasty-looking cresses growing atop every rock including the one beneath me, and saw that the buck was in fact after these.

I changed fishing strategies, dead-drifting a Hare's Ear nymph through the depths of the run. Four times, eight times. Hooked the same nothing. Tried a black Woolly Bugger. More nothing. Added leechlike twitches. Zilch. Tying on another prospecting pattern—a mayflyish invention called a Crippled Emerger this time—I said, "That's it for this spot. Let's head upstream."

Khwaja didn't say boo to this plan. But the browsing buck was so beautiful up there in mid-creek that I wanted to delay the moment I scared him away. So I fetched the water bottle from my pack and took a long drink. The buck watched me, then drank too. I browsed on fig bars. The buck browsed cresses. I took a leak in the creek. So did the buck. Figuring male bonding had reached its zenith, I said, "Here I come, big fella," then started upstream.

False-casting as I strolled, I planned to throw my fly into the uppermost tip of the run I'd just fished. But this riffle-tip, I saw as I neared it, was so shallow and brightly sunlit that I could make out every drowned twig and pebble on the bottom. Obviously fishless. I reeled in my line, intending to splash on past, when something stopped me cold . . .

This was the quintessential Khadir moment, so I'll get as technical as I can: first, it was actually *nothing* that stopped me. But when fishing with Khwaja, one learns to trust certain nothings—certain no-reason starts or stops. What froze me in my tracks this time was an urge to show the barren tip-riffle the same fly-fisherly respect I'd just shown the promising run. Why? There *was* no why. It was naked impulse. Apart from the no-reason chills, naked impulse is the most reliable sign I know that Khadir is transmitting.

The next task, I've learned from long experience, is unquestioning obedience to the urge, even in defiance of reason. My eyes clearly saw the tip-riffle to be as troutless as a city sidewalk. Khadir, it seemed, saw otherwise. *Don't be ridiculous!* huffed my mind. But as Khwaja and I both know, my mind is not my identity, *noumenon,* spirit, *atma, dharma,* soul, *buddhi, anam, nous,* or fishing guide. So fuck it. I proceeded to behave as if the "sidewalk" held the fish of my dreams.

Dropping to my knees to lower my silhouette, I inched silently into casting position, stripped enough line from my reel to preclude the need for fish-spooking false-casts, took another glance at the cress-eating buck, then tried to mimic his calm as I made—with a single stroke of the rod—the lightest possible cast up into the riffle-tip. My fly alit on clear-as-air water not ten inches deep. It had floated a yard or so back toward me when one of the big, canteloupe-colored stones so plainly visible on the bottom turned its entire upstream edge into an enormous white mouth. This mouth gaped clear out of the water, engulfing my fly and a fair fraction of stream with it. I lifted my rod in reply. An animal so huge and strong that I could not believe in its existence began to shake its head, equally unable to believe in me. But the rod throbbed hard. The hook burrowed. Conversion was simultaneous for us both.

The trout shot straight toward me, forcing me to stand, run backwards, and strip line madly, to keep things taut. It then writhed around the far side of a midstream boulder, forcing me to pay out line, dash out into the creek, unlasso the rock. The rest of our combat was comparatively uneventful, if ten or so minutes of pure wonder can be considered an unevent. The huge, glowing, green-gold trout ripped tirelessly up and down the identically green-gold and glowing pool. The cress-eating buck watched us both. As the trout finally drew close, its thrashing body was so big it created wakes. When these wakes hit my legs, no-reason chills rose at the feel of the lapping. Desperate for cover, the big fish finally sought it in my shadow, hovering long, by choice, between my knees. The buck watched. Khwaja's tiny insects moved left to right and right to left in sunlight. Fragrance of pine. Fragrance of wilderness. So many intimacies. For a time, I couldn't move. Then the seven-syllable rumor—*Big Cutthroat in Small Water*—entered my hands: the largest West Slope I've ever seen: a female as beautifully plotted, thick through, and long in the making as a thousand-page novel.

I knew, as I held her, that I'd encountered her solely because of an "irrational impulse" to fish empty sidewalk. But when such urges lead you year after year to fish after fish, how rational is it to keep calling your impulses "irrational"? I'm just a fisherman. As such, I prefer, to any form of reasoning, the catching of even the most unreasonable of fish. I therefore expressed, upon releasing this one, my sincerest gratitude to the unreasonable cause of its capture:

"*Geez*, Khwaja!" I gasped. "*Thanks!*"

The Green One, once he finally starts transmitting, is often surprisingly slow to stop: the way that beautifully plotted West Slope, upon release, did not so much swim as *dissolve* back into the elements that created her; the way her dissolution then made every sunlit, seemingly barren inch of clear-as-air creek feel rife with invisible life; the way this rifeness then filled the clear-as-creek July sky with intimations of life unseen and the no-reason chills smacked me in a wave and my identity swamped and capsized, leaving just enough residue to work a fly rod and forget how to work a pronoun as not-I and I wandered the cusp between inner and outer creeks and granite ridges, inner and outer aspen groves and sun-flares, paintbrush and bear-sign, tamarack, trout-rise and pine, overwhelmed and grateful for the whole fragrant, lit-from-within confusion—all of this, I believe, came of the guidance of the one I call Khwaja.

And not-He and He and not-I and I landed four more West Slopes. All of them preposterously large for that tiny creek. All invisible in the beginning; green, gold, and glorious in the end. All somehow hidden in the same sort of "barren" tip-riffles, so that for the duration of the day our eyes were fed the sight of stones suddenly possessed of fish-mouths, of seens possessed of unseens, of paradigmatic beauties possessed of invisibility, then strength, then form and colors too lovely to do anything but touch, thank, and let go.

The seven miles out sure as shit hurt.

My guide sure as shit didn't give an Arabic hoot.

But after five fish like those, even that braying donkey, my body, had grown soulful enough that a feared inferno never became more than brief purgatory.

We reached my old truck. I paid up with the usual syllables:

"Geez, Khwaja! Beats church! *Thanks!*"

That was it—the whole guide/client transaction.

"Lovers," **said Jalal** al-Din Rumi, "don't finally meet somewhere. They're in each other all along." Maybe that's why the best guide I know isn't visible: he's not external.

The mind stills says, *Did anything really happen? Is anyone but me really there?*

The mind will say this forever. But I mostly fish rivers these days. In so doing, movement becomes stasis, flux is the constant, and *every-thing* flows around, through, and beyond me, escaping ungrasped, unnamed, and unscathed. The river's clean escape does not prevent belief in its reality. On the contrary, there is nothing I love more than the feel of a wholeness sliding toward, around, and past me while I stand like an idiot savant in its midst, focusing on tiny, idiot-savantic bits of what is so beautiful to me, and so close, yet so wondrously ungraspable.

And I said to my heart, there
are limits to you, my heart. . . .
Fish are beyond me.
Other gods
Beyond my range . . .
gods beyond my God.

—D. H. Lawrence

He who thinks this self is a killer and
he who thinks it is killed is deluded. . . .
The soul is not born, it does not die;
having been, it will never not be; unborn,
enduring, constant, primordial, it is not
killed when the body is killed. . . . Weapons
do not cut it, fire does not burn it, waters
do not wet it, wind does not wither it. . . .

—Krishna, in the *Bhagavad Gita*

The Great One, coming up against the current,
    begins thinking of it.
The Great One, coming, putting gravel in his mouth,
    thinks of it.
You look at it with white stone eyes—
The Great One, charging upriver,
    becomes it. . . .

—Haida incantation

20. god

Introduction to a Dream

A summer ago—while researching the plight of salmon for the essay earlier in this book—I was visited by a dream from which I woke overwhelmed and gasping. I have not seen the world in quite the same way since. Though my dream was about a trout, not a salmon, and though everyone to whom I've told it has had a different interpretation, all of them insightful, for me the meaning was never in question: whether I can convey it or not, I woke from this dream flooded by the feeling that a so-called "species"—such as the coho, sockeye, steelhead, chinook—is a gift created in an unending Beginning, and a product less of evolution or natural selection than of unconditional love; I woke convinced that all such species constitute a life-creating force that extends divine generosity to the world as sunbeams create life by extending to us the sun; I woke convinced that these primordial populations of fish bear greater resemblance to what we envision when we hear the words "angel" or "god" than to what we imagine in hearing the embattled term "endangered species"; I woke feeling that to cause the extinction of such beings—as America is now doing under federal mandate—is an act not just of biocide, but of spiritual suicide.

Strange to say, I woke from the same dream with a kind of heightened calm that has guided my salmon work ever since, and even consoles me a little as salmon populations continue to crash. There are beings born of energies that neither industrial folly, nor my own, can harm.

In the dream, I am standing waist-deep in Flathead Lake—the largest freshwater body west of the Mississippi—teaching my friend, Sherman Alexie, how to fly-fish. The water, the air, my outward instruction, my inward strategizing, all feel as real as real. What doesn't, quite, is Sherman. Normally voluble, thoughtful, scathing, hilarious, he is silent today. Focused on his casting. (Not saying a word. Sherman!) His casts are looking good, too. Maybe the fact that fly fishing requires thoughtfulness, and can be scathing and hilarious, has sponged him up and left him lost, already, in what I love about this art: no need for an identity, hardly; certainly no need for words.

There are lake trout in Flathead. Mackinaw. They're not native to these waters, whereas Sherman, a Spokane Indian, is a native fisherman. The world abounds in so many ironies of this kind, though, that I can only hope irony is indigenous. The Mackinaw, in any case, live out in the deeps, normally, and we're boatless, Sherman and I. So I've brought him to where the Swan River runs into the lake: a sheltered bay ringed by boutiques, hotels, restaurants, galleries, tourists; the sort of place I never fish. But Sherman's an urban Indian these days, indigenous to basketball courts, lecture halls, airports, anything but rivers. He's also a new dad, sleep-deprived and punchy. And doesn't swim a lick. One false step on one of my favorite rivers and I'm left to tell my friend's wise-eyed three-month-old that he's an orphan. So this over-civilized, close-to-the-hospital cove looks about perfect to me. I've even seen a few cutthroat cruising the shoals, though today's agenda is simply to show my friend how to wade without drowning; read the water; handle a rod; cast.

When I look his way, though: a miracle! This long-haired whipper-snapper who's never fished in his life is playing a huge lake trout! Bigger than huge! A gargantuan, hook-jawed male. Sherman's even got it tired. I see the Mackinaw starting to give up the fight in clear green water not thirty feet away. I can't *believe* the size. Fifty, sixty pounds. The catch of a lifetime!

Rubberneckers are already collecting behind us, shouting idiot encouragement, idiot advice. I tell Sherman to pretend he's Lot's wife and the people are Sodom and Gomorrah. I tell him to pretend his fly line's an air-tube and the fish is his child and if the connection breaks, the child dies. Sherman's already so focused, though, that he treats *me* like Sodom and Gomorrah. He's handling his impossible fish perfectly, keeping the rod high, merely suggesting, with steady pressure, the direction he'd prefer it to go. And, huge though it is, the trout has about had it.

Looking around for a place to land it, though, I find trouble. We're backed as close as we can get to shore, but are still in belly-deep water, with a head-high seawall trapping us where we are. There's no beach, and no shallows, for hundreds of yards—and probably not a net in Montana big enough to scoop this fish where it swims. Seeing the difficulty, Sherman looks expectantly at me. I feel my instincts kick in. I've landed salmon and steelhead in worse fixes than this. I ask, "Do you want to kill this animal?"

Sherman nods without hesitation. It's Indian tradition. Celtic tradition, too. Fionn McCool did not catch and release the Salmon of Wisdom: he cooked and ate it. That's how he became Fionn McCool.

But what an incredible creature! I say, "You're *sure?*"

My friend nods again. And I don't argue. My catch-and-release habit is a civility necessitated by my country's vast population and lethal industrial ways. The fate of this fish is between it and Sherman. It's Duncan clan code, and an honor, to serve as my friend's gillie.

I tell Sherman to hold the fish's head as steady as he can, near the surface, but to let it run if I frighten it into a fresh outburst. He nods.

I turn to the lake trout and focus. Jesus, what an animal! No way to tail it: my hands wouldn't reach halfway around. I've got no choice, in this deep water, but to grasp it by the gills—a prospect the catch-and-release Yankee in me finds appalling. To grab any salmonid's gills is typically fatal, causing bleeding that eventually kills it no matter how gently it's released. I ask Sherman a third time if he wants to kill this beast. I hear nothing but Indian in his yes.

Okay. I wade around my friend till the trout is directly in front of me, then relax my shoulders, take a slow, deep breath, ease my hands up under the fish's belly where they can't be seen. Within seconds I'm stroking the Mackinaw's cold, smooth, human-sized abdomen. It seems to welcome this, seems to relax down into my hands. *"My God!"* I whisper. *"Look* at it!"

As if Sherman had been looking anywhere else.

Now the necessary treachery. I slide my hands, palms up, along the fish's body till I'm cradling it beneath the head the way a lover might his beloved before a kiss. The Mackinaw gazes downward, the way living trout do. Doesn't struggle. Doesn't even move. I could make my attempt now. Knowing, though, that all hell is about to break loose, and that this creature is strong enough to break my grip if not my fingers, I'm not quite satisfied with the way I'm bending down over it. Every predator it's ever known has attacked from above. I need its trust before I betray it—and after betrayal, I'll need the strength of my legs. I should attack from below. The water's cold. My waders will fill. But this is a once-in-a-lifetime moment. Still cradling the massive head, I take the deepest possible breath, and slip quietly beneath the surface of the lake.

The Mackinaw and I are now face-to-face. Nose to nose. In *its* world, not mine. It regards me with surprising calm. Thanks to the treachery in my heart, I regard it far less calmly. My fingers, though, are in position, just behind its gills. The fish remains motionless. It's time.

With all the speed and strength that's in me, I suddenly drive my fingers deep into the Mackinaw's gills, my thumbs clamping down from the outside like padlocks snapping shut. Blood gushes instantly. The huge mouth flies open. Its eyes, too, fly wide, swing impossibly forward, stare into mine, become too human, gape in outrage. Its head, its body, shake wildly, crimson blossoming around us both. But my grip is in its vitals, its equivalent of lungs. Feeling this, the fish stops shaking completely, locks its eyes on mine, and, to my horror, begins to speak: *"Don't . . . you . . . remember? The . . . elders . . . have . . . forbidden . . . the . . ."*

No! I can't allow this! Fatal wounds are inflicted. Let death be fast. I straighten my legs, rise up into *my* world, rip the huge trout up into it with me. Blood keeps flying, the fish thrashes wildly, but my fingers are eight spear-points driven into its very life. The power soon departs from the thrashing. I feel the creature's surrender, feel a kind of sigh. Movement continues, but it's listless now: a convulsive memory of the lost ability to swim. My fists remain locked.

Unsure of my true feelings, I choose wood for an expression, turn to Sherman, and nod, signaling that the fish is his. Sherman's expression is pure awe. I don't know whether he heard the animal speak. I don't ask. Killing a fish, especially *this* fish, should be a quick, reverent business—and this poor animal is still breathing into my fists. "Pull your prayer together," I say to Sherman. "I want to be quick." He nods, and instantly follows when I heave the fish up over the seawall and scramble up after it.

At the Mackinaw's appearance, a mass exhalation, *Ahhhhhhhh!* is suctioned from the crowd. We climb up and stand. Sherman's godlike trout now lies on an incongruous mowed lawn. It's no longer struggling, but is still gazing with intelligent eyes, its breathing desperate, a sound as distressing to me as was its speech. People encircle us and it, cheer and gawk, pound our backs, do what crowds do. I want them to vanish. The Mackinaw's gasps are unbearable. With no civility at all, I snap, "Someone find a club! *Fast!*"

Most of the people continue to gawk. Those who try to help return with feeble, lightweight sticks. A clueless woman hands me a willow switch. I toss it away. "A priest must be strong, heavy!" I bark. The fish keeps gasping.

A teenager hands me a driftwood limb that might have worked when it was green, but it's been bleached to the density of balsa by the sun's rays. Desperate, I try it anyway. Pinning the fish upright between my knees, I breathe my silent prayer, hope Sherman is doing the same, then strike a blow on the back of the massive skull. The priest snaps like a breadstick. The Mackinaw keeps gasping. "Damn it! Come on!" I tell Sherman.

Lifting the trout by its ruined gills, I take off along the seawall. Sherman follows with our fly rods. The fish is as heavy as a seven-year-old child, and my waders are sloshing, but I try my best to run. We pass coffee shops, galleries, motels, their windows lined with gaping, fist-pumping people. Muffled faces shout at the sight of the fish, leaving steam clouds and nose grease on plate glass. I feel blood running down my forearms, hear the trout's gasps, feel its body weakly swimming against my own, feel utterly sick and wrong.

But we come, suddenly, to a tiny beach bereft of people, curtained off by small willows, littered with driftwood logs and limbs. And I instantly find a heavy, hatchet-length tree remnant, the kind I call a "river tooth." Its iron heft fills me with calm. The perfect priest. I vow to salvage this moment for Sherman, vow to dispatch this magnificent animal with the dignity it deserves.

Laying the Mackinaw on its belly, I again pin it upright between my knees. As I take aim at the shining back of its skull, I notice it's the width of my own, the precise green of the lake's deep waters, and that I can see, as if the skullbone itself were made of water, deep down into its depths.

I draw breath, breathe out my secret word, strike the green skull dead center and hard. The trout shudders all through its body, grows still. I heave a huge sigh. Thank God it's over.

Then the Mackinaw begins, impossibly, to struggle.

Sherman just watches, accepting this sudden nightmare as if he thinks killing big fish must always be this hard. Maintaining focus, I strike the lake trout with all my might. It struggles harder. I hit it again and again. The harder the blow, the harder it fights back. Trying to pray as I pound, trying to hold to a sense of reverence, I administer what comes to feel like a merciless, murderous beating. Darkest red blood pours from the ruined skull, turns instantly black, becomes hair. The more blood flows, the longer grows the hair. Enraged by my own horror, I pound the increasingly broken, increasingly human head brutally, only to feel the body quickening between my legs. The fish's blue-green flesh becomes blue clothes and brown skin. Its fins become fingers, hands, arms. Its tail becomes rapidly lengthening legs. Everything's alive! everything's growing! I'm straddling God's deep magic, Creation's own truth, and hooks, fingers, treachery, priests can't alter, slow, or stop it! The no-longer-green body, strong arms, long legs, become jeans and a workshirt, become my own daily garb, become a much larger, much more powerful creature. *"Wait!"* it groans down into the beach cobble. *"Please! Wait!"*

I drop the river tooth, free the pinned body, stand back. Our quarry lies facedown on the beach, black hair to its shoulder blades, iridescing like magpie feathers where it's not drenched by blood. Its skull wounds are a pulp, pulsing in time to its heartbeat. Yet the sprawled arms move to push its body up. The creature gathers itself, stands . . .

turns to us . . .

It is a man. A beautiful Indian man. Sherman's and my height. In Sherman's kind of skin, my kind of clothes. And he is looking at us. He is looking at us with a face so open, so free of blame or anger or pain despite the deceptions and woundings we've inflicted, that I can't speak, can't think, can't move. His hands are slender and strong, the blue veins beautiful against brown skin. His body is muscular, willowy, perfect. His eyes are as black as night in the center, as white as snow at the rim, and so clear that we feel at once: *he sees things we don't.* This man is no mere man.

The Indian from water is looking around, now, at the world into which he's risen. He is smiling with pleasure as he looks. His looking makes Sherman and me want to gaze at our world, too. The water and sky are brighter, greener, and bluer than we'd remembered. The mountains cup the lake's waters so intricately we see love in the gestures of every slope and stone. The Indian-from-water's face is so appreciative of our world, even despite his wounds, that water rises in my eyes.

He feels this at once: feels the water rise in my eyes, turns to me, and with an expression of love, even gratitude, he smiles: at *me*. The water rises faster, threads down my cheeks. *He forgives me. He forgives me!*

Suddenly his gaze lifts. Seeing something beyond me, his already shining face grows more radiant still. In a voice as deep as a man's but as thrilled as a child's on Christmas, he cries, *"My Father is here!"*

Sherman and I look, see no one, but somehow share his joy. The lake Indian's love is so huge we feel the Father's presence just by gazing at the son. *"Please!"* he says, with almost unbearable gentleness. *"Just let me say good-bye to my Father! Then I'll come with you."*

We nod at once. But we don't *want* him to come with us! We don't want to finish killing him! We've no more wish to take this wondrous being from his Father than to have the hearts ripped from our own chests. We would *refuse* to finish killing him, if it seemed possible. Only: *those wounds* . . .

The water Indian's eyes turn, now, toward the crowd we left behind, on the seawall near the mouth of the Swan. They're specks from here, those people. But his eyes! Again the lake Indian's face fills with uncontainable love. He cries, *"My children! My sons and daughters are here!"*

Hearing this after all I've done to him, I can't help but let out a sob. Yet I also feel myself beaming, see Sherman beaming, too. Because the sons and daughters are here! And his love for them! His willingness to reveal that love even to us! His physical beauty, blazing eyes, refusal to blame! It's all over for Sherman and me. We are Flathead-Lake-deep in love with this being from water. I feel ready to follow him, feed him, fight for him, serve him, drink the lake for him if he asks—and maybe beg him to adopt me, should the occasion arise.

With more affection than I've ever heard in a voice, the water Indian says, *"Just let me say good-bye to my children, and to my Father. Then I'll come with you . . ."*

My eyes stream as I nod. We're so confused. We don't *want* him to come with us! We want his Father and children to keep him forever. We adore this perfect being from water. Anyone with eyes and a beating heart would adore him. But there are strange, unbreakable laws at play here. *Fishing,* I think we call them. So, once he says his farewells, he'll be coming with *us.* How terrible! How wonderful!

Giving Sherman and me—his catcher and attempted killer—a heart-melting smile of gratitude, the lake Indian sets off toward the distant crowd. We follow like faithful dogs, wondering if we can persuade him not to make us finish him off. What a position to be in! *Fishing!* Bloody ridiculous! I can't take my eyes off his back, can't stop staring at his hands. I suddenly notice his clothes are dry, glance at Sherman: he sees the same thing. We notice his hair is in a braid, though he never braided it. Then we notice his skull wounds: they're nearly healed! Our hearts leap at this sight. *Please!* I'm thinking. *Don't make us kill or eat you! Heal! Live forever!* Yet at the same time we're thinking: *But don't leave us, either! Let us live where you live! We'll say hi to the kids, hi to the Father, then all go to* your *world. I'm sure we'll adjust! Let's go!*

But there's a fresh problem. Though the lake Indian is merely walking, he can't wait to greet his family—and he walks like a Mackinaw swims, the strides incredibly fluid. And we're in waders, Sherman and I, mine full of water. We run, or try. But without meaning to, without once glancing back, the lake Indian widens the distance between us. This growing gulf is unbearable—like watching my home burst into flames, like hearing my child has cancer. We try our best to get closer but we're gasping, now, the way the Mackinaw so recently gasped, and the lawns above the seawall are suddenly littered with logs and railroad ties—a wall-repair project, I guess. The Indian-from-water strides down these logs with the ease of a trout gliding over them, but when Sherman and I step on the same logs they roll to the side, making us fall. We jump up again and again, keep falling, lose our fly rods, hurt ourselves, limp on in pursuit, but the lake Indian's workshirt and jeans, his healed head, his shining black braid get farther and farther away.

We're a hundred yards behind when the crowd parts, then closes around him, like water.

We too reach the crowd a half minute or so later, shoulder our way through, search every face, rush around corners, circle the blocks of the town.

We never see the beautiful Indian-from-water again.

And we are so, so relieved.

And utterly heartbroken!

There is one thing we now want as much as we want the lake Indian to live forever, and that's to be with him again—even if it kills him.

When at last I turn to Sherman, I am not eloquent: "You caught a fuckin' *god!*" I gasp.

Sherman stares at me, and nods.

"I may never fish again," I say, hating the words the instant I speak them.

But Sherman just smiles. No nod this time. He recognized at once what I too now realize: we will *never* stop fishing for the one we have just, somehow, released. Not till he's ours. Or we're his.

I wake to a blue dawn, my Montana bedroom open wide to August, the trout stream out the open door silver and singing, the mountains beyond the silver cupping the waters so intricately I see love in the gestures of every slope and stone. My heart pounds and pounds. Like the river-tooth priest just pounded. Maybe it's broken now, my heart. Maybe it's my own heart I just pulverized.

I can't escape this dream's gravitational pull. Nor do I wish to.

There is a faith, called fishing. It is my faith. I am sworn to its service and its gods, and once you swear, you are no longer your own. How can I quit until the gods themselves command it?

There is a faith, called fishing. It's a form of waiting, some say, for that which has never really been seen. I say, whether I've seen him or not, I love him. And gladly go on waiting.

21. Spirit-Fried No-Name River Brown Trout: A Recipe

Like Christ (aka ⌒╳), and unlike most of the rest of us, a pan-fried trout is utterly forgiving. If you use too high a flame, the skin takes the abuse and the flesh is still delectable. Too low a flame and it still makes decent sushi. Even overcooked for hours in British *Babette's Nightmare* simmer-it-to-mush style, the structural integrity of muscle that spent its entire life fighting river current is nearly impossible to reduce to goo.

Secret ingredients? There are none. Indispensable ingredients? There are two. The first? Honest butter. Forget margarine, forget olive oil (the cultural dissonance!), forget *I Can't Believe It's Not Coagulated Petroleum With Yellow Dye!*®, forget cholesterolic and caloric paranoia, period. Wild trout frying is not a meal, it's a rite. You are preparing to eat an animal that gave up its beautiful river and only life for your pleasure. Pleasure ought, therefore, to be maximized. Open your palate to the trout's flavor and your heart to its riverine essence, and that essence will charge through you like spring runoff, flushing every artery you've got. It is never "heart smart" to refuse to open your heart. Butter aside, there are no Trout Frying Commandments. Almonds, garlic, and corn-meal offer interesting counterpoint if you like fried almonds, garlic, and cornmeal; needless distraction if you don't. The flesh under discussion requires no trick additives. If you open your heart and use enough but-ter, a trout fried in a dredged-up chrome fender over an acetylene torch is worth eating.

Due to the chef-friendly equation between ease of prep and splen-dor of result, the trout is considered by many to be an easy fish to fry. It is not. The reason it's not is that butter is only one of the two essen-tial ingredients, and the other is frequently overlooked. What is the mystery ingredient? *The trout itself.*

The cause of this shocking omission is the corporate-spawned delusion that those blotchy, cellophane- and styrofoam-swaddled, dented-Grumman-canoe-colored fish-corpses at the local chain supermarket are, as the label claims, "trout." Don't believe it! The super-market product is mass-manufactured, half-embalmed pond-spawn. Raised on obscene industrial pellets, "toned" by flaccid, poop-flecked waters, these hapless victims of genetic Mcdiddling bear as much resem-blance to wild river trout as does a drug-bloated, shit-smeared, feedlot moo-cow to a wild bull elk. *True trout frying cannot take place until a food-worthy species has been identified and a choice specimen taken.* Trout frying can begin, in other words, only with the catching of a *wild* trout, which can be obtained only after a journey to clean wild water. We have of necessity moved, in a single paragraph, from a tube-lit, corporate-owned refriger-ation unit to the most unspoiled lake, river, or stream within range of your home. This is what I call "Progress"! We're still not quite ready to catch a fryable fish. But we are at least now safe to begin considering their true variety.

Trout species vary from drainage to drainage, as Highland Scots and Indian tribes once did and by choice still do, and as any conceivable long-term, slow-time, sustainable inhabitant of the "Americas" will one day do.

Even the same one trout species takes on surprisingly different characteristics and flavors from river to river. The reasons for this are myriad, sometimes holy, and far beyond the scope of a single human mind, let alone a single human recipe. Suffice it to say that in my little home niche here in western Montana, I catch seven kinds of wild trout (the brook, the Mackinaw, the cutthroat, the rainbow, the bull, the cutthroat-rainbow hybrid, and the brown); that two of these are native to these waters, four introduced from elsewhere, and one (the hybrid) a little of each; that all seven are well able to sustain themselves without human assistance if human ignorance and avarice give them half a chance; and that it is this self-sufficiency that has earned the best of them the beautiful designation "wild."

But, ah, Industrial America! Of the seven local species, the indigenous bull trout is endangered, the indigenous West Slope cutthroat threatened, and the introduced Mackinaw lousy eating, so the first two I release and the third I culinarily ignore. I'm so stunned by the blazing colors of the occasional brookie I catch that I'm as likely to kill it as I am likely to kill a mountain bluebird or western tanager. And almost every time I set the hook to a bread-and-butter rainbow or hybrid cutbow, it pirouettes skyward and so does my heart, so that by the time I land it I'm as likely to kill and eat it as I am to kill and eat a member of the Joffrey Ballet.

Six of seven species landed, six of seven released, and my frying pan still empty. The reader begins, perhaps, to see the difficulty in obtaining that second Trout Fry Essential. Who wants to kill and eat beauty? Who wants to kill and eat one's dance partner? I am one of those people who finds the American rodeo clown a wildly more romantic figure than the Spanish bullfighter, since rodeo clowns not only refuse to mince and posture, but practice—with far bigger, far more dangerous bulls—the art of catch-and-release. I am also, however, one of those people who, like trout themselves, eats flesh. In honor of this unanimity, I now turn, with all the appetite that's in me, to the seventh and last local wild-trout possibility: the brown.

Our Montana brown trout—like most nineteenth-century arrivals—began the long journey westward by crossing the Atlantic in ships. There were two distinct immigrant families. I call them the McBrowns and the Brauns. The more silvery, red-spotted Loch Leven McBrowns originated, like a lot of Montanans (the clans Craighead, McClay, McGuane, Maclean, Doig, Duncan, etc.) in Scotland. The more buttery-colored, orange-spotted Brauns hail from Germany. And to this day, if you gently squeeze the living bellies of either, they let out a croaking sound that brings Scottish broguery and *Deutsch* umlauts to mind.

What I love best about McBrowns and Brauns, though, is not the Old World heritage or remnant dialect: it's the fact that these fish, unlike most European introductees to this land, did not follow the Pioneer/Plunderer, Industrial Robber Baron, Missionary Zealot, or Racist Cracker models. *Mirabile dictu,* brown trout chose the Native American model. From the moment of their release upon this continent, the McBrowns and Brauns opted, belly-croak brogues and umlauts notwithstanding, for sly, adaptable, indigenous ways. And indigenousness, by *Gott,* is what they got.

Moving from oak barrels into America's sweet rivers, lying deep and still when in doubt, brown trout set out not to invade their new continent but to *belong* to it. They carved out a niche among the competing species. They achieved balance with the food supply. They learned to sidestep the pantheon of predators. They learned to migrate elk- or Indian-style to beat the harsh seasons. They survived river-stopping ice-ups, riverbed-scouring ice-outs, multiyear droughts, hundred-year-floods, irrigation overallotment, placer and open-pit mines, 75,000 American dams, generations of polluters, generations of political representation by river-molesting nudniks, generations of bombardment by cow-asses uncountable, generations of bombardment by Sportfishing Huns.

Despite all such assault, they thrive. There are rivers, streams, and spring creeks all over America that have, in a single century, become as impossible to imagine without their wild browns as the waters of the Pacific Northwest were once impossible to imagine without their salmon. There is no veteran fly fisher conversant with the various salmonid species who does not consider browns the Coyote of North American Trout. The McBrown's and Braun's swift transition from Highlander and Deutschlander to ineradicable American Native bypassed the usual Outlander Phase. It took a *fish* to do it, but brown trout are living proof that a gracious and native harmony—to the European immigrant who daily seeks nothing else—is attainable not just in theory, but in body, tooth, and soul.

Another thing to love about browns: There are private "game ranches" in many states, Montana included, where you can hand over a MasterCard, borrow a rifle, use the roof of your luxury sedan to steady your sights, shoot a terrified, fencebound deer, elk, or buffalo, climb back in the sedan, order the beast professionally gutted and cleaned if your shot killed it—professionally executed, gutted, and cleaned if it didn't—then order a haunch of it cooked to specs, on site. For the right kind of money you may even be able to order your haunch profession-ally pre-chewed. So what a pleasure to report that *there is no analogous way to purchase or pretend to dominate or sink your pointy teeth into a wild brown trout.* Brown trout are not for sale. For 99 percent of their lives they're not even visible. Hiring an ace angler to kill one for you is socially difficult and legally illegal. And hiring a professional fishing guide to lead you to one suitable for eating is an excellent way of entic-ing the guide, who is almost certainly a poker-faced, closet brown-trout worshiper, into making sure you get skunked.

The wild brown is, then, as egalitarian a quarry as happiness itself. To catch in order to fry in order to eat one of these indigenous beau-ties, even the most prodigiously portfolioed oligarch in America has to slip into a Gore-tex fartsack and stagger out into a cold, wild river, where, with his brain the size of a canteloupe and fiscal grasp of conti-nents, he'll find the Coyote of Trout, with its brain the size of a pepper-corn, anything but willing to rise up and die.

Even for those of us who live here, plying the rivers for browns over the course of a Montana summer is no way to keep steady meat on our tables or healthy egos on our ids. Brown trout are delicious—to my palate, the tastiest species of my legal local four. But of the local trout species, they wear the most perfect camouflage, have the teeth most likely to cut through a leader, prefer the snaggiest lairs, and almost invariably, when hooked, head for the nearest sunken tree. They have the keenest eyesight and greatest paranoia about what's going on up onshore. They're often nocturnally voracious but uncatchably ascetic by day. Upon achieving trophy size they turn cannibalistic, nearly immunizing them to the efforts of us insect-imitating fly-slingers. And when they *are* rising, they have the subtlest of rise-forms, making them the most difficult trout to locate and stalk. As a result, those who would consistently catch browns must own more than a pedestrian itch to wet a line. Of fly fishers especially, these fish demand not just interest but obsession. Not a pretty obsession, either. In order to become one of the rare maestros who can deceive these beasts at will, one must immerse oneself for years and to the eyeballs in the sort of obsessive fish-speak I've been scribbling this whole past paragraph—

unless one happens to know a wicked secret: *Even the oldest and most sagacious of browns grow temporarily crazed—by sex.* No fooling. Every mature brown trout that swims makes a spawning run in fall. This seasonal change of metabolic and existential purpose transforms the Coyote of Trout into the most imbecilic of impulse shoppers. It's a tragic but all-American malady: you can sell a spawn-minded brown damned near anything.

I'd heard stories, before moving to Montana, about how aggressive browns grow in October. Being from the Northwest coast, I imagined a belligerence akin to that of salmon, who purposefully stand guard, after arriving at the spawning grounds, around their redds. There is no similarity. Like all but the kinkiest humans, a brown wants no other species of creature in its bed of love except other browns. Unlike most humans, the brown considers its *entire visible world* to be this private bed, remains open-eyed and armed (to the teeth) round the clock, and at the sight of trespassers aims to kill. It's a strange behavior to transpose into human terms. If my wife and I were to become the sexual equivalents of brown trout tonight, our foreplay would consist of attacking and swallowing seven pet chickens, five goldfish, a guinea pig, a Dalmation, a pony, and a horse. *Vive la différence!*

I know a gin-clear creek, near a highway I often travel, that meanders through a quarter-mile-long meadow too pretty to pass by. I called it Three Fish Meadow, because the eight or ten times I'd plied it, I caught an average of three pan-sized trout, none of them browns. One crisp day in early October, I stepped into the same meadow, obeyed an impulse to tie on a fat orange jack-o'-lantern of a fly called an October Caddis, cast it into a pool-table-sized pocket behind a wheelbarrow-sized rock, and immediately hooked a nice brown. After landing and releasing the fish, I cast into the same little pocket—and instantly hooked another good brown. This happened five more times. Each of the seven browns raised hell in the pocket, crashing into and dragging line across its cohorts. Each subsequent fish nevertheless savaged my pumpkin fly. Continuing up through Three Fish Meadow, I caught and released twenty-six trout averaging thirteen inches. All but two were sex-crazed browns. The meadow, in spawning season, needs a new name.

I remember, midway through the meadow, a female brown who had claimed as her boudoir a side-channel so shallow I never thought to fish it, and so nearly stepped on her as I came hiking along full speed. *Yet she didn't spook!* At the sight of a seventy-two-inch human splashing down upon her with a hundred-and-eight-inch fly rod in hand, this fourteen-inch creature shot to the foot of her bedroom-sized glide, did a one-eighty, then zipped straight back at me, *as if to scare me off by charging.* If she'd been a few inches longer, it might even have worked!

Since I didn't bolt, the horny she-trout halted in eight inches of water not four feet to my left, and proceeded to glower up at me. I tried to glower back, but her eyes began to unnerve me. *If I lay some eggs in a nest in the gravel here,* she seemed to be thinking, *will you swim over 'em and do your part?*

Deciding we both needed a reality check, I choked up on my fly rod like a baseball hitter who's been given the bunt sign and dropped my big orange fly, *PLONK!* right on top of her head. This was not fly fishing. This was terrorism. I was doing to the little trout about what Brom Bones did to Ichabod Crane in *The Legend of Sleepy Hollow.* A sane trout would, like Ichabod, have fled for miles. My flirtatious friend grabbed the pumpkin fly as if it were a tossed bridal bouquet. I began laughing so hard I lost her—a relief to us both. But talk about sexual aggression! The Chinese ought to be grinding up October browns instead of elkhorn to restore wilted Eros.

Much as I enjoyed catching those browns, and much as I would have further enjoyed eating a few, I encounter a moral quandary with regard to the brown trout's seasonal nincompoopery: What fly-fisherly honor is there in catching and eating a creature whose peppercorn outsmarts our canteloupes forty-eight weeks out of the year, by simply waiting for the sex-drunk four weeks when it couldn't outsmart a fly-fishing Orvis shop mannequin? What honor is there is matching wits with and deceiving a normally inspiredly elusive creature while it languishes in a lovesickness so severe that a fourteen-inch specimen considered *me* a potential mate? Many of us could whomp Shaquille O'Neal at one-on-one basketball while *he* was having sex, too. Is this cause for pride? When a brown in the throes of its own mania to create life slashes my fly in late autumn, it is not a fly-fishing conquest by me: it's a biological conquest of the brown trout by the brown trout itself.

That said, I must make a confession. When it comes to fly fishing, I'm an addict, hence a pretty low-rent guy. My impulse to fish is so strong that I'll admit it: it's *fun* for me to attach my fly to a brown trout's biological conquest of itself. What I must ask myself and all honest fly fishers, though, is whether there is a more and a less honorable way to proceed with this low-rent malady of ours. Is there a sustainable way for us, and for the sex-stoned brown, each to pursue our very different addictions and live to tell the story?

I believe so. I believe the sustainable solution is a recipe: I discovered, one day in late fall, that it is not only possible but enormously pleasurable to spirit-fry and eat a brown trout, then release it unharmed. It happened like this:

One October day I slipped into my waders, drove to a certain never-to-be-named brown-trout river, hiked down to a certain logjam, dropped a fly in the eddy behind this jam, lost sight of my fly when it drifted behind some willows, heard a slurping sound behind the willows, raised my rod at the sound, watched the rod slam downward, and felt the angry headshakes of a solidly hooked fish.

Those headshakes excited me for three reasons. First, I recognized them to be the headshakes of a brown—my fry-pan favorite. Second, judging by the slow authority of the shakes, this brown was sizable: I pictured salmon-sized trout steaks sizzling in *Le Creuset.* Third, the logjam it was hiding in happened to be a logjam I'd built myself earlier in the summer, by chain-sawing and dismantling a dry-docked upstream jam and walking its logs a quarter-mile downstream to this deeper site and getting hung up en route in half-drowned, abandoned barbed-wire fences and driving into Missoula and cruising the hock shops and finding an ancient pair of bolt cutters and dickering the guy down to twelve bucks and driving back to the river and cutting and coiling and removing drowned barbed-wire fencing till I got my hands punctured and shins dinged up and logs right down where I wanted them. This jam was, in other words, an act of indigenous fly-fishermanly madness. And the wild animal on my line was evidence that Mother Nature had noticed my madness, and approved of it.

A big brown in summertime, hooked in the very same place, would have bolted into the logs and snapped my line in short order. The October brown, however, shot directly away from the logs into the snagless center of the run, where nothing good could possibly happen to it, and proceeded to veer from side to side, not as if looking for escape, but as if looking for something to attack and kill. Typical spawning-run brown behavior. I worked my way through willow brush to the hole's tail-out, forded the little river, waded back up to the pool, and waited for the big brown to come up with a new idea.

It never did. It came up with desire, anger, beauty, size, and that was it. After five or six minutes of furious veering, it tired. I led it down to the tail-out, eased it into the shallows in front of me.

I looked at the brown. The brown looked at me. I saw by the oversized, totemic jaws that the fish was a male. I took him in my hands, turned him gently on his side, measured him against the marks on my fly rod: twenty-two inches. Filleted out, quartered, and fried with almonds, he'd sate my entire family. Released, he would create his own.

The little stones in the stream were bronze in the October sunlight. The brown, against those stones, was brilliant yellow, white, and gold. His pelvic fins, translucent amber, were the size of silver dollars. The orange spots scattered down his side shone, as Richard Hugo once said, "like apples in a fog." He was so old he'd developed a gaze like a cougar, a redtail, an eagle. One does not capture an animal like this every day. I was able to pluck out the fly, right him in the water, keep my grip loose so as not to harm him. I was not able to let him go.

I dropped to my knees in the water beside him, my waders fending off the cold. The current swirled around half of me and all of the brown, coming in small, uneven surges that gently rocked my body; it felt like riding a quiet horse. Though I held him captive, the brown stayed perfectly in rhythm with this horse. Since he faced upstream, I turned that way too, and looked in the direction the brown trout was looking. Ours was an eastward-flowing stream. It was evening. The sun was turning orange before us in the west. Mountains veed to the water on both sides of the river, the northward-sloping ridges green and white with pines and new snow, the southward-sloping ridges yellow with last summer's grass. As the flow swirled down toward us, reflected sun turned its surface into a blinding sheet of orange-flecked silver. As the silver came closer, reflected sky turned it into broken shards of blue. Closer yet, the blue vanished, the water went as clear as air, and the sunlit stones beneath us became a bed of shining gold. All this beauty, all these riches—and I was *still* not sure what I would do with my brown.

Then I noticed, right in front of us, a fresh-dug, trout-length excavation in the bed of gold. It was his redd. Or hers. His paramour's. And as I stared at this redd, beaten into the stones by a seemingly departed female trout's body, I realized for the first time in my life just who the animal in my hands would truly be making love to. Not to his mate. Hardly to a mate at all. She'd dug the redd, laid her eggs. But he would never touch her. All he would ever touch was this water and these stones. He was making love, as was his mate, to the blinding silver, the broken blue, the shining gold.

I touched his side with my finger. A drop of milt spilled from his vent and vanished downstream. He was in the throes, even as I held him. I saw why I'd considered spawning browns stupid. I saw it was I who was stupid. I saw that, at a certain time of year, the rhythm of the river becomes impossible for these creatures to resist; that the mere act of swimming, mere caress of cold water, becomes a long slow copulation; that their entire upstream journey is an arduous act of sex. The dip in the gravel, nest of eggs, spraying of milt, was just the culmination of that weeks-long act. I looked again at the mountains veeing down toward the water. The gravel beneath us was made of fragments of those mountains, the current flowing past made of their melted snows. The brown trout I held was making love to the mountains and snow.

I realized that, in consuming this fish, I'd be consuming part of everything that made him. I realized that everything that made him was precisely what, or who, he was making love to. I realized that this same everything is who we, too, are made of; who we, too, are submerged in; who we, too, daily eat; who we, too, seek to love and honor. The trout in my hands let me feel this. He was, through no intention of his own, a spiritual touchstone. And one takes such stones not to stomach, but to heart.

One doesn't want to kill beauty, one doesn't want to kill a dance partner. But one doesn't want to let them go, either. I held that brown way longer than I should have. Held him till my hands began to burn. I've said it before: I must say it once more: *there is a fire in water. There is a flame, hidden in water, that gives not heat, but life*. I held a trout, and my own two hands, in that fire. The cold flames ran through and past us. And I was fed, I was sated, I'd had all the nourishment and flesh I needed when at last I opened my heart, opened my hands, and let my beautiful brown trout go.

Appendix

The blithe industrial eradication of salmon is a spiritual and cultural disaster not only for the Pacific Northwest's tribes, but for all traditional salmon people. Medieval Christian songs and poems revere salmon as embodiments of Christ-likeness. And pre-Christian Scandinavian, Celtic, Russian, British, central European, Alaskan, Inuit, Icelandic, and other legends and myths revering salmon are as ancient as the cultures themselves. To cite a single passage from one of these marvelous traditions, here—as rendered by Irish author/raconteur James Stephens in *Irish Fairy Tales* (Macmillan & Co., 1924)—is the salmon chapter of

The Lives of Tuan Mac Cairill

I had been a man, a stag, a boar, a hawk. . . . Then I grew old, and in my Ulster cave close to the sea I dreamed my dream, and in it I became a salmon. The green tides of Ocean rose over me and my dream, so that I drowned in the sea and did not die, for I awoke in deep waters, and I was that which I dreamed. . . .

In all my changes I had joy and fulness of life. But in the water joy lay deeper, life pulsed deeper. For on land or air there is always something excessive and hindering; as arms that swing at the sides of a man, and which the mind must remember; and the stag has legs to be tucked away for sleep and untucked for movement; and the bird has wings that must be folded and pecked and cared for. But the fish has but one piece from his nose to his tail. He is complete, single, and unencumbered. He turns in one turn, and goes up and down and round in one sole movement.

How I flew through the soft element! How I joyed in the country where there is no harshness, in the element which upholds and gives way, caresses and lets go, and will not let you fall. For man may stumble in a furrow, the stag tumble from a cliff, the hawk, wing-weary and beaten, with darkness around him and the storm behind, may dash his brain against a tree. But the home of the salmon is his delight, and the sea guards all her creatures.

I became the king of the salmon, and with my multitudes I ranged on the tides of the world. Green and purple distances were under me, green and gold the sunlit regions above. In the deeper latitudes I moved through a world of amber, myself amber and gold; in the upper latitudes, in a sparkle of lucent blue I curved, lit like a living jewel; deep again, through dusks of ebony, all mazed with silver I shot and shone, the wonder of the sea. I saw the monsters of the uttermost ocean go heaving by, and the long lithe brutes that are toothed to their tails; and below, where gloom dipped down on gloom, vast, livid tangles that coiled and uncoiled and lapsed down steeps and hells of the sea where even the salmon could not go.

I knew the sea. I knew the secret caves where ocean roars to ocean, the floods that are icy cold, from which the nose of a salmon leaps back as at a sting, and the warm streams in which we rocked and dozed and were carried forward without motion. I swam on the outmost rim of the great world, where nothing was but sea and sky and salmon, where even the wind was silent, and the water was clear as clean grey rock.

And then, far away in the sea, I remembered Ulster, and there came upon me an instant, uncontrollable anguish to be there. I turned, and through days and nights I swam tirelessly, jubilantly, with terror wakening in me, too, and a whisper through my being that I must reach Ireland or die.

I fought my way to Ulster from the sea. Ah, how that end of the journey was hard! A sickness was racking in every one of my bones, a languor and weariness creeping through my every fibre and muscle. The waves held me back and held me back. The soft water seemed to have grown hard, and it was as though I was urging through a rock as I strained towards Ulster. So tired I was! I could have loosened my frame and been swept away; could have slept and been drifted and wafted away, swinging on grey-green billows that turned from the land, heaving and mounting, surging to the far blue water.

Only the unconquerable heart of the salmon can brave that end of toil. The sound of the rivers of Ireland came racing down to the sea and came to me in the last numb effort: the love of Ireland bore me up: the gods of the rivers trod to me in the white-curled breakers, so that I left the sea at long, long last; and I lay in sweet water in the curve of a crannied rock, exhausted, three parts dead, triumphant.

Delight and strength came to me again, and now I explored all the inland ways: the great lakes of Ireland, and her swift brown rivers.

What a joy to lie under an inch of water basking in the sun, or beneath a shady ledge to watch the small creatures that speed like lightning on the rippling top. I saw the dragonflies flash and dart and turn, with a poise, with a speed that no other winged thing knows: I saw the hawk hover and stare and swoop: he fell like a falling stone, but he could not catch the king of the salmon: I saw the cold-eyed cat stretching along a bough level with the water, eager to hook and lift the creatures of the river. And I saw men.

They saw me also. They came to know me and look for me. They lay in wait at the waterfalls up which I leaped like a silver flash. They held out nets for me; they hid traps under leaves; they made cords of the colour of water, of the colour of weeds—but this salmon had a nose that knew how a weed felt and how a string. They drifted meat on a sightless string, but I knew of the hook; they thrust spears at me, and threw lances which they drew back again with a cord. Many a wound I got from men, many a sorrowful scar.

Every beast pursued me in the waters and along the banks; the barking, black-skinned otter came after me in lust and gust and swirl; the wild-cat fished for me; the hawk and the steep-winged, spear-beaked birds dived down on me, and men crept on me with nets the width of a river, so that I got no rest. My life became a ceaseless scurry and wound and escape, a burden and anguish of watchfulness—

and then I was caught.

The fisherman of Cairill, King of Ulster, took me in his net. Ah, that was a happy man when he saw me! He shouted for joy when he saw the great salmon in his net.

I was still in the water as he hauled delicately. I was still in the water as he pulled me to the bank. My nose touched air and spun from it as from fire, and I dived with all my might against the bottom of the net, holding yet to the water, loving it, mad with terror that I must quit that loveliness. But the net held and I came up.

"Be quiet, King of the River," said the fisherman. "Give in to Doom," said he.

I was in the air, and it was as though I were in fire. The air pressed on me like a fiery mountain. It beat on my scales and scorched them. It rushed down my throat and scalded me. It weighed on me and squeezed me, so that my eyes felt as though they must burst from my head, my head as though it would leap from my body, and my body as though it would swell and expand and fly in a thousand pieces.

The light blinded me, the heat tormented me, the dry air made me shrivel and gasp; and, as I lay on the grass, I, great salmon, whirled once more my desperate nose toward the river and leaped, leaped, leaped, even under the mountain of air. I could leap upwards, but not forward, and yet I leaped, for in each rise I could see the twinkling waves, the rippling and curling waters.

"Be at ease, O King," said the fisherman. "Be at rest, my beloved. Let go the stream. Let the oozy marge be forgotten, and the sandy bed where the shades dance all in green and gloom and the brown flood sings along."

And as he carried me to the palace he sang a song of the river, and a song of Doom, and a song in praise of the King of the Waters.

When the king's wife saw me she desired me. I was put over a fire and roasted, and she ate me. And when time passed she gave birth to me, and I was her son and the son of Cairill the king. I remember warmth and darkness and movement and unseen sounds. All that happened I remember, from the time I was roasting on the iron until the time I was born. I forget none of these things. . . .

So far the story of Tuan the son of Cairill.

And no man knows if he died in those distant ages, when Finnian was Abbot of Moville, or if he still keeps his fort in Ulster, watching all things, and remembering them for the glory of God and the honour of Ireland.

About the Photographs

The photograph at the head of the section "Wonder Versus Loss" was taken in April 1940, by Everett Olmstead (1887–1973) at Celilo Falls, Oregon. The Indians are Wyam, Wasco, and Wishram, from Celilo Village, just right of the camera's view. They pose with the Union Pacific *Streamliner,* an articulated locomotive built in 1939 to work the Chicago to Portland route. Both Falls and Village, after 11,000 years of consecutive human habitation, were submerged in 1957 by the slackwater from The Dalles Dam. The fish is a wild steelhead, likely bound for Idaho when it was dip-netted by the tribes, who at Celilo captured an estimated one in twenty migrating salmon. Although the Bonneville Power Administration and Army Corps were correct in claiming that their dam would "protect salmon" from this Indian fishery, the BPA's eight Corps-built Columbia/Snake dams now kill an estimated four in ten Idaho-bound adult salmon, and an estimated nine in ten ocean-bound, migrating smolts. And "kill" is hardly the word: the fish are simply wasted—harvested and eaten by no one.

The morose-looking chief on the left is Henry Thompson, son of legendary Wyam chief and eloquent dam opponent Tommy Thompson, who oversaw the fishery at Celilo for decades during which 16 million wild salmon a year passed through Celilo. In the best of years now, a few thousand wild fish pass through. The residents of Celilo Village were paid $3,494 apiece as compensation for the flooding of their 11,000-year-old home. Good dip-net fishermen at the time made $1000 to $4000 a week catching salmon. Tommy Thompson was 102 years old, living in a rest home far from Celilo, on the day the Falls were submerged. As Celilo began to vanish, he cried to his wife, "Bring me more blankets. I can feel the waters rising. They are covering me up. I am shivering with cold."

The Corps and NMFS remain in charge of "salmon recovery" under the Endangered Species Act, and insist in defiance of all science but their own that Columbia/Snake salmon migration is "safer than ever" with all eight dams intact.

The postcard image of the ecstatic Japanese fisher and leaping carp is the last message Henry Bugbee ever mailed to me. He sent it in response to a prose-poem I'd written about a trout's leap, which I dedicated to

Henry and published in *River Teeth*. The painting, titled "Ebisu Catching a Carp," is by Kawanabe Gyōsai (1831–1889), Edo period, Ukiyo-e school, from the Freer Gallery of Art at the Smithsonian Institution. Henry once wrote, "Let us wade right in and keep fishing where we are, with our fingertips touching the trembling line. It is just in the moment of the leap we both feel and see, when the trout is instantly born, entire, from the flowing river, that reality is knowingly defined."

The aerial photograph heading the section titled "Activism," by Emmet Gowin, depicts the mile-wide Columbia River near its confluence with the Snake, and the abandoned nuclear waste disposal trenches, foundations, and streets of Hanford City, Washington. This Cold War metropolis of more than 30,000 Americans produced the nuclear reactors and chemical separation plants that refined the plutonium triggers of every U.S. nuclear warhead built since 1945. Abandoned forty years ago, this city was the principle reason why the four Snake River salmon-killing dams were approved by Congress in 1955. Five hundred thousand gallons of high-level liquid radioactive waste have since leaked from underground storage tanks into the aquifer and Columbia. Two hundred ten billion gallons of "lower level" radioactive waste were also poured into gravel-lined beds that filter directly into the soil, aquifer, and river. A subterranean current of deadly tritium, iodine, strontium, and plutonium isotopes flows from Hanford into the Columbia to this day, creating problems the federal government has deemed insurmountable. At the same time, all that unmanageable radioactive waste has prevented the

Hanford Reach from being dammed by the Army Corps and converted to slackwater. The highly ironic, beautiful result: this thirty-mile, free-flowing stretch of wild river and riparian today supports the most complete array of indigenous wildlife, the most productive salmonid spawning habitat, and the largest surviving population of wild chinook salmon left in the entire Columbia/Snake River Basin. As Emmet Gowin has said, "Even a devastated place is sacred. If we know what it once was, we may begin to understand what its possibilities are."

The photograph heading the section titled "Fishing the Inside Passage," by Douglas Frank, depicts one of thousands of creeks I've waded since boyhood. A great thing about such streams is what Einstein did not at all mean by "the relativity factor": after you've splashed a few miles along such a stream, your interior calibrates itself to the scale of life around you. In this intimate environment, the rise of a trout of even, say, twelve inches disturbs the entire stream's surface, and at the setting of a hook the whole world seems to erupt. To create a similarly impressive disturbance on a river surface like the Columbia's, a fish would have to be the size of a barge. The rare small-stream encounter with a twenty-inch trout or thirty-inch salmon thus feel impossible, "like something in a dream." And in a dream, all the actors, and the stage as well, are something inside of you.

All photos are copyrighted and used by permission.

THE PHOTOGRAPHERS' WORKS ARE AVAILABLE AT THE FOLLOWING:

Everett Olmstead:
Thomas Robinson
Photo Research Group
441 NE Jarrett St.
Portland, OR 97211-3126

Emmet Gowin:
Pace MacGill Gallery
32 East 57th Street
New York, NY 10022

Douglas Frank:
1845 SE Exeter Drive
Portland, OR 97202

Acknowledgments

To He and Not-He, the Target of my interior compass, the Maker and Keeper of the incomparable planetary ménage à trois between two *H*'s and an *O: Jeez! Thanks!*

To the people who helped shape, inspire, and enable this book—especially Steve Pettit, Sherman Alexie, Bill Thomas, Michael Snell, Danny Moses, Emerson Nsnaha'cwɛyt'u Blake, Pattiann Rogers, David Cates, Graham Chisholm, Bill Bakke, Pat Ford, the Yakama, Warm Springs, Nez Perce, and Umatilla people, Brian Bad Whiskey Doyle, Karen Knudsen, Geoff Smith, Ken White, Colleen Colby, Emmett Gowin, Annick Smith, David James (Jim) Dodge, Robert Michael Pyle, Rick Bass, Bill Kittredge, Dick and Tracy Stone Manning, Henry Bugbee, Sally Moore, Derek and Sophie Craighead, Sam Alvord, Tom McGuane, Peter Matthiessen, Gentleman Jon Jackson, Coleman Barks, Paul Koberstein, Joseph Cone, my spiritual siblings (Melissa Madenski, Casey Bailey, Jane Hirshfield, Carl and Judy Ernst, Doug and Marnie Frank, John Bussanich, Phil Aaberg, Tom Crawford, Frank Boyden, the Missoula Babarians, Phil and Jules), my daughters Celia and Ellie, son and friend, Tom, mom and friend, Donna, and before, after, and above all, Adrian—more jeez and more thanks.

To the countless good souls who asked about this book after the many readings and lectures that borrowed from it, only to have me direct you to it by the titles *How the Pacific Makes Love to the Rockies* and *Necessary Hooky* and *Extreme Fly Fishing* and *My Life as a Sequel to the Mayonnaise Chapter* and *Standing by the Always-So* and *Big Church No Preacher* and *Rethinking Water*: sorry! I'm still just learning this confounded language.

Finally: how can I thank the objects of my lifelong obsession, fish, except to chase, torment, touch, eat, and sing of them as long as I can and, after that, still burble and point. Krishna says: *"Know this Atman, unborn, undying, never ceasing, never beginning."* Jesus says: *"Take. Eat. This do in remembrance of Me."* Krishna again: *"Surrender all action to Me in sacrifice. The pervading infinite spirit is ever present in rites of sacrifice."* Though this sort of thing sounded promising from the start, to a thickwit like me it also felt unlivably abstract—till I started fishing. Endless thanks, then, to the salmonids I love, take, and occasionally eat, for being not abstract symbols but living, wounded, gasping embodiments of sacrifice, again and again placing me—kneeling as I should be, in water as I should be, stunned with gratitude as I should be—in the presence of pervading infinite spirit.

To Liam Wood, who left us while so kneeling; to Rob Ball, whose courage in the valley of the shadow takes my breath away; to the three Warren brothers and their people; this, not from me, but from the *Taittirīya Upanisad*—a scripture composed, say the rishis, by no one; a scripture self-created, found floating like mist, or the bands of a rainbow, in the primordial forest air:

> *He who is here in a man and he who is up there in the sun—they are one and the same. After a man who knows this departs from this world—he first reaches the self (ātman) that consists of food, then the self that consists of life-breath, then the self that consists of mind, then the self that consists of perception, and finally the self that consists of bliss; and, eating whatever he likes and assuming whatever appearance he likes, he continues to travel across these worlds and to sing this Sāman chant:*
>
> *O wonderful! O wonderful! O wonderful!*
> *I am food! I am food! I am food!*
> *I eat food! I eat food! I eat food!*
> *My name never dies, never dies, never dies!*
> *I was born first in the first of the worlds,*
> *earlier than the gods, in the belly of what has no death!*
> *Whoever gives me away has helped me the most!*
> *I, who am food, am the eater of food!*

I have overcome!
He or she who knows this shines like the sun.
Such are the laws of the mystery!

The author thanks the editors and publishers of the following publications, in which some of this work first appeared, or was later serialized or anthologized, usually in very different form.

Periodicals: *Harper's*, "Birdwatching as a Blood Sport"; *Outside*, parts of "Valmiki's Palm" and "In Praise of No Guide"; *Sierra*, "The War for Norman's River," part of "A Prayer for the Salmon's Second Coming," and "Beauty/Violence/Grief/Frenzy/Love" (published as "Man of Two Minds"); *OE Journal, Cascadia Times*, Earth Ministry's *Earth Letter*, and the Patagonia clothing catalogs, parts of "A Prayer for the Salmon's Second Coming"; *Whole Terrain*, "River Soldiers"; *Open Spaces*, part of "Valmiki's Palm" and "River Soldiers"; *The Sun* and *The Colorado Springs Independent*, part of "Who Owns the West?: Seven Wrong Answers"; *The Sun*, "god"; *The Los Angeles Times Sunday Magazine*, parts of "Lake of the Stone Mother" and "Spirit-Fried No Name River Brown Trout"; *Portland, Talking River Review, The Drake*, and *Talking Leaves*, parts of "Native"; *Orion*, "Khwaja Khadir," "Strategic Withdrawal," and part of "Native"; *The New York Times*, part of "The War for Norman's River"; *The Missoula Independent*, "In Praise of No Guide"; *Big Sky Journal*, "Spirit-Fried No Name River Brown Trout," "Idiot Joy," and part of "Six Henry Stories"; *Gray's Sporting Journal*, "Fearless Leader"; *Northern Lights*, "The Non Sense of Place; *River Teeth: a journal of narrative nonfiction*, "Valmiki's Palm."

Books: *Notes from the Field: Great Writers and Adventurers on Life Outside*, published by Patagonia and Chronicle Books (2000), part of "Tilt"; *A River Called Home*, published by The Clark Fork Coalition and Mountain Press, part of "The War for Norman's River"; *Getting Over the Color Green: Contemporary Southwest Environmental Literature*, University of Arizona Press (2001), "Lake of the Stone Mother"; *When Philosophy Becomes Lyric: Reflections on Henry Bugbee's American Classic*, University of Georgia Press (1998), four of the "Six Henry Stories"; *The Gift of Birds: True Stories of Avian Spirits*, Traveler's Tales Press (1999), "Birdwatching as a Blood Sport"; *Best American Sports Writing*, Houghton Mifflin (1998), "Birdwatching as a Blood Sport"; *Off the Beaten Path: Stories of Place*, The Nature Conservancy and Farrar, Straus and Giroux (1998), "The 1872 Knee-Mining Act & Your Exciting Financial Future!"; *Heart of the Land,* The Nature Conservancy and Pantheon Books (1995), "Lake of the Stone Mother."

Thanks, finally, to the Montana Arts Council for their support.

Grateful acknowledgment is also made to the following for permission to reprint previously published material:

Sherman Alexie, for the poem "Prayer," at the end of "A Prayer for the Salmon Second's Coming"; from *The Man Who Loved Salmon,* © 1999 by Limberlost Press; reprinted by permission of Sherman Alexie;

Tenshin Reb Anderson, for "In my middle years . . ." by Wang Wei, translation © 1989, reprinted by permission of Reb Anderson;

Wendell Berry, for five lines from his poem "The Country of Marriage," from the book *Collected Poems: 1957–1982,* published by North Point Press © 1987; reprinted by permission of Wendell Berry;

Tom Crawford, for his poem "Fish," from *The Temple on Monday,* published by Eastern Washington University Press, © 2001; reprinted by permission of Tom Crawford;

Jim Harrison, for eight lines from "Cabin Poem" and fourteen lines from poem 2 in the section titled *Geo-Bestiary,* both from *The Shape of the Journey: New and Collected Poems,* published by Copper Canyon Press, © 1998; reprinted by permission of Jim Harrison;

Jane Hirshfield, for three lines from the poem "Given Sugar, Given Salt," from the book *Given Sugar, Given Salt* © 2001 by Harper-Collins & Co. reprinted by permission of Jane Hirshfield;

W.W. Norton & Co., for six lines from "The River Now," from *Making Certain It Goes On: The Collected Poems of Richard Hugo,* published by W.W. Norton, © 1984; reprinted by permission of W.W. Norton.

About the Author

DAVID JAMES DUNCAN is the author of two novels, *The River Why* and *The Brothers K,* and *River Teeth,* a collection of stories and memoir. *The River Why* ranks thirty-fifth on *The San Francisco Chronicle* list of "The 20th Century's 100 Best Books of the American West." *The Brothers K* is an American Library Association Best Books Award winner and a *New York Times* Notable Book. Both novels won the Pacific Northwest Bookseller's Award. David has read and lectured all over the United States on wilderness, the writing life, the nonmonastic contemplative life, the fly-fishing life, and the nonreligious literature of faith. He lives with his family on a Montana trout stream, where he is at work on a comedy about reincarnation and human folly, called *Nijinsky Hosts Saturday Night Live.*